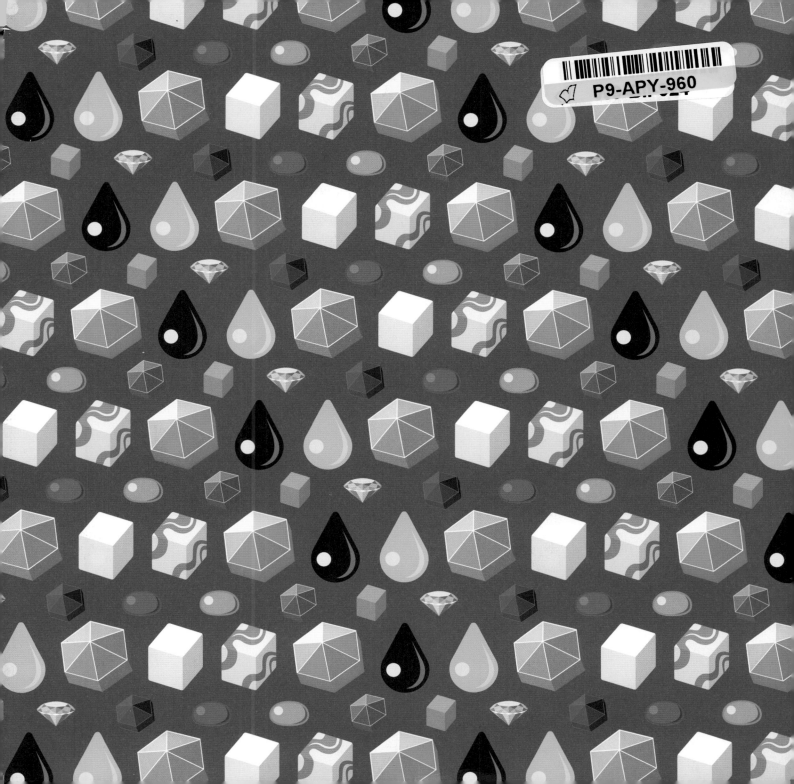

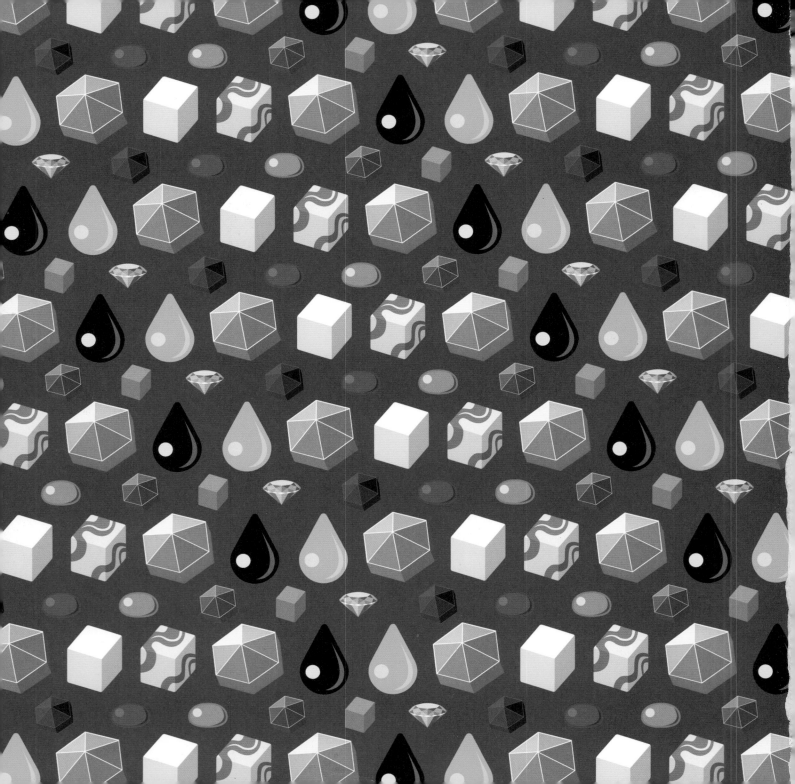

BY ANDREW HUSSIE

BOOK 3

PART 1

ACT 4

Act 4
"Flight of the Paradox Clones"

💎 -1,000

ACT 4
FLIGHT OF THE PARADOX CLONES

GATE 1

Welcome to Book 3, which obviously starts with Act 4, which obviously starts with Gate 1. I mean...obviously? Glad that's obvious to everyone. What's also PAINFULLY obvious to anyone looking at this page, no matter who they are, is that this is a loading screen. Hot Flash Content is being piped directly into your book, right now, at the speed of bullshit. We're off to a great start here in the author notes section. Hey, remember Flash loading screens? From the internet? Those were the days. You needed SOMETHING to look at while untold KILOBYTES were crawling through your ethernet cables. In this case, I chose to dazzle you with a hypnotically morphing spirogaph. You quickly went into a trance of fascination. The suspense built. Cue the music. And then.......magic.

Okay, no magic here. No music or movement, because it's a book! All you get is my goofs. Sorry, sucker. Let's talk about this animation. It's pretty damn enchanting, really. We finally get to see what's under those gray clouds. It's a bunch of fireflies, and a blue landscape with phosphorescent flora and black oily rivers. Act 4 marks the official beginning of the scenery porn era of *Homestuck*.

Land of Wind and Shade

Or "LOWAS," as becomes the model for further nomenclature in reference to *Homestuck*'s lands. These "lands," of course, are fairly small planets. Hard to say how big exactly. I don't think I ever really did any due diligence on the cosmological scale of these bodies. They're big enough to explore and get lost in but not so huge as to be hopelessly unchartable. I guess I always pictured them being like a small state in the US. Like if Rhode Island or Connecticut were wrapped around a sphere. Literally doing so would make for a fairly lackluster land, suitable for a pretty bland player of *Sburb*. (I suppose such as...every resident of those particular states? Why...why am I alienating these people already? It's only the fourth page. Oh well, forty-eight states to go, I guess.)

6

OKAY LET'S CUT THE SHIT AND TALK ABOUT THIS FLASH! It's a playable game. That turned out to be a thing in HS. As a Flash loaded, readers would wonder...is this going to be a GAME? (Virtually always: no. But sometimes...sometimes, yes!) This one is similar in style to the game when John first enters the Medium and can wander around his house, but this time there's ACTUAL battle mechanics. You can bonk imps with a hammer, collect grist and items—all rather pointlessly, I should add. But you *can* do it, is the point. Why? I really couldn't fucking tell you, to this day. I think I was legitimately insane? This, with perfectly brutal honesty, I must admit now strikes me as something a crazy person would do.

7

NANNASPRITE: I am still in the house, dear! I'm afraid I cannot accompany you on your journey. But I can talk to you like this, if you ever need me to provide a puzzling half-answer to one of your questions!
JOHN: oh, ok. thanks, nanna.
NANNASPRITE: You should begin exploring and talking to locals! They will be able to provide you with some new insight into your quest, and may illuminate some matters on which I have remained coy to this point! HOO HOO!
JOHN: yeah, what's up with that, nanna? did the game make you all coy and prankstery when you became a sprite or were you always like that when you were alive?
NANNASPRITE: Oh, wouldn't YOU like to know, dear! HOO HOO HOO HOO HOO!
JOHN: ha ha ha... ok.

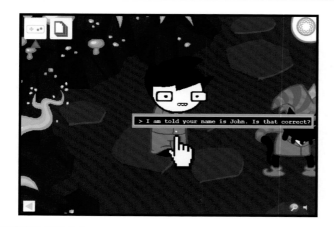

I suppose the upshot of the game format is that it lets the player wander around this fantastical new land and discover its mysteries just like John is doing. Actually, YOU don't get to. You get to thumb through this very thick book with your grubby fingers while I struggle through a borderline state of dementia, heroically trying to remember what I was thinking when I made this. But some people sure did get to do that. Anyway, this is what happens when you click that icon in the upper right. John gets to talk to Nanna, like...there's some sort of comm system back to his sprite? Sprites technically can't go far from the house after their player enters the Medium. That's the strict rule of *Sburb*. Until much, much later, when it stops being all that strict, for reasons that are unlikely ever to be explained, even by the WISEST of sprites.

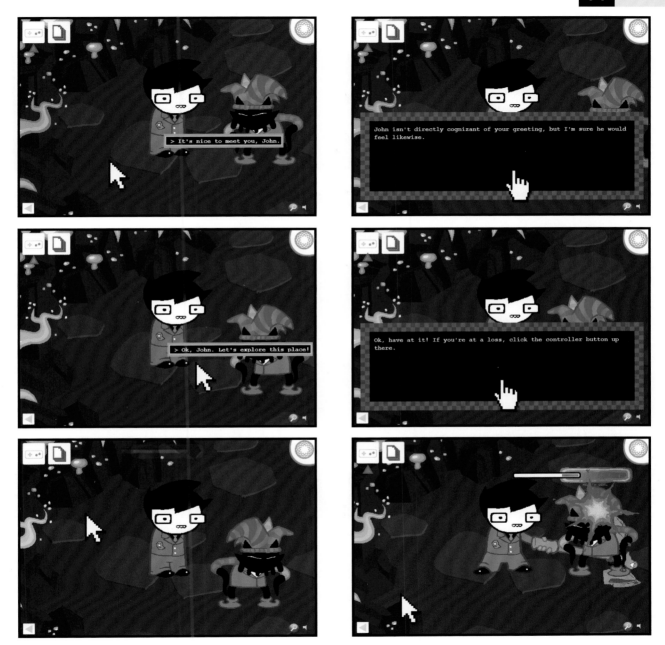

Here's a little taste of the gameplay. You click on a thing and a menu pops up, which includes what is...technically a text command that is being entered by...the player of *Homestuck*? (Who has at this point been revealed to be any given exile, operating the post-apocalypse *Sburb* station.) It's pretty esoteric. But you don't need to think about any of this to play the game, get a sense of John's rad land, meet some scurrilous foes in need of a bashing, and feel like a cool hero.

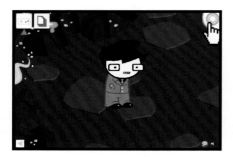

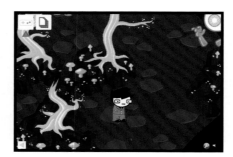

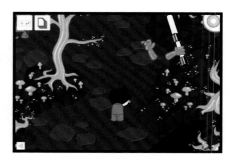

You have deactivated your GHOST GAUNTLETS for the time being. It gets pretty distracting flailing them around all the time when all you're trying to do is explore.

The ghost gauntlets holding that ridiculous paisley hammer are just a fixture of the environment in this game. I didn't want them to be an item you could use, because that would have been complicated to implement. It was a little attention to detail on my part, by which I mean my inclination to consider how John could wield this huge hammer in his inventory. Specific items that are accrued by the players become a lot less relevant much later in the story. Because it stops being a thing about a Guy In A Game You Are "Playing," and starts being more about a bunch of Characters In A Story You Are Reading, Who Are Sad All The Time.

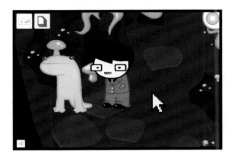

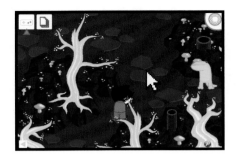

"GLUB GLUB! Sure is windy here! Often, wind skims the voids of the Pipes, as if grazing the hollow of a cut reed, or say, a plundered Parcel Pyxis. It is a lovely sound and brings back fond memories of my childhood. Which was a couple days ago."

Here were meet a "consort." Or, a salamander, in the case of John's planet. All planets have consorts, usually a different kind of amphibian or reptile for each. Why amphibians or reptiles? Didn't I cover this already in another book note? Oh. You don't remember either? Well, guess we're in the same boat then. (Consorts have very short life spans, which is the joke here.) And a parcel pyxis is like a pipe mailbox they throw shit in to send places. They have a whole pipe-based civilization, but the pipes are all clogged with oil, and... You know, I did a much better job with this worldbuilding stuff by letting you understand it all in the game through exploration and inference. Too bad you're not playing it now, so you get remedial lore for boneheads down here.

"Look at this! Another Cherished Idol profaned! Such sacrilege has become commonplace with the recent glut of Underlings. It would bring a tear to my eye if I were not so clearly fit to be tied with these hyperactive mannerisms and severe attention deficit oh my god look a bug."

12 This salamander laments the desecration of a glorious village frog idol. (Frogs are sacred. This fact will be as important as it is frequently repeated.) He talks about the underling swarm dedicated to destroying and oiling up such idols as a "recent" event, as if this village has existed for hundreds of years and only now have the underlings emerged to wreak mischief. This is in keeping with the strange paradox of planets in the Medium: the fact that they were just created instantly through booting up the game, and yet have always existed with entire smorgasbords of ready-made lore and quests for the players to engage with.

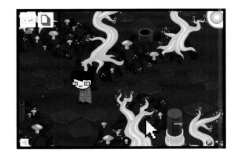

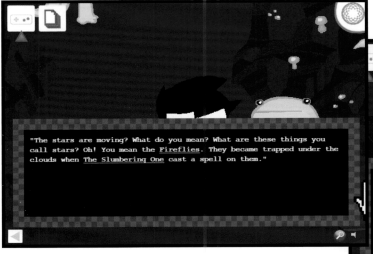

"The stars are moving? What do you mean? What are these things you call stars? Oh! You mean the Fireflies. They became trapped under the clouds when The Slumbering One cast a spell on them."

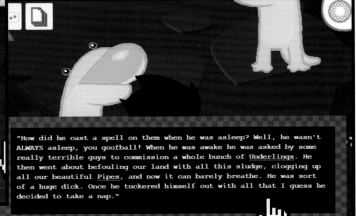

"How did he cast a spell on them when he was asleep? Well, he wasn't ALWAYS asleep, you goofball! When he was awake he was asked by some really terrible guys to commission a whole bunch of Underlings. He then went about befouling our land with all this sludge, clogging up all our beautiful Pipes, and now it can barely breathe. He was sort of a huge dick. Once he tuckered himself out with all that I guess he decided to take a nap."

Here this sassy salamander alludes to an alliance that John's denizen seems to have formed with the agents of Derse. Those are the "terrible guys" who commissioned the underlings. The denizens aren't really the bad guys of this game. They're more like ornery yet neutral gods of these planets, who can help or harm depending on the circumstances. Derse agents are the formal bad guys, whose designated role is to obstruct the progress of the heroes, vandalize frog statues, antagonize frog enthusiasts, and dislike frogs in general.

13

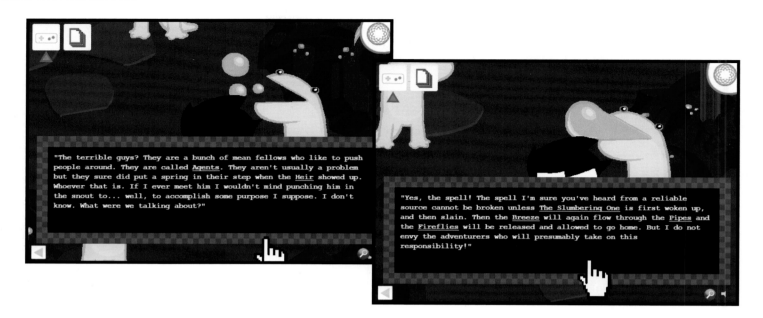

"The terrible guys? They are a bunch of mean fellows who like to push people around. They are called <u>Agents</u>. They aren't usually a problem but they sure did put a spring in their step when the <u>Heir</u> showed up. Whoever that is. If I ever meet him I wouldn't mind punching him in the snout to... well, to accomplish some purpose I suppose. I don't know. What were we talking about?"

"Yes, the spell! The spell I'm sure you've heard from a reliable source cannot be broken unless <u>The Slumbering One</u> is first woken up, and then slain. Then the <u>Breeze</u> will again flow through the <u>Pipes</u> and the <u>Fireflies</u> will be released and allowed to go home. But I do not envy the adventurers who will presumably take on this responsibility!"

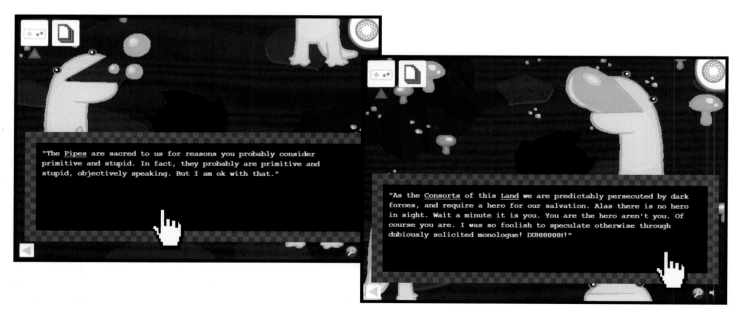

"The <u>Pipes</u> are sacred to us for reasons you probably consider primitive and stupid. In fact, they probably are primitive and stupid, objectively speaking. But I am ok with that."

"As the <u>Consorts</u> of this <u>Land</u> we are predictably persecuted by dark forces, and require a hero for our salvation. Alas there is no hero in sight. Wait a minute it is you. You are the hero aren't you. Of course you are. I was so foolish to speculate otherwise through dubiously solicited monologue! DUHHHHHH!"

Are you thrilled about sifting through layers of worldbuilding as conveyed through the expository bubblings of enthusiastic amphibians? Then this is the page for you. It's a pretty straightforward outline of John's formal quest on this planet. Wake the monster, kill the monster. Clean the pipes, release the Breeze. The Breeze clears the clouds, the fireflies go free. That's the goal. What does it all MEAN? That is for YOU, the reader, to boggle over, forever. It's worth noting that when John actually gets around to doing all this, the meaning of completing this quest and the thing that it actually accomplishes are radically different than what the present stakes of the story are understood to be at this point. There is, throughout this tale, an ever-present tension between the hero's quest as presented at face value and the hero's True Quest—the mysterious journey overlaying and superseding the shallow journey described by consorts, sprites, et al—which the kids must come to grips with.

"Farmin' these goddamn mushrooms. Fuckin' pain in the ass."

This is a pretty good procession of salamanders talking about important stuff, which perhaps makes you think it's all leading up to an encounter with some sort of regal presence in the village. Perhaps a tribal leader. But no, it's just this fool, farming all these goddamn mushrooms. The Mushroom Farmer is just notable enough of a salamander to be known to fandom as the Mushroom Farmer, and would probably be credited that way in the end credits if this were a movie. Same goes for the fellow below wearing the hat. He's known as Crumplehat. Trust me on this.

See? I told you his name was Crumplehat. Maybe try to fucking believe me next time I tell you stuff.

16

"Hey, nice suit, champ. I will buy it from you for 1 Boondollar."

Sell suit for 1 Boondollar? Y/N

NO

"I should have known only a shrewd business man would wear such a garment. I have been chagrinned in ways I never imagined possible."

There are two reasons why John can only say no to this offer. First, I would have had to program an alternate path where he gives up the suit, as well as change the sprite to reflect that, and permanently introduce a fork in the story where John either sells the suit or doesn't. The second reason is it's just a straight-up dogshit offer. Giving someone a boondollar for something is like offering them a penny you found in the toilet.

17

"I am freaking out here. Do you know what this is??? It is a huge log of Cruxite. More than I have ever seen. It is the most precious material in existence. Why if I had access to a means of producing an unlimited supply, I would be the richest salamander in the Land."

"Just kidding. It's completely worthless. Here, you want it? It's free."

Salamanders are pretty good at trolling, actually. So are lots of figures in *Homestuck*. Like John's nanna, his dad, John himself, all his friends, and also all the characters who are literally called trolls. I guess there are a lot of characters who like to troll each other because that is my forte, you could say, as a storyteller? This could also explain why characters who are actual trolls entered the story. They simply manifested as an extension of the story's nature.

"I am a secret wizard. Behold my robes."

Behold Robes? Y/N

YES   NO

Oh Christ, the Secret Wizard. I forgot about him. Yeah, him too. He's also a really big-deal salamander. (Just joking, he's actually a small deal.) He's a simple man. All he really wants you to do is behold his robes. That's it.

You wonder what the hell a secret wizard is. This guy is making you a little nervous. You don't think you'll ask him for your bedsheet back.

John's bedsheet will show up again later as well. It makes quite a trip through the story, actually, and appears in a surprising number of panels. Specifically, every single panel that WV appears in. Surprised? No? Oh. Well, let's just say you are, and move on. (Okay, wait, before we move on I should clarify something. WV's shroud is actually the *dream* version of John's bedsheet. The Secret Wizard just keeps this oily, shitty one forever, and then starts some sort of cult. Okay, NOW we can move on.)

"This thing right here? You have never seen a <u>Parcel Pyxis</u>? Incomprehensible! Ok I'll play your pretend game for a minute. It is a receptacle connected to our network of <u>Pipes</u>. We use them to send stuff to different places. They are fully intertwined with our customs and social practices.

If there is something we want, we chisel it on a <u>Minitablet</u> and drop it in. Who receives it? Hard to say! But if you encounter...

...a <u>Minitablet</u> and you possess what is chiseled on it, it is considered only polite to drop it in the <u>Pyxis</u>!

Similarly, if you encounter a <u>Parcel Pyxis</u> that has a prize in it already, you are obligated to keep the prize for yourself! Consider it to be a gift to you from the <u>Breeze</u>. This is just the way things work...

Whenever one of us is standing near one of these, we feel compelled to give this little speech about it."

So in other words, their entire mail system revolves around putting shit in the pipes, having it sent to completely random places, and whoever gets it gets it. This sounds pretty stupid, but I guess it's part of their religion or something. So you have to respect it.

21

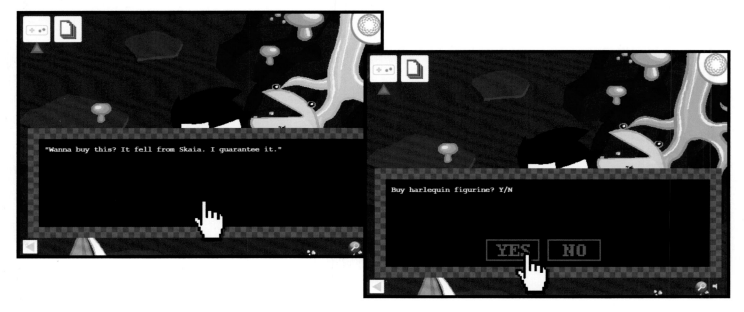

"Wanna buy this? It fell from Skaia. I guarantee it."

Buy harlequin figurine? Y/N

YES   NO

When you're playing through this game, I guess one of the more low-key, gradually unfolding jokes is how it slowly becomes apparent that all the garbage from John's house that he carelessly launched out windows and fumbled over cliffs ended up down here to be scavenged by a bunch of enterprising salamanders who try to pawn all the items back on him. Or just keep them as incredible new accessories.

"Ok that will be 5,000,000 <u>Boondollars</u>. Oh what you don't have that much? Ha ha ha of course not no one does! It's impossible."

"Wanna buy this? It fell from Skaia. I guarantee it."

Buy harlequin figurine? Y/N

YES   NO

Five million boonies really isn't all that much, tbh.

"Fine I'll just be over here sitting pretty with this choice clown thing or whatever it is. And you will be there wallowing in pitiable destitution."

I'm glad we dedicated an entire page to the choice John makes in refusing to buy back his own shitty clown statue from this guy.

Look. This is my ART, people. It needs room to BREATHE.

"GLUB!!! That's my way of saying go over there and check it out. 'GLUB' can basically mean anything I want it to mean. It's really cool having a bullshit language."

Maybe you should try using your TELESCOPE here.

Maybe one of the strangest traits of salamanders is how acerbically self-deprecating they are. Maybe they hate themselves? They'd be far from the only ones in this tale. Also, here's a nice, snap game-design thing I thought of on the fly, when this game was being "developed" over a span of literally about forty-eight hours. Just put a damn bubble with a telescope in it hovering at exactly the place where the player needs to use the scope. That way, they use the scope, and they don't NOT use the scope. So you can see what's in the scope, over there. Incredible.

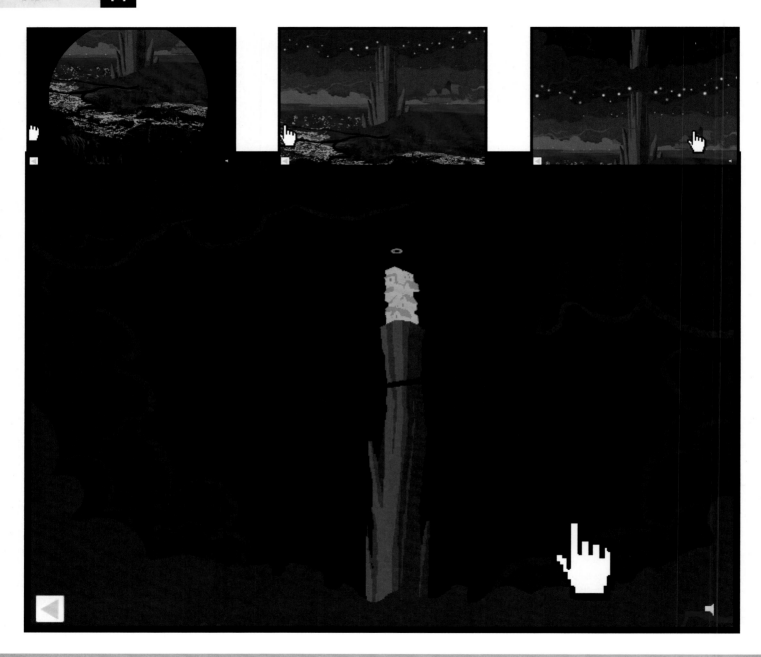

Here's what's in the scope: a view of John's house up on a tall rock-spire plateau, way off in the distance. This view gives you a sense of how far John traveled by going through his gate, the relative proximity of his house, and the fact that the house is inaccessible for a while at least. It also reveals a little more about gate logic and the distances they can send you, and helps you start to imagine hopping all around this world via gates to complete your quest. Oh, and I guess this is kind of a cool shot? Sure.

"nanna, are you there?"

JOHN: i just saw my house from below. what gives? why did the gate take me down here?
NANNASPRITE: All the gates do, John. To ascend, each time you must first descend!
JOHN: huh. alright. so i guess i scramble around down here until... uh, until what?
NANNASPRITE: Until you find the next gate. It is hidden somewhere in the Land.
JOHN: ok, so i get to that gate and go in. then what? where does it take me? uh... further up maybe? but i haven't even built that high yet.
NANNASPRITE: So you see why you had to build in the first place, John? You must have a little faith in your dear old nanna!
JOHN: yeah, well, i do nanna but i'm still not really getting it. does the next gate down here take me back up to the house or something?
JOHN: (please don't say hoo hoo hoo)
NANNASPRITE: HOO. HOO HOO.

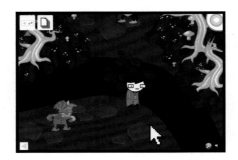

And here Nanna basically explains some stuff I just explained on the previous page. The point, obviously, is to browbeat you with explanations of *Sburb* game logic fundamentals until you start crying. Here's another thing I guess I haven't mentioned yet: walking through this game gives you a pretty good appreciation of the variety of imps, now that there's been another pre-entry prototyping. Remember Rose entering the game just as John goes through his gate? Now we get to observe all these imps in princess gear, or with tentacles, or cat parts, or some permutation of all three.

"nanna, there are more imps than ever down here, and they seem to be getting stronger."

NANNASPRITE: Yes, dear. There are plenty of imps up here too. I had to start giving them cookies because I baked too many. I hope you don't mind!
JOHN: no that's ok. also they look different.
NANNASPRITE: That is because a new prototyping has taken place.
JOHN: huh?
NANNASPRITE: Your pretty young friend has joined you in the Medium!
JOHN: whoah, wait, rose is here? where is she? will i find her down here somewhere???
NANNASPRITE: (oh, settle down, all of you. there are more than enough cookies to go around.)
JOHN: nanna! dammit, will you stop messing around with those stupid imps for a second!
JOHN: nanna? sigh...

> Peer into large opening?

You think you can make out a very faint noise below. Is it... snoring?

And once again Nanna steals my thunder by explaining a thing I just explained. Damn it, Nanna. I feel your pain, John. She's absolutely brutal.

28

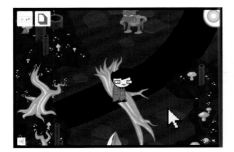

"Not long ago all these <u>Underlings</u> started creeping out of the pipework, and they have been a nuisance to say the least. But just a few moments ago they began spilling from the <u>Land</u> in greater supply, wearing more flamboyantly preposterous outfits than ever. Why you ask? On account of a series of mysterious and arcane wytchkraft-majyspelles. Ha ha just kidding. I have no idea."

More sass from one of these bastards. I feel like I'm getting fucking roasted every time they open their mouths. I'd look up at the sky and ask "Why, God?" but it's not that mysterious. I'm just getting roasted by my past self and his snarkyass writing. If he wasn't trapped back in 2010 or so, I'd ask him why he wrote these damn lizards to be such a bunch of wiseasses. "That's just all I know," he would probably say. Yeah, I feel you man. I mean, don't get me wrong, they're funny as hell. But, why? I don't... Oh, never mind. Now I sound like a person who is insane. I'll try to do better.

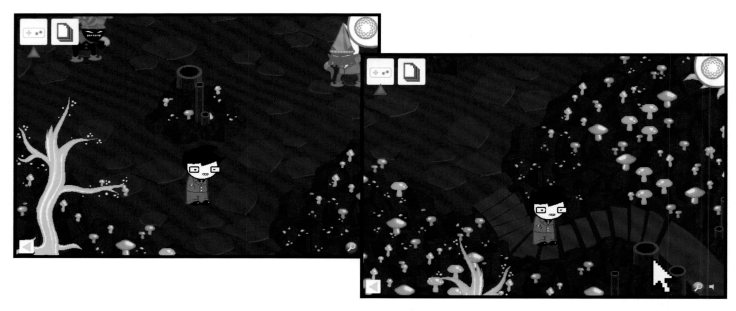

> In a future settled askance of the present...

Oh, here's the end of the game. That game was a single panel of *Homestuck*. And here we are, on...page 30? Thirty pages' worth of annotations just to cover the first panel of Act 4. I think I need to lie down.

Collateral desecration mars the sacred/illicit.

 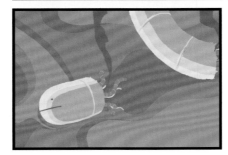 

/Sprawls on floor like useless piece of shit for about seven seconds. Gets back up./ Anyway, back to the Aimless Renegade. Because that's obviously the scene change that makes the most narrative sense. Everyone agrees. Look, more harrowing frog desecration. The confounding question herein: is AR pleased that the frog was beheaded, because as a Dersite he reviles the illegal iconography? Or is he enraged, because the sentry worm has just destroyed evidence of a crime? Ah, the contradictions one faces as an officer of the law.

31

The first thirty pages of this book were used to convey one panel of the story, and now one page has been used to show nine panels. This soothes my wretched soul, very slightly. So, what's actually happening here, you ask? It looks like AR recognizes the dog-head-shaped carving on the pumpkin. It's as if he's seen it before, and knows to fear it. How mysterious.

> In the mystic ruins of an era pre-desecration...

An ancient TIME CAPSULE has blossomed. You find nested in its petals a juice-stained SBURB BETA once belonging to one of your friends.

What will you do?

> Jade: Take the discs.

You captchalogue the SBURB BETA. It uneventfully tucks itself into your sylladex.

You think you're getting kind of bored with this fetch modus. You like to mix it up now and then.

Maybe you'll peruse your selection and try out another one.

> Jade: Switch to Jenga modus.

That's right, in the End of Act 3 animation we saw this big flower blooming, and Dave's copies of the game were inside for some crazy reason, and now we need to check back on what's up with that. All right, nice, I set up the scene for you. Now to add commentary to further elaborate on this fact...

Ummmmmm, iunno. The game is in the flower. And then she takes it. Good work, Jade. And good work, me, on another phenomenal annotation.

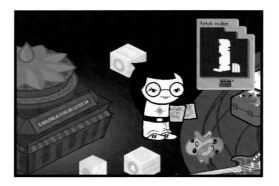

You swap your modus to JENGA, ejecting your sylladex in the process.

Looks like the TIME CAPSULE has reset itself. It is sprouting a new bud. Presumably something else will come out when it blooms again in about 400 years.

Too bad you won't be around to find out what it is!

Your modus grabs the 18 cards needed to set itself up. It divides each card into three CAPTCHALOGUE BLOCKS.

You begin picking up your items. The item is captchalogued, chopped into three blocks, and distributed randomly into the block tower.

You gather up the rest of your items. Might as well try it out!

You go for all the blocks containing your TANGLE BUDDIES.

Careful... careful...

Jade. There's no reason to be doing this at all. Please. Be serious.

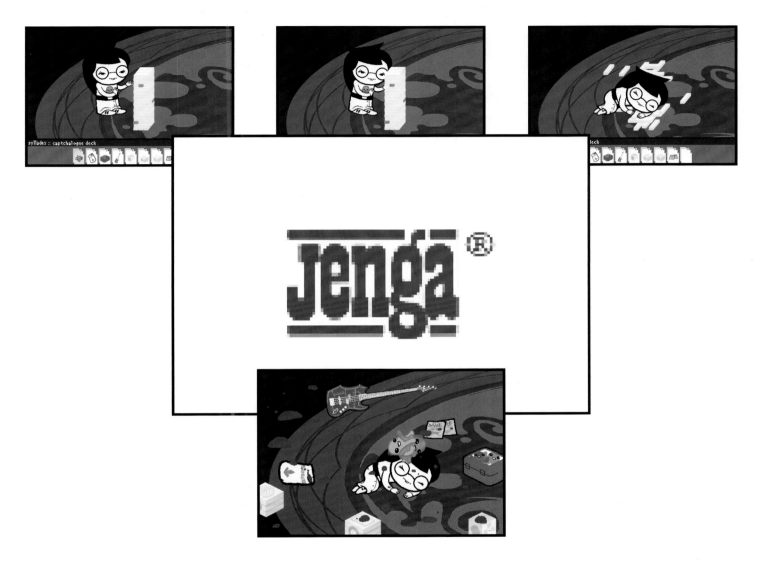

> Jade: Switch to Pictionary modus.

Another example of how, more often than not, I regret that the book doesn't show the short, silly GIF animations more than I regret it not showing the bigger, more complicated ones. Jade wobbling then toppling over onto this Jenga stack was a little gem. Anyway, the moral of the story is: Jade is fucking useless.

Yeah, that one's obviously not going to work.

You switch to PICTIONARY, a choice based on a strong whim from the mysterious ethers of democracy.

> Jade: Try out new Pictionary modus.

Ok, you start by trying to grab your LUNCHTOP.

After you ditch an unwelcome solicitor first, that is.

You've got to concentrate here!

> Jade: Draw Lunchtop.

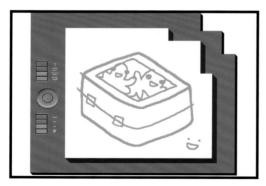

You draw a really nice looking Squiddle lunchbox on the CAPTCHALOGUE SCRIBBLEPAD.

> Jade: Pester John.

The modus recognizes what you were trying to draw and snaps it right up. Nice going!

> Jade: Captchalogue the beta.

The top panel is a nice one to stop and admire. Just think: probably less than a minute ago, Jade grabbed copies of the game out of a big flower and was all set to get some important stuff done. NOW look at her. Pretty embarrassing. No wonder Karkat decided to chime in just now and start grilling her. He saw the whole thing. He probably watches her fuck up a lot.

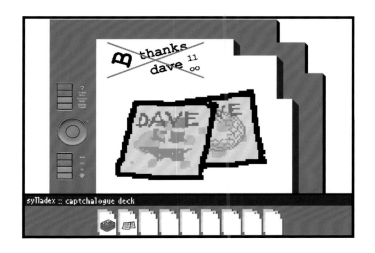

Look at these fabulous beta envelopes you just drew!

Your sylladex thinks they are fabulous too!

YEAH!!!!!!!!!!!!!!

> Jade: Quick! Random scribbling!

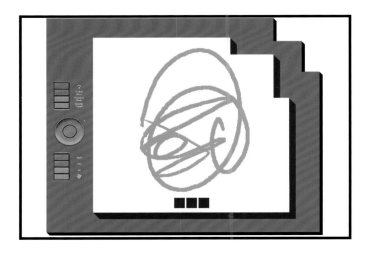

You do a very quick doodle of nothing in particular.

The SCRIBBLEPAD appears to be processing the shapes.

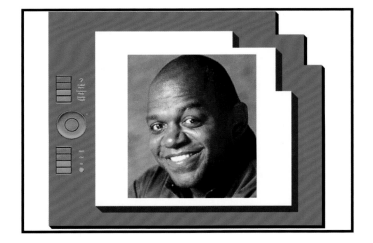

Is that...

Is that Charles Dutton?

Why, yes, that is Charles Dutton. The algorithms for the Scribblepad lean very generously toward Dutton-recognizing patterns, thanks to Jade. The Scribblepad is definitely one of the more fun types of fetch modi. Maybe the most fun. It does quite a bit to show that captchalogue technology really can be ANYTHING, and also does a bit more to hint at the underlying logic of *Homestuck*'s universe. It's a universe not so much of physics as of discrete ideas, and devices that trade in these platonic concepts can understand nothing else. When the user scribbles something, the system will search for not only that which it knows, but that which can ONLY be known, to anyone. There's nothing in between, nothing more subtle. Of course, Dutton knows all this. You can just tell.

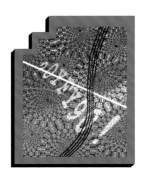

Since you do not actually have a DUTTON PHOTO lying around, the pad captchalogues a DUTTON PHOTO GHOST IMAGE. It is not a tangible item, and can never be used ever. It seems to be more of an imprint on the card itself, like a watermark.

However, the back of the card does seem to contain a viable CAPTCHA CODE for a real DUTTON PHOTO, for whatever it's worth.

Which is very little.

> Jade: Draw a pumpkin.

You sketch a beautiful, succulent PUMPKIN, knowing perfectly well that a PUMPKIN GHOST IMAGE will be captchalogued, because you are quite sure there is not a PUMPKIN in this room, and there surely never will be.

Another interesting feature of the Scribblepad: you can draw things to pick them up if they're lying around nearby (how convenient), but if they're not, the Scribblepad just grabs the item's "ghost image." This is another indication of the fact that the device is dealing in ideas, not material constructs. The ghost image still provides the code for the real item on the back of the card, which means this is an incredibly powerful tool here. You can get a code for any item you can think of, as long as you can draw it pretty accurately, and if you have the code and some grist, you can make it.

You captchalogue a PUMPKIN GHOST IMAGE.

At least you have the CAPTCHA CODE for it on the back in case you ever want to replicate a real one.

oh nooooooo

> Jade: Get the rest of your items.

Another disappearing pumpkin gag. Hard to go wrong with a classic. Except here the gag extends even further, revealing that pumpkins, in addition to being wildly ephemeral objects, also don't even seem to have captchalogue codes. They truly are Gourds of the Void. The vegetable perfectly embodying the cryptic strain of goofy nihilism that pervades everything in this story.

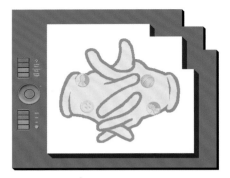

You start by drawing your TANGLE BUDDIES.

But... it looks like it's having trouble understanding the shapes?

Darn! You wanted those!

> Jade: Captchalogue bass on card with Dutton ghost image.

It's not up to you to say what card it goes on! The modus decides! All you get to do is draw.

Anyway you try sketching your ECLECTIC BASS. It's kind of hard to draw accurately.

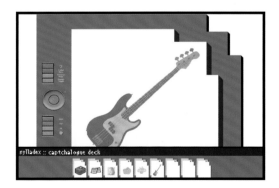

No, that's just a ghost image of an ordinary bass. That's not right.

You try again, focusing on getting all the mechanical details just right.

The pad is kind of a stickler for recognizing a drawing of two cephalopods gleefully entwined, so its best guess is two gloves with pennies and buttons for eyes. Admirable try. I do like how Jade instantly resigns herself to not being able to pick up her cherished toys, rather than just switching to a different modus.

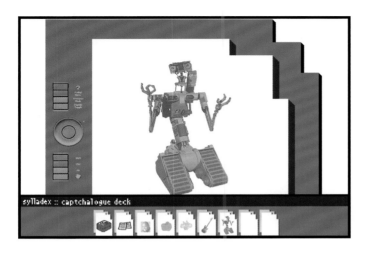

ARGH!

OH NO BUSTED.

The jig is up.

Upon further investigation, it turns out the Scribblepad is actually kind of a piece of shit. Mistaking her carefully drawn ECLECTIC BASS for Johnny Five is too funny not to be an indication that her pad is trolling her. So that's probably what's going on here. There are two things absolutely fundamental to this reality: platonic idealism-based physics and trolling. Everything that ever happens in the story is some combination of those two elemental properties.

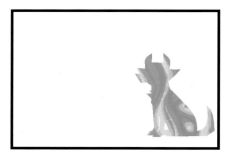

You are returned to your bedroom without the rest of your loot. You doubt you'll have time to go back and get it. You guess you have inadvertently left your own time capsule there for whatever party may find it in the future. Lucky bastards!

> Jade: Install Beta.

You get started installing both discs. Might as well get a jump on it to avoid the sort of future drama that results from poor time management decisions.

> Jade: Pester chums.

Thanks, Bec. This is not only an example of what a good boy and fine guardian you are, but also how you're a great help to us in moving the story along, by getting Jade off her bullshit. We also got to see how all that junk got left there for AR to find, which is very gratifying.

In the meantime you decide to touch base with your pals.

Ugh, no, not those pals. The TROLLSLUM can just sit tight for now.

> John: Pester Rose.

-- ectoBiologist [EB] began pestering tentacleTherapist [TT] --

EB: rose?
EB: are you there?
EB: i went through the gate, nanna said you might be here too.
EB: are you in kind of this spooky glowy place with oily rivers and stuff?
EB: let me know ok.

-- gardenGnostic [GG] began pestering ectoBiologist [EB] --

Looks like Vriska's online. Vriska's always online, isn't she. She, like Karkat, spends an inordinate amount of time monitoring Jade, but for different reasons. (WHISPERS: SHE'S CAUSING HER NARCOLEPSY.) Gamzee's online too, but honestly, who gives a fuck at all about that.

GG: john hi!!!!!
EB: hi jade!
EB: guess where i am.
GG: are you on the ground below the clouds yet?
EB: yeah!
EB: wait how did you know that's where the gate goes...
EB: did you talk to rose? can she still see me while im down here?
EB: she won't answer.
GG: no i havent talked to her yet but id like to soon
GG: ive got a lot of catching up to do with all of you!
GG: sorry ive been so scarce ive just been so busy running around like crazy and looking after my dog and stuff all day!!!!
GG: i think he just locked me in my room actually :\
EB: oh man.
EB: he sounds like such a handful.
GG: yeah
EB: but it's ok, i think he is mostly just looking after you.
EB: like a guardian angel or something.
EB: if i were you i would take him out behind the woodshed and give him a big hug.
GG: :D
GG: hey john can you hold on i have to talk to dave and start playing this game with him
EB: oh? what game?
GG: sburb!!!! duh what else!
EB: what, i thought you didn't even know what sburb was!
GG: oh jeez i was asleep when i said that silly!
GG: of course i know what it is
EB: oh ok.
EB: where did you even get it?
GG: from the ruins
GG: its daves copy
EB: wow.
EB: the thing you just said doesn't even make the slightest bit of sense.
GG: i know right! hehehe
GG: oh!!!!
GG: that reminds me since im setting the game up with dave to be his server you are going to need to do the same thing for me
EB: oh really?
EB: this is news to me.
GG: can you see from where youre standing the place your dads car would have fallen?
EB: oh yeah, i think so. it'll be kind of a long walk though, this place is huge.
GG: you should go there and get your copy of the server and set up with me.....

John and Dave have drastically differing opinions on what they'd like to do to Bec behind the woodshed. Rose is the only one who hasn't weighed in yet. You don't even want to KNOW what she would do to him behind the woodshed. (She would read him her wizard fic. Why, what did YOU think I was implying here?)

```
GG: oh and also get your package!!!!!! :)
EB: okay.
EB: wait, how did you know my dad's car fell down here?
GG: johhhhn will you stop trying to trap me!!!
GG: you TOLD me the car fell remember?
GG: jeeeez
EB: jeeeeeeeeeez!
GG: JEEEEEEEEEEEEEEEEEZ!!!!!
EB: ok fine well color me suspicious anyway.
EB: miss knowitall mcpsychicpants.
GG: john im not any more psychic than you though
EB: ok sure i am convinced.
EB: you have convinced me.
EB: (PSYCHIC PSYCHIC PSYCHIC)
EB: also i told you the package was in the car but i never mentioned that the game was
there too.
EB: so kind of totally busted i guess.
EB: GIVE ME A P
EB: GIVE ME AN S
GG: hahahaha oops ok!
GG: i mean i know lots of things but im really serious its no more information than what
you have access to
GG: but you dont know it yet
GG: anyway we can talk more about it soon.....
GG: i wont have to be so coy with you anymore because im pretty sure most of the stuff
that was supposed to happen has already happened
GG: i couldnt tell you about it because it would have messed it up!
EB: ok, that is fair.
GG: just give me a few minutes while i set up this game!
GG: and say hi to the salamanders for me
GG: <3
```

oh shiiiiit

> Dave: Pester Rose.

Jade is right, she isn't psychic. But that makes her pretty much the only psychic in the story who isn't technically psychic. The rest of the psychics literally are all technically psychic. There are like fifteen of them. At least.

-- **turntechGodhead** [TG] began pestering **tentacleTherapist** [TT] --

TG: hey
TG: will you open your laptop already
TG: see
TG: this is why you need a phone or something
TG: that alerts you to important messages
TG: instead of leaving them trapped
TG: under three inches of fucking yarn
TG: laptops dont need cozies
TG: nothing needs cozies
TG: cozy is a goddamn adjective
TG: maybe ill crochet myself an iphone snuggly
TG: what is this place anyway
TG: what are you doing
TG: i can see your whole damn house here if you want to get filled in or something im sort of the guy with the big picture here
TG: dont make me bop you on the head with a wizard
TG: ill do it
TG: ok no i wont
TG: yet
TG: i guess ill bone up on the faq for a while
TG: so i dont do anything stupid and deploy like 10 crux flangers and fuck up the whole game
TG: oh my god
TG: so many words
TG: do you think like the pulitzer committee is secretly scouring the dregs of the gamefaq archives or something
TG: damn
TG: i cant read this shit im sorry

-- **gardenGnostic** [GG] began pestering **turntechGodhead** [TG] --

GG: yo yooooooo!!!!!!!
TG: whoa ok hey
GG: so youre finally playing the game with rose?
TG: yeah
TG: but she wont answer me

Dave's aesthetic is long conversations with himself. You should know this by now. It never stops being true.

GG: shes probably just exploring im sure she will come around soon....
GG: but its great that you got her out of there in time!!!
TG: pretty much you have no idea how much i fuckin own at this game
TG: i bested no less than three flaming tornados and broke a huge wizard
GG: so how does it feel to be a BIG TIME HERO
GG: mister braveybrave mcheropants
TG: it feels like
TG: i am in sports
TG: all alone
TG: and i am the star
TG: its me
TG: and then the big man comes
GG: hehehe
GG: but it turns out to be CRAZY what kind of basket ball this man plays!
GG: ummmm......
GG: the HOOP IS ON FIRE...
GG: ok i forget how it goes
TG: no you got it
TG: we're good
TG: reference secured
GG: yes!!!!!!
GG: so now it is my turn to be the star!
GG: i will be your hero
GG: its me
TG: wait what
GG: i installed the game!
GG: im connecting to you as the server player
TG: oh man
TG: this is ridiculous
TG: i just set this shit up with rose and now i got to do like
TG: some double duty thing
TG: i mean i own at the game and all but cant i just relax for half a second
GG: dont worry!
GG: you can keep playing with rose while i just set up a few things
GG: i figured id get a good head start to avoid all the drama you guys are always getting into
GG: such a bunch of drama queens!!!
TG: what
TG: look i was getting my ass handed to me by my bro on the roof for like an hour and a half

It's great conversations like these that stoked the passions of Dave x Jade shippers. And maybe, in many ways, they had a point. The only problem with the pairing was its overwhelming heterosexuality attribute. As such, it was not to be.

TG: i got served like a dude on butler island
GG: (DRAMA DRAMA DRAMA)
TG: wait does this mean theres a big meteor coming soon
GG: yes!
TG: when you activate the thing will it start the countdown and summon the meteor
GG: itll come when it comes regardless of what we do
GG: the timer really just lets you know when its coming
TG: are you totally sure about all this
GG: yes look here it is!
GG: http://bit.ly/d7kXrQ

TG: ok yes that image is definitely conclusive proof of something and is 100% understandable by anyone who looks at it
TG: how big is this thing
GG: it is REALLY REALLY big
TG: like the size of rhode island or texas or what
TG: i need some context to know how much crap i should be shitting into my pants
GG: ok i dont actually know :(
TG: well as if like one the size of a bus wouldnt kill me anyway
GG: hehe yeah....
TG: wait hold on rose is finally opening her stupid laptop
TG: so do your thing i guess
TG: have fun
GG: thanks i will! <3

> John: Answer troll.

Getting "served like a dude on butler island" is a great line. I mean, they're all great lines. What do you want from me? I can use this margin any way I want, including to just say, "Oh, that thing I did was great. Ha ha, that one too. Ooh, there's another good one." Would it really be so terrible if that's all I did down here?

P.S. Butler Island turns out to be real later. Jake lives on it.

carcinoGeneticist [CG] began trolling ectoBiologist [EB] --

CG: HEY JOHN.
CG: CALM THE HELL DOWN.
EB: aaaaaauuuuuuuuuuuuuuuuuuuugggghhhhhhhh!!!!!!!
EB: how did you find me?????
CG: FIND YOU?
CG: WHAT DO YOU MEAN.
EB: i changed my chum handle to ditch you guys.
EB: how did you find me?
CG: OH.
CG: HA HA!
CG: HA HA HA HA HA HA HA!
CG: THIS IS THE LITTLE WORD HUMANS SAY REPEATEDLY WHEN SOMETHING TICKLES THEIR ABSURDITY
PALATE, RIGHT?
EB: uh...
EB: lame.
CG: WE NEVER LOST YOU.
CG: YOUR RUSE DIDN'T FOOL US.
CG: IT JUST SO HAPPENS WE DIDN'T PARTICULARLY GIVE A SHIT ABOUT TALKING TO YOU IN THAT
TIMEFRAME.
EB: what, the last few months?
CG: WE HAVE THE ENTIRE CONTINUUM OF YOUR EXISTENCE TO CHOOSE FROM WHEN CONTACTING YOU.
CG: THE PERIOD WAS UNREMARKABLE.
CG: SORT OF LIKE YOUR WHOLE LIFE. BUT I GUESS I MEAN IT WAS ESPECIALLY UNREMARKABLE.
CG: THIS HAS BEEN EXPLAINED TO YOU SO OFTEN IT WOULD MAKE ME SICK TO MY HUMAN STOMACH IF I
HAD ONE OF YOUR HUMAN STOMACHS.
EB: ok, this time i'll believe you that you aren't human.
EB: because the skepticism center of my brain is starting to wear kind of thin i guess.
EB: but you're still a major asshole and i don't actually want to talk to you, so bye.
CG: WAIT.
CG: BUT I'M NOT HERE TO TROLL YOU THIS TIME.
CG: WE'RE FRIENDS OK?
EB: hahahahahaha!
EB: oh man, look at this outburst of little human words i'm saying!
EB: from my human mouth!
CG: FINE YOU CAN THINK I'M A FUCKING DOUCHE AND MAYBE I AM BUT HERE'S THE FACT, IDIOT.
CG: I'VE ALREADY HAD LOTS OF CONVERSATIONS WITH YOU.
CG: IN THE FUTURE. I MEAN YOUR FUTURE.

I would never claim the absolute ability to recall *Homestuck*'s entire text word for word, but I feel quite confident this is the one and only time the troll biology term "absurdity palate" is ever used by a troll, or by anyone else, for that matter. Which leads one to wonder whether it really is a troll biology term, or if it's just one of the many things made up by these guys to mess with humans and sound more alien to them? A number of the phrases and concepts trolls use seem to invite the reader to wonder this. In fact, you could argue that almost every worldbuilding feature of trolls and their culture invites the reader to wonder the same thing about the author.

CG: I'VE KIND OF BEEN WORKING BACKWARDS HERE FOR A WHILE.
CG: AND IT'S A LITTLE FRUSTRATING.
CG: EVERY TIME I GO FURTHER BACK YOU KNOW LESS AND LESS, AND YOU DON'T REMEMBER ANYTHING I SAID BECAUSE IT HASN'T HAPPENED YET.
CG: AND I HAVE TO REPEAT MYSELF A LOT.
CG: AND I'M GETTING PRETTY FUCKING SICK OF IT.
EB: that's the dumbest thing i've ever heard.
CG: WELL IT'S NOT LIKE I MAPPED OUT THIS TROLLING ONSLAUGHT VERY WELL IN ADVANCE.
CG: I MEAN, WHEN YOU TROLL SOMEONE YOU JUST SORT OF DO IT. YOU DON'T START DRAWING FLOWCHARTS AND DIAGRAMS AND STUFF.
EB: wait...
EB: you have something to do with this game, don't you?
EB: i should have known.
CG: OH GOD.
CG: NOT AGAIN.
CG: NO, FUCK NO, I AM JUST NOT GOING TO EXPLAIN THIS TO YOU AGAIN.
CG: YOU'LL GET PLENTY OF DIRT ON ALL THIS FROM ME IN FUTURE CONVERSATIONS.
CG: TEDIOUS CONVERSATIONS.
CG: ONES I'VE ALREADY HAD WITH YOU.
CG: WHERE YOUR DEMEANOR WILL GRADUALLY BECOME INEXPLICABLY AND REVOLTINGLY FRIENDLY TOWARDS US.
CG: AND SO I GUESS IT JUST WAS KIND OF INFECTIOUS AND NOW WE'RE ALL BUDDIES I THINK.
CG: IT'S REALLY WEIRD.
CG: THIS HUMAN EMOTION YOU CALL FRIENDSHIP.
EB: friendship isn't an emotion fucknuts.
CG: SEE, THAT IS WHAT I'M TALKING ABOUT.
CG: YOU'RE MUCH MORE TOLERABLE A GUY THAN I THOUGHT AT FIRST, OK JOHN?
EB: why are you kissing my ass?
EB: what do you want? why don't you just tell me what's going on.
EB: are you in the medium?
CG: OK, FINE. YES WE ARE.
EB: like, here in this land, with the clouds and oil and stuff?
CG: MORE OF THIS NARCISSISM.
CG: YOU ALWAYS THINK EVERYTHING REVOLVES AROUND YOU.
CG: WE HAVE NOTHING TO DO WITH YOUR DUMB LITTLE WINDY PLANET OR YOUR PETTY LITTLE QUESTS.
CG: OR FOR THAT MATTER YOUR ENTIRE GAME SESSION.
CG: YOU AREN'T THE ONLY ONES PLAYING THE GAME.
CG: EVERY GROUP OF PLAYERS GETS THEIR OWN DISTINCT, BLANK SLATE SESSION.
CG: AS WILL BE EXPLAINED TO YOU MANY TIMES.

Here's where Karkat first cops to the fact that he stupidly railroaded himself into having a backwards conversation with John. It's pretty challenging to write a conversation like this over an extended series of exchanges, where one person has full knowledge of future conversations that haven't even been written yet. But that didn't stop me from just diving right into this idea like a fool, just like our boy here, Karkat Vantas himself. It's tough doing something like this in an improvisational manner without really charting it out first, because by the nature of the task you just have no idea at this point how these future conversations went. You just know, as Karkat alludes to, that they start becoming friendlier, which is an outcome likely precipitated by the fact that Karkat tells John that's what's going to happen, and therefore starts saying friendlier things himself. This is how everything works in the story from now on. Things turning out to be the cause of themselves, especially when it comes to the content of stupid conversations. See, this is why you needed a good time-travel primer during the Midnight Crew Intermission.

```
EB: so why don't you just explain it again so i know...
EB: so i don't ask so much in the future???
CG: NO.
CG: FUCK THIS SHIT, JUST NO.
CG: I'M ENDING THIS CONVERSATION BECAUSE I'VE SAID IT ALL TOO MANY TIMES.
CG: AND BECAUSE YOU CAN'T UNDERSTAND.
CG: BECAUSE YOU ARE DUMB.
EB: wow, yeah you're totally not trolling me, bro!
EB: i see now we are bffs forever.
CG: THE FACT THAT YOU ARE DUMB
CG: IS AN IMMUTABLE FACT I AM STATING FOR THE RECORD.
CG: IT DOES NOT MEAN ANIMOSITY IS WHAT IS TAKING PLACE HERE.
EB: oh, ok.
EB: so what do you want.
CG: I NEED YOU TO TELL YOUR FRIEND JADE TO TALK TO US.
CG: SHE WON'T ANSWER OUR MESSAGES IN THIS TIMEFRAME.
CG: IT'S IMPORTANT.
EB: yeah, i don't blame her for not answering.
EB: she pretty much can't stand you guys.
EB: because of all the trolling you did before.
EB: remember?
CG: OK, OUR BAD ON THAT.
CG: JUST TELL HER WE'RE SORRY.
CG: AND TO GET HER GROSS AND TOTALLY UNATTRACTIVE HUMAN BUTT OFF HER UGLY HUMAN HIGH HORSE
AND ANSWER MY MESSAGES.
EB: maybe.
EB: we'll see.
EB: i'm still not really sold on this friendship thing yet.
EB: but i've got to go now and get on with my petty little quests.
EB: so talk to you in the future i guess.
EB: jerkface.
```

> John: Search for your father's car.

/Pulls up to the Jadekat Fuel Station, beeps horn twice for fast & friendly Full Service./ :)

It's going to be a hike.

There's something up ahead through the forest.

> WV: Settle this dispute in a rational, diplomatic manner.

You settle the dispute in the only way you can presently imagine how to settle a dispute. With cans of lukewarm sugary liquid and centuries-old rations.

If only you had access to some means of heating things up.

But it matters not. You warm yourselves in the glow of this human emotion called friendship.

Ah-ha! That little tiny bit of white, with a blue glow just above the rock face on the right. That's some retcon nonsense. Just keeping you on your toes, folks. Oh, and below we have another joke about how Tab is a sugary beverage. This is, without a doubt, the absolute worst running joke in *Homestuck*.

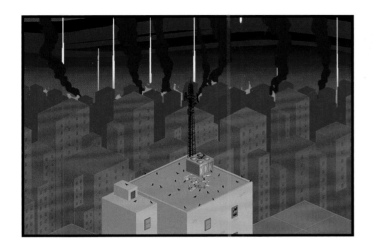

> Jade: Deploy alchemiter.

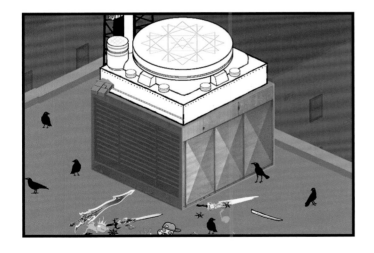

It's almost as if this broken AIR CONDITIONING UNIT was scaled to be a perfect fit for the ALCHEMITER all along.

WEIRD!

> Jade: Deploy cruxtruder in Dave's room.

This here is a pretty dry joke about the fact that I intended to put the alchemiter on top of the AC unit all along. So when I was designing Dave's roof, I made sure to scale the AC block so that the device would fit perfectly on it when the time came. It's not like...a *great* place for the alchemiter? But it sure does fit, I'll give it that.

TG: do you think like the pulitzer committee is secretly scouring the dregs of the gamefaq archives or something
TG: damn
TG: i cant read this shit im sorry
TT: Hold please.
TG: hold what
TG: i see you at your computer typing
TG: what are you doing
TG: dang
TG: hold on
TG: no seriously stop talking to me for a second it looks like jade is dropping the doomsday tube thingy in my room
TG: brb gotta make sure she doesnt break all my shit
TG: hey wait

GG: these darn birds are in the way!
GG: what are they doing in your apartment anyway!!!
GG: also they are adorable
TG: i always keep birds in here its sort of my thing
GG: ohhhhhhh
GG: kind of like all those silly naked puppets are your bros thing?
TG: no no thats irony this is like
TG: sincere honest to god psychosis
TG: im training to be a lame gothy supervillain

I guess if we work REALLY hard at it, we could construe Dave's reference to becoming a lame, gothy supervillain as foreshadowing Davepeta? On second thought, it would probably be an absolutely horrible idea to even consider mentioning Davepeta this early, so forget I said anything.

```
GG: also i think i cant put it down because of the wires on the floor.....
TG: ok
TG: well maybe you should take the opportunity to put it somewhere that isnt stone cold
retarded
GG: i wish i played more games
GG: this is hard!!!!
TG: no its not
GG: :P
```

> Jade: Move Dave's bed to the roof.

```
TT: Jade is connected with you?
TT: Where did she get the discs?
TG: i dont know how does she do any of the loopy batshit nonsense she does
TG: maybe she pulled them out of the volcano over there on bloodmonkey mountain
TT: Wait.
TT: So you mean to tell me she was able to connect with you in a timely fashion, without
waiting until you were on the brink of annihilation?
TG: we went over this
TG: i was a little bogged down
TG: in the epic swaddle of legendary puppet taint
TT: I've done nothing but wait for boys to play this game with me all day.
TT: First John lollygagging with the client, and then you with the server, downright
filibustering my existence with unending fraternal melee.
TT: And yet a girl, one who didn't even own the game, was able to connect with you minutes
after you connected with me.
```

Welp, he did it. The madman did it. He said "retarded." That's not so hot to say in media these days. Maybe it never was? Probably not. But at some point on the cultural continuum between our present year and, let's say, sometime in the '90s, it gradually drifted from being sort of an edgybad thing for a shitty teen to say, to something legitimately unacceptable even for fake teens to say in a thing that entertains people. Anyway, the point is, let's throw this very bad boy under the bus where he belongs, and leave me sitting spotless as always, upon my Perch of Exoneration. (Also, a few demerits to Jade for failing to call him out. Wow, what a bitch!)

```
TG: whoa wait
TG: what the hell is she doing
TG: shes taking my bed what the hell
TT: And there she goes.
TT: She HAS the karma.
```

> Jade: Deploy the cruxtruder in its place.

```
TG: so seriously what were you doing just now
TT: I was talking to someone.
TG: who
TT: You remember the trolls?
TG: yeah
TT: One of them messaged me, so I indulged him/her/it for a moment.
TG: oh i see you opted to chat up one of those dbags instead of talk to the guy who saved you
from a swirling shitstorm of angry flaming wizards
TG: i was worried your priorities might have been out of whack but no i was dead wrong
TT: I also took a moment to check on John.
TG: how is he
TT: I can't see him anymore. Just his empty house.
TT: But I did talk to him briefly.
TG: i should probably text him soon
TG: see whats up
TG: because
TG: i love him
TT: I know.
TG: so this place youre at now
TG: its the same place hes at right
TT: It's hard to say for certain.
TT: But I think I like it here.
```

> Jade: Replace television with totem lathe.

Rose. Come ON. It's "him/her/they." It is SO hard haggling with fake teens trapped in 2009 about problematic language in media. This is going to be the death of me. Thank god I teach them a lesson later in the story, by killing them all repeatedly.

> Jade: Organize Dave's puppets.

This whole place is a disorganized mess. It kind of reminds you of your room but full of weird and ironic stuff instead of cute and great stuff. Your stuff is so much better.

You're pretty sure these are all Dave's BRO'S puppets. You better not mess with them. Frankly his brother makes you a little nervous.

> Jade: Tidy up Strider's apartment a little.

I wonder what it is about Dave's bro that makes Jade nervous? If I had to make a guess, I suppose it would be all the savage beatings he deals to his thirteen-year-old brother on a daily basis. It could also be something else though, I'm not sure.

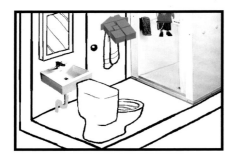
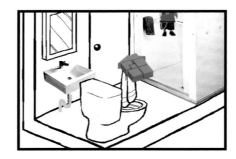
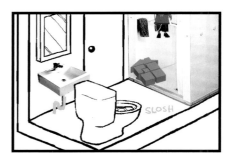

What the apartment needs is a woman's touch. You grab a TOWEL you found lying around and dampen it with water from the toilet. This is how ordinary people clean ordinary houses, right?

Oops, you dropped it.

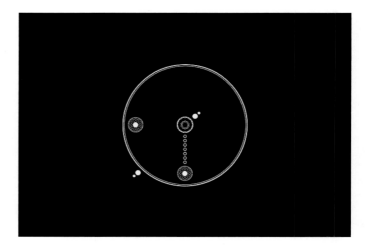

GG: oh fuck!!!!!!

> [S] ==>

Girls in *Homestuck* have problems with toilets, and with bathroom fixtures in general. They just can't seem to help themselves.

LAND OF LIGHT AND RAIN

Here's the second new land animation in the Act 4 series of scenery porn, introducing us to LOLAR. In this animation those clouds whip by so fast and flicker so wildly that they're a little hard to appreciate. They're nicely slowed down here, though. FROZEN IN TIME, you could even say. I'm not going to sit here and brag, like some big piece of shit. But I will say I've never seen anyone slander me for my cloud-drawing abilities.

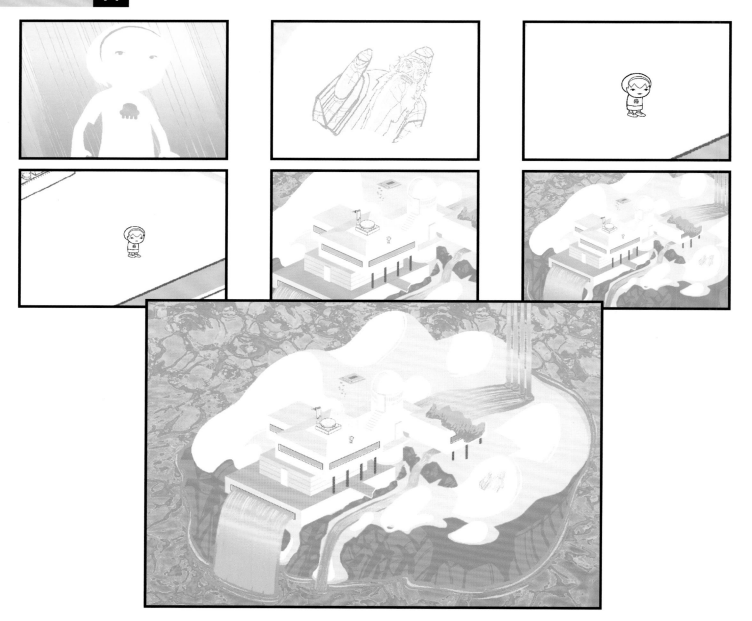

> AR: Cautiously drink TAB.

A note re: the Land of Light and Rain. Light is Rose's actual aspect, and the only one of the kids' aspects that appears in their planet names, oddly enough. And rain? Well you see, that's water. Water continues the pattern of each kid's planet involving a natural element of sorts (wind, water, fire, ice). This theme is extended in a much more literal way with the Alpha Kids (the nobles), who have noble gases (a.k.a. elements) as the theme for their planets. Huh!!!!!!!! Never stop thinking about this story. I won't allow it.

Blech. Too warm. Need to find something
to chill this down with.

Something to heat up your delicious
GRAVY would be nice too.

> AR: Retrieve mysterious artifacts from
ruins.

You excuse yourself for a moment and retrieve a few
of your personal belongings. These should really
impress your visitors.

That musty old toy on the floor ought to make a nice
peace offering for the feisty tall one too. You
are quite certain that ladies like squishy useless
things like that.

> WV: Introduce new friends to John.

Have you ever tried washing down lukewarm gravy with lukewarm Tab while attempting to court a tall, beautiful woman? Then you know the Aimless Renegade's
troubles, my friend.

The yellow bandaged fellow seems to have slogged off
somewhere. But the tall mail carrier with the lovely
white complexion would probably get a kick out of
your big computer with the weird boy on it.

You show her inside.

The hole blown into the the station by the caution
guy's rocket leads into the third room, which had
been locked.

Unsurprisingly there is another sort of gizmo in
here and you have no idea what it does.

The station is very low on power so you don't think
you'll be able to find out.

All in one frame here we have a fairly esoteric setup for a series of payoffs that all take place in the noted *Homestuck* animation known as **[S] Cascade.** This thing
needs power. How does it get power? Uranium! Where's some uranium? In WV's belly! What's this thing do? It's a transporter! Who shows up here to use it later,
taking the uranium from WV's belly and using it to power the thing? It's Jack! Where does it transport to? To either the session this station came from (the kids'
session), or the session that created the current universe (the trolls' session), depending on which way that frog dealie is pointing! The culminating series of events
almost seem predictable in hindsight. It's all so simple, really. Why is anyone ever confused by this story? I'll never know.

You unlock the third room from the inside, and go to the computer room.
There he is! The funny boy you were talking about. His name is John.
You encourage your alabaster friend to say hi to him using the human keypad communication system.

But instead she takes note of your nice chalk drawings and pays you a compliment.

You are somewhat mystified by the fact that she is be more impressed
by your silly drawings than your amazing technology.

Maybe simple things are the key to the heart of a lady. You do not know because you do not know anything
about ladies really. They are a riddle draped in a mystery wrapped in post-apocalyptic shroudwear.

WV: Never mind John. Use that computer to go to your favorite website, www dot reddit dot com slash red pill, to learn more about the mysteries of women.

You decide to give her the chalk. She is grateful for the colorful present and thinks it looks like fun.

Suddenly a powerful aroma hits your nonexistent nostrils.
Someone is cooking something delicious. It demands investigation.

WV: Go investigate the freshly baked pie cooling on the windowsill of the frog temple.

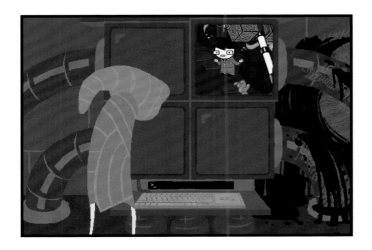

You stop and examine the kind mayor's device. It is quite similar to the one in your station, before the unfortunate accident. The one with the familiar looking girl on it. Perhaps this one is best left alone.

Still, there is something familiar about the boy on this monitor too.

> I am told your name is John. Is that correct?

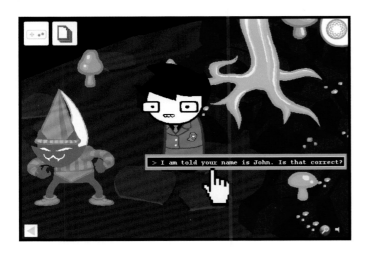

Yep. That's right.

> It's nice to meet you, John.

John isn't directly cognizant of your greeting, but I'm sure he would feel likewise.

> Ok, John. Let's explore this place!

Here we retroactively learn that it was PM issuing the commands all along during the game at the start of this act. We should have guessed, since her diction is so much better than WV's keymashing. The first walkaround game in John's house established the precedent that—since the reader of the story is now directly controlling John and therefore can't be issuing commands in the usual sense—the commands inside the game are being issued by an in-story character known as an exile, from a terminal appropriate for that purpose.

65

001419-001420

Ok, have at it! If you're at a loss, click the controller button up there.

This may or may not mean anything to you depending on your current perspective.

> This is great! Something is in there. Take a look.

You got a MINITABLET!

> There is nothing inside. Should we put something in?

Now, unlike while playing the game, we get to read the narrator's below-panel responses to the commands PM is typing, since they're now being presented through the typical story format of the site. This is some wild stuff, guys. Revisiting a game we just played in the form of a series of static panels is really, really... Well, whatever the hell it is, it would probably be even more so if we hadn't already experienced the game as a series of static panels which had to be presented that way for the sake of printing this book. Hmm...

> There is nothing inside. Should we put something in?

You drop in one of your precious SHOES. You hate to see it go, but you
have to follow the custom and give it what the tablet asks for.

> This one's empty. Perhaps a delivery is in order?

Same with this one you guess. At least this HAT
didn't technically belong to your DAD. You made
it yourself.

> Introduce yourself to the local amphibious
fauna.

Now PM is controlling John to intentionally make him do certain things that the player wouldn't necessarily have made him do, thereby forcing those previously optional
actions to become etched in canon and ensuring they happen for the sake of future story events which depend on them happening.

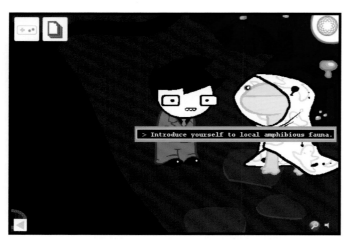

"I am a secret wizard. Behold my robes."

Behold robes?

Y/N

> Y

You wonder what the hell a secret wizard is. You don't think you'll ask him for your bedsheet back.

> Hooray! This one contains a prize!

You got an UNCARVED MINITABLET!

> Open it! Open it!!!

I distinctly remember enjoying this series of updates because they were so easy to do. All I had to do was play a game I'd already made and take a few screenshots of certain moments. Boom, instant panels. When people wonder how this site ballooned to 10,000 pages, that's when I hastily sweep panels like these under the rug and go, "Oh, you know...no reason, really. Hey, look over there."

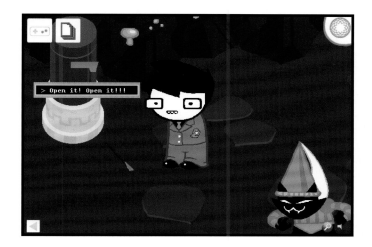

You got a CHISEL.

> How exciting! A parcel for you. Retrieve it!

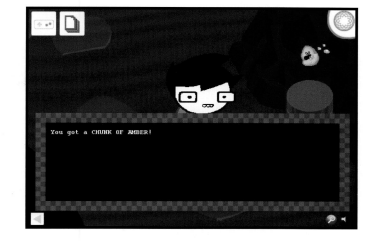

You got a CHUNK OF...

Why am I repeating myself?

> Converse.

He has renamed himself Crumplehat. He has dishonored his ancestors
beyond comprehension with this frivolous accessory.

> A good place to keep lookout?

"Why am I repeating myself?" Hey, man. You asked for this. You made the story this way and included these choices for some reason. Don't look at me. I'm just the guy talking some shit in the gutter of these books like, seven years later.

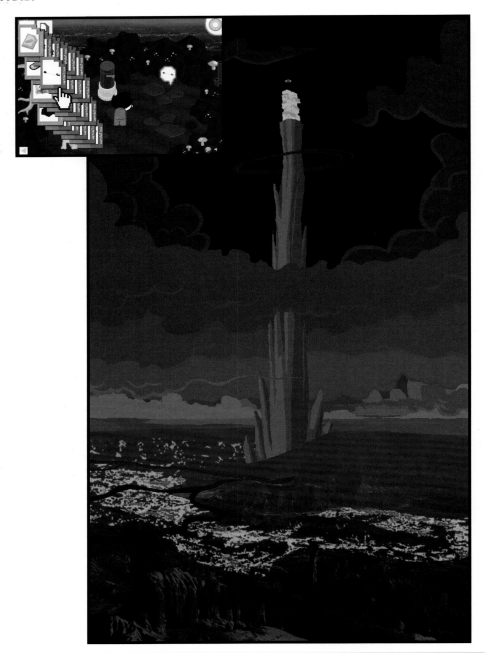

JOHN: nanna, are you there?
NANNASPRITE: Yes!
JOHN: i just saw my house from below. what gives? why did the gate take me down here?
NANNASPRITE: All the gates do, John. To ascend, each time you must first descend!
JOHN: huh. alright. so i guess i scramble around down here until... uh, until what?
NANNASPRITE: Until you find the next gate. It is hidden somewhere in the Land.
JOHN: ok, so i get to that gate and go in. then what? where does it take me? uh... further up maybe? but i haven't even built that high yet.
NANNASPRITE: So you see why you had to build in the first place, John? You must have a little faith in your dear old nanna!
JOHN: yeah, well, i do nanna but i'm still not really getting it. does the next gate down here take me back up to the house or something?
JOHN: (please don't say hoo hoo hoo)
NANNASPRITE: HOO. HOO. HOO.

This page is a pretty cool way to handle this particular layout. I guess that's all I'll say here. No wait, I'll say something else. This page is a fucking waste of time because we already read this during the game. All right, moving on.

> Seer.

> Seer, can you hear me?

Okay, this is a cool thing. We just confirmed the pattern that these commands, when specifically presented like this, are the product of an exile typing at a station terminal. So now we've got this super fancy font talking to the "Seer." The correct logical leap for the reader is to wonder who this exile is. My guess? Personally? I don't want to give anything away. But I suspect it's someone fancy.

71

Apparently she can.

Though usually she goes by Rose.

> Have a look around, Rose.

> You have much to discover.

Seers get talked to by queens. So do Light players, I guess. Rose is both. She's really the perfect queenbait. Oh damn, I did it, didn't I. I gave it away. All right, you got me. This fancy broad talking to Rose is the White Queen. The queen is guiding her upon entry, in a sort of motherly way. It's quite nice.

> John: Go over the river and through the woods.

> Jade: Drop the toilet in Dave's room.

Pretty cool teal silhouette of John there. It's probably one of the first forays into what would later be termed the "hero mode" art style? By this point it got to be a little monotonous, as well as time consuming, to always stay on model and adhere to the established art style. So I would start messing around and pushing the stylistic boundaries a little, especially where I felt like it could save time and create a striking look. Often I played with silhouettes, which had little or no linework to waste time on. I could just quickly block in a few key shapes with solid colors, and compensate for the over-simplicity by using some snappy color choices, like those bright orange lighting effects. Throw in a few simple details—like a tie, gloves, and a few basic tree shapes back there—and you've got yourself a panel. This probably took me...ten or fifteen minutes? Finding ways to save time with a "performance story" like this is everything.

73

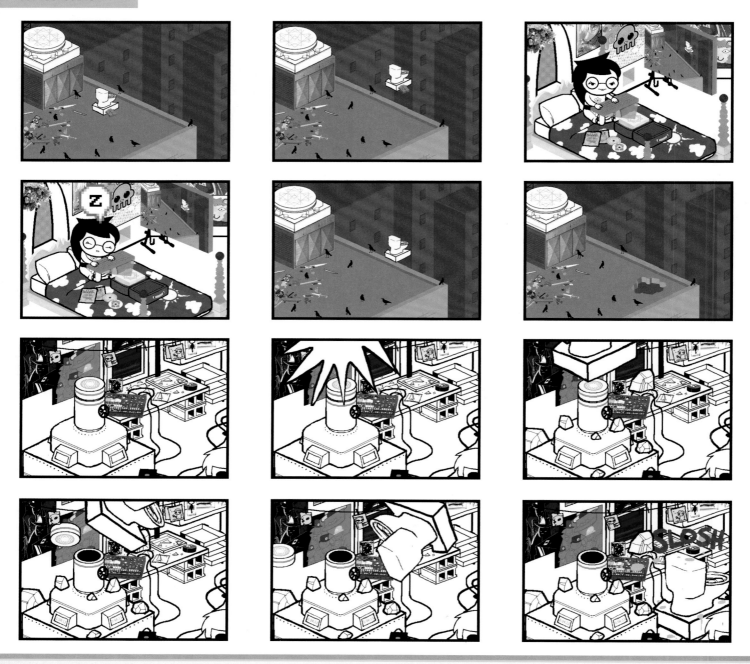

Through the first four acts Jade seems to accomplish more actions of relevance by either falling asleep, or being asleep, than she ever does when she's awake and trying to be productive.

```
TG: this is the worst shitting thing ive ever seen
TG: the thing that just happened
GG: hi dave!!!!
TG: jesus
TG: and the worst thing is
TG: all that juice i drank
TG: i mean
TG: you just HAD TO FIGURE all that juice was going to come back to haunt me
TG: like frankensteins incontinent fucking ghost
TG: it was like
TG: chekhovs juice
GG: hehehe what??
TG: let me be perfectly clear
TG: what i am trying to say is
TG: its like fucking christmas up in my bladder here
TG: and where do i find my toilet
TG: oh look here it is
TG: amputated in my room
TG: gagged with a towel like a fucking prison hostage
TG: and now the cruxploder is counting down
TG: 4 hours oh i guess thats not that bad
GG: 4 hours until what?
TG: what
TG: oh god
TG: are you asleep
```

It's fine, Dave, a bit of urine deposited into a disembodied toilet bowl sitting in the middle of your disaster of a bedroom isn't going to make it much more of a disaster than it already is. I'm sure all the crows will be polite and turn around while you go.

```
GG: ummm....
GG: i...............
GG: i think i might be!
TG: ok
TG: ok lets just
TG: not panic here
GG: im not panicking i feel fine!
TG: lets try to play it cool
TG: and not break all my shit
TG: also dont put anything weird in the seizure kernel
TG: im going to go find somewhere to pee
TG: dont watch me ok
GG: <_<;
TG: like i know you dream about me enough already
TG: lets keep some shit left to the imagination ok
GG: i wont look ok jeez!!!!!
TG: the last thing i need is for your weird brain webcam to be snapping shots of my dong
TG: your grandpa was a sick fuck why would he build a voyeurbot for a little girl
TG: fuck
GG: stop being a huge baby and go peeeeee!!!!!!!!!!!!
```

> Dave: Use now empty apple juice bottle as pee receptacle.

You begin to hatch
a brilliant plan.

Here's a spicy meatball for you JohnDave shippers out there. Note how he withers at the thought of his perfectly viable potential heterosexual partner, Jade Harley, catching a glimpse of his willie through her voyeurbot. And how quickly his imagination pivots to thoughts of forcing his very good boy buddy, John Egbert, to imbibe a fresh, warm bottle of his pee. Kind of makes you think. Think about John and Dave, kissing each other, I mean.

Once you're done you'll captchalogue the bottle and send the code to Egbert and tell him it's something really important. Then he'll make it and be like, oh man yes apple juice I am so thirsty!!!

But he will not be drinking delicious juice, oh no. He will be choking down a world of hot piss and it will serve him right for liking all those dumbass movies unironically.

But that all sounds like a big waste of time so you just go in the shower.

> Dave: Kick that puppet out of the shower.

A melancholy bit of subtext here is how naturally it seems to come to Dave to quickly contrive contingencies for how to surreptitiously urinate. Almost as if it's not the first time he's considered peeing in an empty bottle in his bedroom. Not wanting to venture out to the rest of the house and risk another beating from his bro has probably conditioned him to think this way. He possibly even breaks out in a cold sweat involuntarily any time he has to pee. Whoa, I'm bumming everybody out!!! Ha ha, look at that funny drawing up there of John covered in piss.

```
GG: oh noooooooooooooooooooooooooooooooooooo
GG: :(
GG: dave
TG: what
GG: :(
TG: what is it
GG: dave this poor bird
TG: what bird
GG: the one with the sword through it!!!
TG: i wouldnt know anything about that
GG: but isnt this your sword?
TG: that could be anyones sword
GG: :|
TG: what does it look like
TG: is it a cheap piece of shit
TG: cause i only bother with high quality blades
TG: forged by stoic asian masters
TG: hells of rude kinds of expensive
GG: all i know is........
GG: its sharp and its through a bird and its a sword
GG: end of story!!!!!!
GG: i am going to help the poor bird
TG: wait
TG: what do you mean
TG: dammit hold on a minute
```

> Jade: Retrieve Dave's copy of Sburb and the impaled crow.

I would argue "that could be anyones sword" is a good line to overhear in literally any context.

> Jade: Put something weird in the seizure kernel.

Here you go, Dave. This is why one version of you has to live as a sad, half-impaled birdboy for the rest of eternity. It was always Jade's fault, wasn't it? No wonder she gets so messed up about bird Dave.

TG: wow awesome
TG: so now i guess instead having of a wise or helpful spirit guide sprite thing
TG: im stuck with this brainless feathery asshole
GG: what do you mean i just brought the cute birdie back to life!!!
GG: isnt he great?
TG: we need to wake you up
TG: youre not very logical like this
TG: kind of dumb really
GG: gosh im SOOOO SOOOORRY!!!!!!!!
GG: i was tired!
TG: yeah but come on you sleep like 20 hours a day
GG: well you are out of luck.....
GG: i will wake up when im good and ready!

> Jade: Wake up.

At least it's not Calsprite. Dave needs to count his blessings. Really, there are so many terrible sprites you can end up with. Just ask the Alpha Kids.

```
TG: where are you sitting
TG: are you on your bed
GG: yes why
TG: what side
GG: ummmmmmm....
GG: the right side...
GG: why??
TG: ok heres what i want you to do
TG: just humor me
TG: raise your left hand
GG: okaaay......
TG: now
TG: just kind of swat the air to your left
GG: ...
```

> AR: Use gunpowder and empty crates to make a campfire.

There's a very good chance Karkat saw all this, and it made him horny.

> AR: Win over that fine carapace in grey.

The fact that WV and AR have stains on the part of their headdresses covering their mouths implies a few things. First, that they have been attempting to eat their respective meats and vegetables by bringing the food up to their mouths, only to realize their mouths are covered by cloth or caution tape. They've possibly made this mistake more than once in this sitting. It also implies that in order to successfully take bites of the food, which they have, they realized they needed to pull the mouth-coverings down a bit, then take a bite, then lift the mouth-coverings back up in between bites. It also implies that it either doesn't occur to them to remove their headdresses completely while dining, or they just don't want to. Maybe they don't fully trust each other yet? I'm really sorry for explaining this small, stupid detail so thoroughly. I have probably five or six more paragraphs' worth of material on this topic, but I've decided to keep it to myself out of respect for you, the reader.

The soap opera is heating up. AR clearly has designs on PM. But does WV as well? What does the fact that he's torn between thinking about PM and AR imply? To what extent should we be factoring in your gay WV headcanons? One thing is unambiguous: Serenity is heartbroken that WV has eyes for anyone other than her. Probably the saddest thing in Sadstuck history, right there.

You are vaguely reminded of something. It's hard to remember. It was so many years ago.

> So many years ago, entrenched in the temporally oblique...

Try not to forget that these carapacians can live a really long time. They don't technically age, or suffer degenerative consequences of age. So when PM thinks back to years ago, we're talking maybe a couple hundred years ago, when she wandered the desert wasteland? She could live plenty longer than that, too. Carapacians are supposed to live a long time, since each chess person has the potential to become an exile and thus wander around forever until they figure out how to rebuild civilization like Jack did as Slick. In this sense, they're a bit like anti-consorts, whose lifespans are tragically short. The game has no use whatsoever for any individual consort. They are a supremely nonindividualist society.

What have we here? An illegally parked vehicle.

You sure hope this guy's got a swollen porkhollow. He just landed himself in citation city.

This looks much more orderly. Public safety has been assured. Your sworn duty as an AUTHORITY REGULATOR has been upheld.

> AR?: Surround the scene with caution tape.

> AR?: Write the owner of this vehicle a ticket.

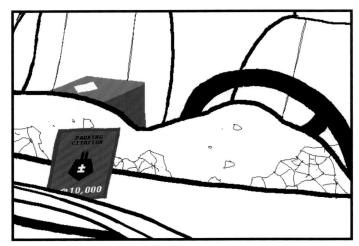

Hello. What have we here?

There's nothing at all that isn't funny about what's happening here. There's so much implied by this citation. Like AR's zeal for issuing it, and the fact that he's even patrolling this mystical land in the first place to ostensibly...issue parking citations? Who else is driving cars around here? *Are* there even cars? We know there are shuttle-like things on Prospit and Derse. Maybe agents make frequent trips to the lands in their kingdom-sanctioned shuttles to cause some mischief, or just for leisure. But apparently you can't just park cars anywhere??? Certainly not on top of a perfectly good tree.

You discover a couple of UNAUTHORIZED PARCELS
in the cabin of the vehicle. You confiscate
them immediately.

You are a simple PARCEL MISTRESS on one of your
routes. Today is another day of uneventful but
highly satisfying deliveries.

You stop in your tracks. It is a dangerous
AGENT from the enemy kingdom. Perhaps
you should avoid him.

But you notice he is holding two parcels.
You recognize one of them. You have spent
a long time looking for it.

It looks like you are going to need to
get that package from him somehow.

> John: Activate ghost gloves.

That's a pretty saucy mail lady ensemble she's sporting. Showing off a bit of carapace midriff. No wonder AR loses his shit.

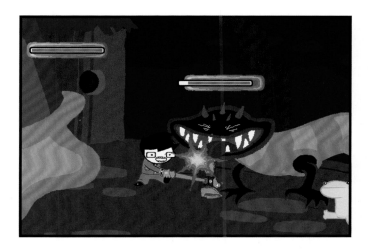

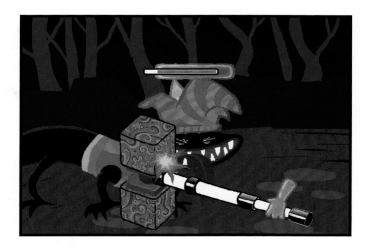

Sons of bitches are harder to kill than you thought they'd be.

Here John is going about his business as if this really were a video game that involves routine bouts of combat with actual foes, rather than an environment in which to cry about your teen problems with your friends. Try to enjoy this ephemeral moment. It doesn't look like John is.

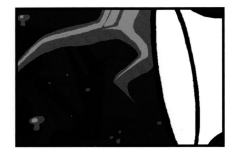

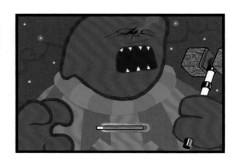

The giclops absconds.

Look, Grandpa Jake Harley doing something useful and kind on behalf of one of our young heroes. One can only assume he just wanted to shoot some monsters and didn't actually realize he was being helpful.

You could have sworn that strange man was
holding your copy of Colonel Sassacre's.

> WV, PM, AR: Stargaze.

It is a clear and peaceful night. A delicious meal has been shared with new friends.
The glow of the ammunition fire gradually subsides. All is well.

But you can't shake the feeling there is something familiar about all this.
There is something you are forgetting.

What's a joke? Sometimes it's just a small phrase included in a sentence, with no fanfare. You just let it go by, it's ridiculous, nothing else needs to be said. Unless you're writing book notes. Ammunition fire? Yeah, let's just burn some fucking live ammunition guys. We need to start a fire, what do we have around here? How about all these bullets I found? Sounds great. Really good idea.

Of course. Now you remember.
You must deliver a message to John right away.

WOMEN.

> PM?: Retrieve package.

That left bottom panel there works better when you can tell she's frantically scampering into the station. The boys here? They don't understand women. They don't get how sometimes you need to take a previous commitment, albeit one made centuries ago, seriously. What does this have to do with gender politics? Why are we even talking about gender? What IS gender? I don't know. And these smitten idiots clearly don't either.

You conclude you have no choice. You will march right up to him and ask politely for the package.

Wait a minute...

What's this?

It is a carved MINITABLET.

The carving is not especially clear to say the least. But your wealth of delivery experience allows you to decipher it immediately.

It is the other parcel the agent is holding. It appears you will need to acquire both from him now. It is your sworn duty.

> PM?: Ready sword.

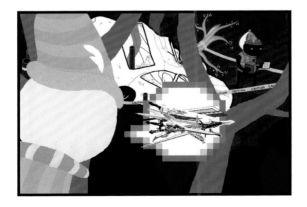

You do not have a sword. You are quite sure it would never occur to you to carry a sword or resort to violence under any circumstance.

You will have to take a more diplomatic route with this fellow.

> AR?: Doff your hat to the attractive female.

I'm glad SOMEBODY understands the mail delivery system on this planet, because I sure don't. And I was the one who invented it. PM must be pretty smart.

You doff so furiously you are in danger
of starting a HAT FIRE.

Probably not the best idea around all this
oil. Especially without any sort of flame
suppressant handy.

> PM?: Retrieve both parcels.

He cannot give them to you. They are
ILLEGAL CONTRABAND, and if you wish to
petition for their release, you must
consult with his superiors.

You show him the carved MINITABLET.
As he can plainly see, you have signed
authorization to deliver one of the
parcels.

He gives you the ENVELOPE. But he
retains the PACKAGE.

Because it's not animated here in the book, you can't see how fast he's doffing his hat. But it's really, really fast. This is a measure of his sexual arousal.

You quickly drop the ENVELOPE into an
empty PYXIS. It is out of your hands now.
THE BREEZE will know where to take it.

You follow the agent. You must not
lose track of that parcel.

> John: Chase the man, you want your
book!

You have some questions for that guy,
whoever he is.

But the village is still burning. You've got to
help these salamanders put out this fire.

> John: Save the lizards!

Ok you JUST SAID they were salamanders.

Anyway, thank goodness for your BARBASOL BOMB. The
cooling lather should work its magic in no time...

Turning a key item over to the whims of the Breeze is quite a brilliant way for me to say, "All right, we won't see this thing again until the exact moment I decide it's important to the plot for it to show up out of nowhere, without needing to contrive any sort of logical explanation."

OH GOD HOW CAN SHAVING CREAM BE SO FLAMMABLE

A big gust of wind conveniently comes
along and blows out all the fire.

It is really convenient.

The townspeople rejoice and are more than willing
to give you all the credit. You suspect it is
probably because they are not all that smart.

> John, the uncarved tablet you retrieved.

I'm not sure if shaving cream is flammable at all, actually. It probably isn't. It's just a funny idea to insist that it is, repeatedly, without any clear reason why. Along the same lines as stubbornly insisting Tab has sugar in it.

Why yes, it appears you do.

> Great! I would like you to carve something on it.

You seem amenable to this request. It's a little wobbly up on top of all these dancing lizards though.

Not that it matters because you suck at drawing anyway.

> Rose, find your sprite.

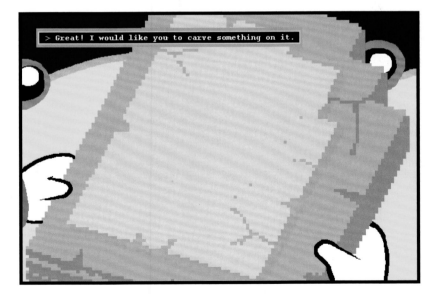

Influencing character actions through the command prompt turns out to be a fairly interesting form of meta-mind control. You can tell a character what to do, but they seem to reserve a certain right of refusal. A command usually has to line up with something they'd be inclined to do anyway, or have some rational reason for deciding to do on their own even if they weren't told to. Here, John seems to be willing to just randomly start chiseling something on this tablet because PM asks him to. Maybe it's because she asks so nicely? In contrast to how WV was putting more aggressive, blunt commands in John's head, which seemed to rankle him and make him less likely to cooperate.

> Your deceased pet.

Rose gets an incredibly warm welcome to her land compared to John. John didn't have the slightest idea what was going on, found his house was full of oil smears and minus his father, and the only "psychic" guidance he received was from an idiot chessboy filling his head with total nonsense in all caps.

96

JASPERSPRITE is nowhere to be found. He always
was a little cagey, even when he was alive.

> Is it not why you are here?

Someone is pestering you. But you are oblivious to
the message because your laptop is buried under
three inches of fucking yarn.

There are footprints in the white sand.

> Follow them.

It looks like they lead out back to the mausoleum.

> Examine your pet's tomb.

The white sand is very fine and powdery. Fun fact: it's actually chalk dust.

The mausoleum was destroyed by the explosion. The secret passage remains.

You have no idea where it leads, but it sure isn't the lab anymore.

> Enter.

The focus is, of course, on Rose as a hero of this story, but finally entering the Medium is a significant moment for Mom Lalonde as well. She clearly knew this day was coming. Spent most of her life doing whatever she was doing in that lab behind the house, as well as raising her daughter for this day. When the time comes, she slips out the back and gets on a boat to who knows where. She's finally free. By leaving the martini glass there, is she indicating she's finally kicking the habit too? Why don't we just call it the prelude to Roxy's sobriety arc.

It seems someone has recently untied a boat.

> A mother will do whatever is best for her children.

> WV: Become the mayor of Exile Town.

You build a bigger and better town to preside over. All expatriates are welcome, no matter what happened in the past, regardless of professional persuasion or metallurgical affiliation. You cut the town's ribbon with an official JUDICIAL BAYONET, which is stuck inside a grenade but you are kind of nervous about removing it.

This should catch the eye of the tall nice lady.

The grumpy yellow guy thinks this is dumb.

Exile Town looks suspiciously like Can Town, with just a lot more garbage around. The more time we spend with exiles, the more we see that the main thing to being an exile is figuring out how to deal with massive amounts of boredom.

He thinks it is dumb because any town without a proper militia is as good as conquered.

As such he prepares one begrudgingly. It's a dirty job, but someone must be charged with the defense of the innocent.

> WV: Fondly regard desert night.

 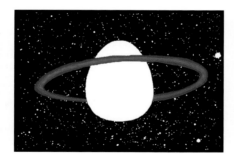 

The stars twinkle over the freshly christened EXILE TOWN. It is a beautiful evening and the future is so full of promise you can't imagine what could possibly oh my god a huge eggy looking thing just appeared in the sky.

Exile Town's military industrial complex is already completely out of control.

> Jade: Give Dave punch card of an eggy
loking thign [sic].

There's a lot of egg stuff suddenly happening all at once. Why? Is it all coincidence? Not really. Remember that the designs of the exile stations are related to the
entry items of the players (apple, cork from a big wine bottle, etc.).

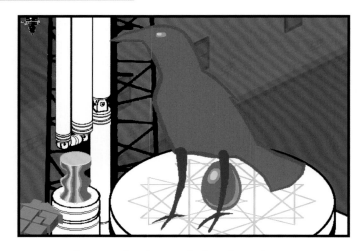 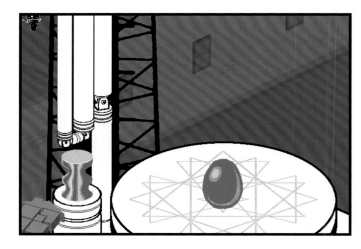

Ok, you do that and then he makes a totem with it and then some other stuff happens and then...

EGG!

> Dave: Pester Jade.

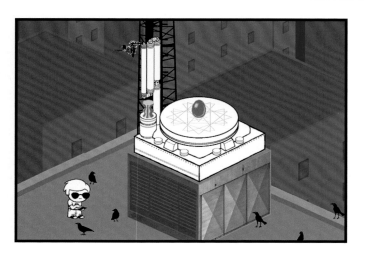

```
TG: oh man
TG: awesome
TG: its awesome where you put that
TG: i was worried we were on the verge
of getting some shit done
GG: duuurrrrr dave i was going to build
some stairs up there durrrrrhhhhhh
TG: well where are they
TG: you say there will be stairs
TG: and yet
TG: i see no stairs
```

"EGG!" is used as a sound effect a lot of times in the story, actually. I forget how many times. But it's a lot. "EGG!" isn't really a sound anything can make. Except maybe a guy shouting the word "EGG" at the top of his lungs, I guess.

GG: gosh i dont know i guess i didnt find the time to make them because i keep getting punched in the face by robots and stuff!!!!!!!
TG: sorry
GG: ;p
TG: am i supposed to break that thing
TG: or hatch it
TG: or what
GG: i dont know!
TG: also what happened to all my shit
TG: the stuff scattered all over the roof
TG: did you put it somewhere
GG: nope....
TG: i mean not that i care
TG: it was a lot of mostly useless garbage
GG: what was it doing up here?
TG: i was going to use it to fight my bro with
TG: but i guess i forgot in the heat of battle
TG: also he was too fast

> Dave: Make the world's largest omlette.

Whoops, looks like that dumb
idea isn't going to happen!

A brainless feathery asshole swoops
down and carries the egg away.

Dave mentions all the useless crap he stuffed in his sylladex before he came up to the roof, and how he intended to use it in his battle with Bro but "forgot." That's basically me saying I specifically gave him all that crap as sylladex ammunition to use in his strife with Bro but never really got around to using it. It just seemed like a waste of time to do all that animation work, making Dave "hashrap" all of the junk like cherry bombs and shitty swords out of his 'dex at Bro, when really the thrust of the battle is: Bro beats the shit out of Dave, flies away like a mysterious cool man, and that's really all there is, and ever will be, to say on the matter.

103

TG: ok so
TG: the egg is now in a nest made of shitty swords and soft puppet ass
TG: please advise
GG: i think your sprite wants to hatch it!
GG: awww
TG: do you think thatll take more than four hours
GG: hmm...
GG: i dont know it looks like its pretty warm where you are
TG: its hot as the sizzle side of the steak
GG: maybe not too long then????
GG: i guess we'll find out!
TG: maybe i should try to get it back
TG: and put it in the microwave
GG: :(

> Jade: Deploy Punch Designix.

All of the entry items represent certain challenges or themes. Dave's involves waiting for a ridiculously inaccessible and stubbornly guarded egg to hatch, which is a challenge that relates to patience. What does this "mean"? You, the studious reader, will have to crunch the numbers on that.

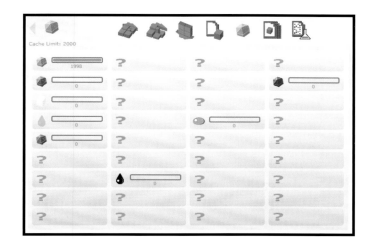

You can't! You'll need some SHALE for that.

> Jade: Check unknown objects.

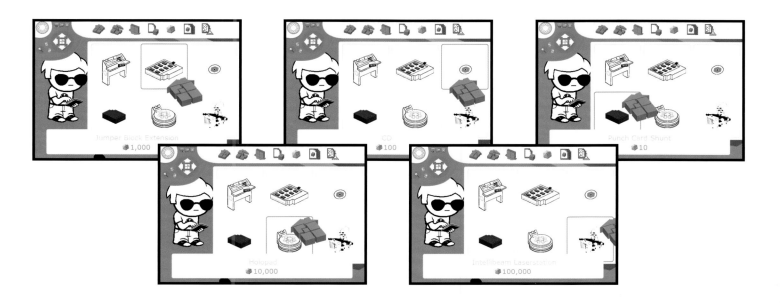

Dave (or really his server player, Jade) has some new stuff to mess with now. We don't know what any of it is yet. Just that a lot of it is probably kind of dumb. How do we know that? Why, we know that because one of the things is called the "Intellibeam Laserstation."

```
GG: ok some of these things we can deploy but some things we dont have nearly enough grist
for!
TG: you mean the jumper block thing
GG: no no weve got enough for that.....
GG: but its still pretty expensive
TG: wait what
TG: the thing costs 1000 for me
GG: yeah me too!
GG: and we have 2000 to work with
GG: ok 1998 ._.
TG: what
TG: man i only got 200 to splash around with in roses rainbow world
TG: what the hell
GG: ohhh...
GG: how much did rose start with? when she was playing with john?
TG: hang on ill ask
GG: k
TG: she says 20
GG: i guess we keep getting more with each server/client connection!
TG: yeah
TG: so i guess you can buy everything now
GG: no!!!!
GG: i cant buy the holopad thingy and the intellibeam laserstation
TG: ok now i know youre making this shit up
GG: hahahaha no theyre right here!
GG: they cost a fortune
TG: well all i got here is the designix which i cant deploy cause i dont have any purples
TG: and the expensive as hell jumper thing and the cheap shunts which i assume do dick all
without the jumpers to put em on
TG: oh also this cd which is 100 but i didnt drop cause it seemed like a stiff allocation of
resources for now
GG: yeah ive got that too!
GG: i will deploy it
TG: so with each new connection in our player chain i guess new weird deployables are
introduced
GG: yes i think that is how it works
GG: when john connects with me he will probably get some cool new things too!
TG: hey look we're learning stuff
```

> Jade: Deploy green and white compact disc.

I would explain how these things work, but the kids just did. They figured it all out through constructive dialogue and teamwork. What do you need me for?
Well, the fact is, you don't, and possibly never did. All you need are my OCs. They're all you need on your lonely journey through life, truth be told.

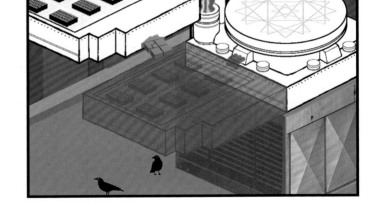

TG: what should i do with these beta copies
TG: i dont really need them anymore
GG: i suppose just hang on to them for a while........
GG: and then later
GG: just do whatever you are naturally compelled to do with them!
TG: wow that was a weird answer
TG: but ok

You take the BETA and the CD.

> Jade: Deploy circuit board looking thingy.

It was obviously labeled as the JUMPER BLOCK EXTENSION.

It appears to be deployable only as an extension to the ALCHEMITER. Looks like you're going to have to move it.

Damn, and it looked so nice up there!

Jade has a horrible poker face when it comes to pretending she doesn't know things about the future or pretending she's not clumsily manipulating people into doing the things she knows they need to do. What she means is, she knows that Dave will eventually be naturally compelled, in some totally inexplicable way, to put the beta copies in a giant flower in the ruins near her house, or to do something that will eventually lead to them being put in the giant flower by someone else. It's so obvious that's what she's up to.

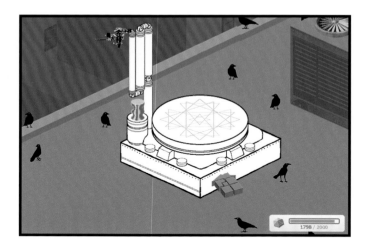

You expend another relatively affordable
100 BUILD GRIST to relocate it.

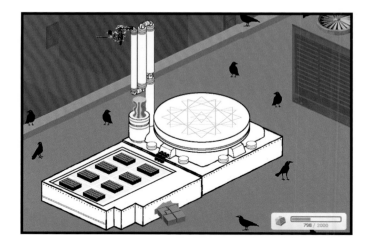

You then pay the steep fee of 1000 BUILD GRIST
to deploy the JUMPER BLOCK EXTENSION.

> Jade: Attempt to deploy catchalogue disk drive.

Again, the name of the thing was right there
in plain sight.

You deploy the PUNCH CARD SHUNT for peanuts.

Looks like a captchalogue card is supposed to
fit in the slot.

> Dave: Insert card with the CD on the slot.

We're coming very close to the point where the *Homestuck* "suggestion box" was permanently closed to the public. So all these cool commands where the readers don't have the slightest idea what they're talking about, like "deploy captchalogue disk drive," are about to come to an end. R.I.P. forever, the preposterous notion that anyone ever really had much control over this story at all.

You put the card in the slot and stick the shunt on the jumper pins.

Nothing happens. You might need to stick a punched card in there, probably allowing the holes in the card to affect the flow of current through the circuits. And to punch cards you'll need to get a designix somehow.

> Dave: Insert disc into computer.

> Dave: Install software.

You can see from Dave's desktop that in the middle of all this action he was still finding time to work on *Sweet Bro and Hella Jeff* comics. He's working on the "NANCHO PARTY" arc. He no doubt was seized by inspiration and had to drop everything to bring his vision to life. I find this content to be relatable, you may be stunned to discover.

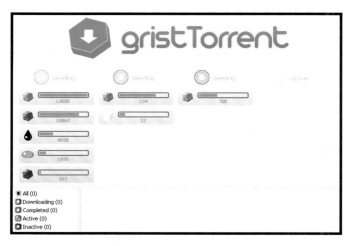

GRISTTORRENT is now running.

> Dave: Illegally pirate some of John's shale.

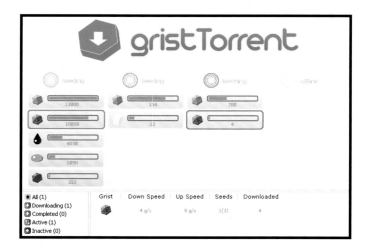

You start leeching off John's SHALE at a pace of 4 g/s.

Not the fastest download rate, but then again you don't need a whole lot. In one second you already collect enough for a PUNCH DESIGNIX.

> Dave: Download a bunch of grist from John. He has plenty.

GristTorrent is like BitTorrent. Remember BitTorrent? Actually, I'm not sure even I remember BitTorrent at this point. Do people still use that? Well, GristTorrent is like that, but for grist instead of illegal shit. It's the perfect way to turn a great team of friends who get along famously into a group of grist-grubbing pickpockets, sniping each other's grist caches right out from under their noses. It can be a handy tool if everyone's willing to be civilized about it, but my guess is a lot of teens would end up getting into shouting matches over it and eventually just uninstall it to protect their grist from thieving pals.

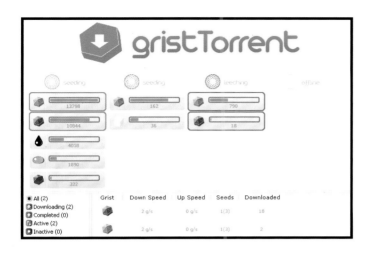

You set the application to leech off John's BUILD GRIST because he's obviously got too much for his own good.

It cuts the download rate in half though.

> You guide the Heir. Consult with him.

-- ectoBiologist [EB] began pestering tentacleTherapist [TT] --

EB: rose?
EB: are you there?
EB: i went through the gate, nanna said you might be here too.
EB: are you in kind of this spooky glowy place with oily rivers and stuff?
EB: let me know ok.
TT: I guess one could use those words to describe it.
TT: If armed with a predilection for the inapt.

On the topic of the suggestion box and how it's about to shut down, I remember the "exile takes control of the commands" conceit being a really valuable tool to take control away from the gnashing horde of wackadoos clamoring for me to get John to eat his shoes or fuck his pogo ride all the time. It was a pretty neat trick for steering the focus toward something more productive. It was also a way to introduce mysterious characters (like the queen here), lend a bit of indirect characterization to them, and deepen the lore by another tick or two. All that good stuff. And it all comes from the basic acknowledgement that readers really shouldn't have any input on the things they are reading at all. Who would have guessed!

EB: bluh bluh bluuuuuhhhhh.
EB: ok, what words would you use, miss wordypants mcsmartybluh.
TT: Eerily iridescent?
EB: umm...
TT: I certainly don't see any oily rivers.
TT: There's an ocean though.
EB: i haven't found an ocean yet.
EB: but i dunno, the place is really big.
EB: it's like a whole planet down here.
EB: oh man, which reminds me.
EB: i just got hounded by a troll.
TT: Yes, one of them is bugging me now.
TT: I thought it was odd timing.
EB: yeah well, they say they want to be friends, also they're playing sburb but like not the same session as ours or something.
EB: oh also they're moving backwards in time, which sounds really retarded, but whatever.
TT: Color my curiosity piqued, I guess.
EB: yeah, i guess answer him if you want. or not.
EB: but anyway, it's great you made it here alive and stuff!
EB: so dave came through?
TT: Eventually.
TT: Pardon the envy I'm about to vent in your direction.
EB: for what?
TT: For finding yourself at the mercy of a rational orchestrator.
EB: oh, haha.
EB: yeah, i'd feel kinda weird if dave was watching me too.
TT: You don't feel weird when I watch you?
EB: rose i feel weird when you're just TALKING to me, when you're watching me it's just like the weird frosting on the big weirdo cake.
TT: I can't see you now, for what it's worth.
EB: yes i'm freeeeeeeeee :D
EB: ok, i'm going to go over this river and through these woods.
EB: you talk to your troll i guess.
EB: we'll compare notes later.
TT: Ok.
TT: Bye, John.

> Who is this bothering you?

John, I just lectured Dave on problematic language. Do I have to have a talk with you too? These idiot children will be the death of me. Also, not all trolls are having a conversation "backwards in time," as John assumes. Only Karkat was that dumb. Most are being relatively linear. Except Kanaya, who gets way too cerebral about it while macking on Rose. Anyway, enough of this cute banter, Terezi's calling.

-- gallowsCalibrator [GC] began trolling
tentacleTherapist [TT] --

GC: H3Y L4LOND3
GC: STOP CRY1NG 1N YOUR MOMS B3V3R4G3
GC: SH3 H4T3S YOU 4ND H4S L3FT YOU FOR3V3R
GC: H3H3H3H >8D
TT: Now I'm confused.
TT: On the surface, this appears to be another
contrivance from a troll desperate to offend.
TT: But John said you wanted to be friends.
TT: And if you knew me, I suppose your remark could be
construed as a ploy to elicit agreement.
TT: And soon, rapport.
TT: Not that it would actually work.
GC: GOD
GC: YOU R34LLY DO T4LK TOO MUCH
TT: So which is it?
GC: OOOOOOOOOH
GC: YOUR T3XT SM3LLS GOOD
GC: 1S TH4T L4V3ND3R
TT: You smell words?
GC: YOU DONT???
TT: Right. Aliens, I forgot.
GC: Y3S 1TS 34SY TO FORG3T
GC: G1V3N OUR "R4PPORT"
GC: 4ND HOW MUCH W3 R34LLY H4V3 1N COMMON
GC: 1 FORG3T TH4T YOU HUM4NS 4CTU4LLY COMMUN1C4T3 W1TH SP33CH 1NST34D OF R3L34SING CLOUDS OF
FR4GR4NT G4S3S
GC: 4ND SM3LL1NG 3ACH OTH3RS S3NT3NC3S
TT: Gross.
GC: 4H4H4H4 SO GULL1BL3
GC: YOULL B3L13V3 4NYTH1NG 1 T3LL YOU
GC: OF COURS3 W3 T4LK DUMMY >8]
TT: Still not sure if I'm being courted or trolled here.
GC: 1M GO1NG TO GO W1TH TH3 LATT3R
GC: 1 H4T3 YOU 4LL QU1T3 4 LOT
GC: BUT 1 TH1NK
GC: TH3 OTH3RS W1LL 3V3NTU4LLY R34L1Z3 TH4T 1TLL B3 MUTU4LLY B3N3F1C14L FOR US 4LL TO WORK
TOG3TH3R
GC: 4ND SO TH3YLL PROB4BLY B3 4LL FR13NDLY L1KE L4T3R ON

Right here, this is it. This is when the story blasts off with virtually nonstop troll interaction. It pretty much never looks back. In hindsight, the complete takeover of the story by troll stuff was inevitable. Because of the way they're being introduced slowly—a mysterious conversation here, a wild and colorfully eccentric new character there—they all seem pretty intriguing at this point. It's easy to take trolls for granted as almost the center of the story when you already know about them and have been exposed to them before even reading HS. But man, when this was all just emerging for the first time, through fast and loose storytelling methods, this was Hot Fucking Stuff, let me tell you. People were psyched.

TT: By later on, you mean now?
GC: Y34H
GC: TH4TS PROB4BLY WH4T JOHN W4S H34RING
GC: 4ND M4YBE TH3YLL 3V3N M34N 1T 4ND W4NT TO B3 FR13NDLY
GC: BUT 1 1NT3ND TO ST4Y P1SS3D 4T YOU FOR3V3R
GC: 3V3N 1F 1 S33M H3LPFUL
TT: Then you're in luck.
TT: Because you don't.
GC: H3H3 NO BUT 1 W1LL BE
GC: TH3 F4CT TH4T 1 W1LL B3 H3LPFUL
GC: 1S 4N 1MMUT4BL3 F4CT 1 4M ST4T1NG FOR TH3 R3CORD
GC: 1T DO3S NOT M34N FR13NDSH1P 1S WH4T 1S T4K1NG PL4C3 H3R3
TT: John was told you were moving backwards through time.
TT: Was he gullible to believe this?
TT: Or is the fact that I'm asking just further indication of my own gullibility?
TT: Feel free to continue shifting the definition of the word to suit your convenience.
GC: W3 H4V3NT 3V3N B33N T4LK1NG TO YOU FOR LONG
GC: L1K3 4 F3W M1NUT3S FROM MY P3RSP3CT1V3
GC: 1F TH3R3 4R3 SOM3 OF US WHO D3C1D3D TO ST4RT T4LK1NG TO YOU 4T TH3 3ND OF YOUR 4DV3NTUR3 R1GHT OFF TH3 B4T
GC: 1NST34D OF 4T THE B3G1NN1NG L1K3 WH4TS LOG1C4L
GC: TH3N TH4TS TH31R STUP1D BUS1NESS
GC: 1M ST4Y1NG L1N34R
GC: C4US3 W31RD T1M3 STUFF G1V3S ME A H34D4CHE
GC: OH 4LSO 1TS PO1NTL3SS
TT: Alright, let's continue milking my human gullibility and say I believe you. You're the sensible one who's decided to communicate with us in linear lockstep with our timeline in order to help us out.
TT: How can you help me?
GC: YOU JUST 3NT3R3D YOUR M3D1UM R1GHT
TT: Yes.
GC: OK
GC: DO3S 1T S33M L1K3 TH3R3 1S A SUBTL3 VO1C3 1N YOUR H34D URG1NG YOU TO DO TH1NGS
TT: Yes.
TT: It's not so subtle, actually.
GC: Y3S!!!!!!! >8O
GC: FOR M3 TOO 1T W4S MOR3 LOUD 4ND CL34R TH4N FOR TH3 OTH3RS
GC: YOU S33 W3 4R3 M34NT TO B3 B3ST H4T3FR13NDS FOR3V3R
TT: A beautiful soulgrudge this cosmic was surely authored by the constellations.
GC: TH3Y 4LL THOUGHT 1 W4S CR4ZY
GC: BUT H4H4H4 1T TURN3D OUT W3 4LL W3R3 1N OUR OWN W4YS

By saying "authored by the constellations," I really wonder if Rose, clever person that she is, already picked up on the fact that the twelve losers in her trollslum are zodiac-themed? I know a bunch of readers picked up on it from just a few of the troll handles. Seeing all twelve handles at once makes the theme pretty obvious, but only seeing a few at a time takes a bit of deductive reasoning. It's not instantly evident that "gallowsCalibrator" could be referencing the mechanics of a scale, or that gallows are associated with harsh justice. Or even "adiosToreador." You had to think, like, hmm... Oh, I see, bullfighting. Something about a bull... Oh, I get it now—scales, bulls, Libra, Taurus, twelve characters, it's the damn zodiac. This is how puzzles work. GET IT?????

GC: TH4T H3LP3D US R34LIZ3 TH3 P4RTICUL4R D3ST1N13S THE G4M3 PUT TOG3TH3R FOR US
GC: 1N TH3 VOC4BUL4RY OF L1K3
GC: TH3 HYP3R FL3XIBL3 MYTHOLOGY 1T T41LORS TO 34CH PL4Y3R GROUP
TT: You mean, for instance...
TT: If a player were to learn she was a "Seer"?
GC: Y34H 3X4CTLY! S33R OF M1ND P4G3 OF BR34TH KN1GHT OF BLOOD M41D OF T1M3
GC: 3TC 3TC 3TC
GC: 12 FOR US BUT OBV1OUSLY 4 FOR YOU
GC: 3V3RY S3SS1ON 1S D1FF3R3NT
TT: And this voice?
GC: OH Y34H
GC: 1TS 4N 3X1L3
TT: Exiled from what?
GC: 1T TOOK US FOR3V3R TO F1GUR3 TH1S OUT
GC: B3C4US3 TH3Y 4R3NT M34NT TO B3 4N OBV1OUS 4SP3CT OF TH3 G4M3
GC: TH3YR3 ON YOUR D34D PLAN3T
GC: JUST L1K3 TH3YR3 ON OURS
GC: Y34RS 4FT3R 1TS R3CKON1NG
GC: TH31R ROL3 1S TO H3LP YOU ON YOUR QU3ST 1N SOM3 W4YS
GC: TH3 OBV1OUS W4Y 1S BY D1R3CTLY GU1DING YOUR 4CT1ONS
GC: BUT M4YB3 TH3 MOR3 1MPORT4NT W4YS 4R3 TH3S3 L1TTL3 TH1NGS TH3Y DO PROB4BLY W1THOUT 3V3N R34L1Z1NG 1T
GC: 4CT1ONS TH4T COMPL3T3 LOOPS 1N TH3 T1M3L1NE
GC: COGS 1N P4R4DOX SP4C3
TT: Paradox space?
GC: OH H3LL
GC: L1ST3N TH3 UN1V3RS3 W1LL 34T P4R4DOX3S FOR BR34KF4ST
GC: 4ND SO W1LL TH1S G4M3
GC: G3T US3D TO 1T
GC: BY NOW YOU SHOULD R34L1Z3 TH1S WHOL3 M3SS W4S 4 B1G S3LF FULLF1LL1NG CLUST3RFUCK
GC: A HUG3 ORG14ST1C MOB1US DOUBL3 R34CH4ROUND
TT: I'm starting to see that.
TT: So the exiles are on Earth? Does that mean our goal is to get back there too? To resurrect it somehow?
GC: NO NO NO
GC: S33 1RON1C4LLY TH3Y G3T TO DO TH4T
GC: 4FT3R TH3YR3 DON3 H3LP1NG YOU TH4T 1S
GC: YOUR JOB 1S OF GR34T3R CONS3QU3NC3 TO S4Y TH3 L34ST
GC: BUT P4RT OF TH31R JOB 1S TO R3BU1LD L1F3 4ND C1V1L1Z4T1ON TH3R3
GC: 4ND 1F TH3YR3 SUCC3SSFUL 1N THOUS4NDS OR M1LL1ONS OF Y34RS TH3 T3CHNOLOGY 1S UN34RTH3D 4ND TH3 PL4N3T 1S R1P3 FOR S33D1NG 4LL OV3R 4G41N

This one section contains a huge payload of lore being revealed. Points that could have been roughly deduced earlier are now being explicitly confirmed, along with the introduction of some entirely new ideas. There's important stuff here, which maybe bears reading a couple times to make sure you've got it all. Thank god it's being conveyed through leet speak in all caps.

```
TT: You never answered the question. Where were they exiled from?
GC: FROM TH3 TWO K1NGDOMS 1N TH3 1NC1P1SPH3R3
GC: 3XP4TR14T3D DUR1NG TH3 R3CKON1NG
GC: FORM3R 4G3NTS
TT: What are agents?
GC: 1 TH1NK
GC: TH1S W1LL B3 MOR3 CONSTRUCT1V3
GC: 1F 1 CONT4CT YOU 4G41N 1N 4 L1TTL3 WH1L3
GC: WH3N YOU KNOW MOR3
GC: 4ND 1 DONT H4V3 TO 3XPL41N SO MUCH
TT: When?
GC: 1N 4 COUPL3 OF S3CONDS
GC: FOR M3
GC: BUT NOT FOR YOU
GC: SUCK3R

-- gallowsCalibrator [GC] ceased trolling tentacleTherapist [TT] --
```

> Meanwhile, the past pulls a mean double reacharound...

Terezi was the only one who went about this in a fairly sensible way. I guess once Vriska got around to her trolling stunts, she was pretty logical and effective about it too. It's just too bad her actual goals were destructive, vainglorious, and kind of stupid. That's her brand, though: cooking up smart, cunning ways of achieving incredibly ill-advised goals.

116

ghostyTrickster [GT] began pestering gardenGnostic [GG]

GT: hey, happy birthday jade!
GG: yay thank you john!!!!! :D
GT: whew ok, i got your present in the mail JUST on time.
GT: plus i sent rose's and dave's too.
GT: why do your guys'es birthdays got to be all bunched together like that??? you are running me ragged!
GG: heheh i know but it is nice of you to think of us all like that!
GT: i can't wait for you to see what i got you. i don't want to spoil it or anything but hopefully it will help you solve those problems you've been having lately.
GT: MYSTERIOUS WINK ;)
GG: im sure it is great, i cant wait either!!!!!
GG: it might take a while to get here from there but it will be worth the wait!
GT: oh man.
GT: i am such an idiot, i forgot about how long it takes you to get stuff.
GT: ARGH.
GG: john thats ok really! im sure will get to me exactly when it needs to and it will be a nice surprise when it does!
GT: ok well i hope so.
GG: <3......
GG: uhhhh hold on

carcinoGeneticist [CG] began trolling gardenGnostic [GG]

CG: WAIT GOD DAMMIT DON'T BLOCK ME.
CG: I MEAN NOT THAT BLOCKING ME WOULD DO ANYTHING.
CG: BUT JUST LISTEN.
GG: what do you want?????
CG: I JUST HAVE TO DELIVER A MESSAGE AND THEN I'LL GO.
CG: IT IS A MESSAGE FROM YOU, SO YOU PROBABLY OUGHT TO LISTEN.
GG: this is nonsense
GG: every time i believe something you say you laugh at me and call me a gullible human!!!!
GG: its so childish
CG: OK FINE I ADMIT IT, I COMPLETELY SHIT THE BED HERE.
CG: I GET THAT.
CG: AND I CAN'T PROMISE I WON'T KEEP TROLLING YOU.
CG: CAUSE I WILL, IN WEEKS OR MONTHS OR WHATEVER.
CG: I'LL KEEP GIVING YOU A HARD TIME, BUT SEE THAT WON'T BE PRESENT ME.

Hmm, more fascinating mysteries. The nonlinear nature of the troll dialogue really sucks you in because of exchanges like this. Karkat wants to deliver a message to Jade...*from* Jade? Why does she tell him that, and when? What happens between now and then? It's maddening. Conversations from the future are always planting little seeds like this. We now know certain things need to happen, but we aren't sure exactly what they are, or under what circumstances they'll take place. A lot of the time I already knew what this stuff was, so I planned it out and left breadcrumbs like this in conversations for foreshadowing purposes. Other times, I didn't know exactly what something was, or precisely how it would happen, so it was like introducing a little puzzle for myself to solve along the way.

CG: THAT'S PAST ME.
CG: FROM LIKE A HALF HOUR AGO OR SO, WHEN I WAS MORE HOT AND BOTHERED ABOUT ALL THIS, OK?
GG: D:
GG: i dont know what youre talking about at all.....
GG: its another prank
CG: WHATEVER, FINE, THINK IT'S A PRANK.
CG: AS LONG AS YOU REMEMBER THIS CONVERSATION.
CG: SEE WE'RE TRYING TO TALK TO YOU IN THE FUTURE, AND IT'S IMPORTANT, BUT YOU WON'T ANSWER US.
CG: SO WE TALKED TO YOU WAAAY IN THE FUTURE TO ASK HOW TO GET IN TOUCH WITH NOT-SO-FUTURE YOU.
CG: ARE YOU FOLLOWING?
GG: no
CG: SHE SAID TO TALK TO YOU NOW AND TELL YOU THIS.
CG: YOU KNOW YOUR ROBOT?
GG: you mean the robot you think is stupid?
GG: the one youve mocked me for having on a number of occasions???
CG: YEAH, WELL I STILL DO THINK YOUR ROBOT IS STUPID.
CG: BUT THAT'S BESIDES THE POINT.
CG: LATER ON IT WILL BLOW UP FOR SOME REASON. IT DOESN'T MATTER WHY.
GG: this is the worst prank youve ever pulled!!!!!!
CG: QUIET.
CG: ANYWAY, WHEN IT HAPPENS YOU WON'T KNOW WHAT TO DO.
CG: THE THING TO DO IS TO CONTACT US.
CG: AND WE'LL TELL YOU WHAT TO DO.
GG: why should i do that?
CG: BECAUSE THAT'S WHAT YOU TOLD US TO TELL YOU.
CG: WHATEVER, BELIEVE ME, DON'T BELIEVE ME, I DID MY JOB.
CG: I'M OUT OF HERE.

carcinoGeneticist [CG] **ceased trolling gardenGnostic** [GG]

GG: ok im back sorry
GG: i had to tell someone to go away!
GT: oh god.
GT: the trolls again?
GG: yup :o
GT: they have been such a pain in the ass lately.
GT: it seems like there are so many.
GT: there are either like fifty of these retards or it's one guy with a lot of alt accounts.
GG: ive never had any sort of feeling about them or what they want which is kind of weird!!!
GG: but it seems to me like they are probably all different people and not one guy

118   I wonder if Karkat also thinks Aradia's robot body is stupid? Aradiabot is like...right there. In the same room with him, right now. That's her actual, physical body. Does he think it's stupid? Kind of ableist of him, since that's all she's got. Or maybe he's full of shit and just looking for any reason at all to give Jade a hard time.

```
GG: i have counted twelve
GT: what do they want with us!!!
GG: some people just like to needle others for some reason john
GG: it is like a game i guess. they are like pranksters!!
GT: oh hell no, shittiest pranksters ever.
GG: but i think they are mostly harmless
GG: every so often they manage to get through my block filter and hassle me. its been going
on for years! actually some of them are kind of funny i think hehe
GT: oh wow, what? years??
GT: ok, well i am sick of them.
GT: i've been thinking of changing my pesterchum handle to throw them off.
GT: so...
GT: i guess i'm gonna do that.
```

Is there anything more useless than the Pesterchum block filters? Oh, it's Karkat. We've already seen him, at the end of the last intermission, but it still feels a bit like we're meeting him for the first time here. We meet a bunch of trolls for the first time like this: hunched over a keyboard, looking either surly or extremely pleased with themselves over the CYBER HAVOC that they have just wrought.

The package from your pen-pal appears again. You've been wondering when it was going to show up. It has been months since you last worked on it!

Hopefully your friend has made the final modifications you require. You'll have to mail it soon so it reaches John in time!

```
-- gallowsCalibrator [GC] began trolling
ghostyTrickster [GT] --

GC: H3H3
GT: uuuuugh
GC: H4H4H
GC: H3H3H3H3
GT: ?
GC: LOL!
GC: H3H3H3H3H3H3H3
GC: >:]
GT: well
GT: i guess you're not too bad a troll
if this is all you do.
```

Just because we're gradually introducing all these mysterious new trolls doesn't mean we can't take a moment to seed yet another long, slow-boiling mystery that will eventually lead to the introduction of an entirely different roster of new characters. That's what the "Jade's pen pal" plot thread is, which doesn't yield dividends until Act 6. Is this actually an intriguing morsel in the context of everything else that's going on? Are we suffering from intrigue overload yet? Hell if I know. My policy was, when in doubt over whether to throw more shit into the story: throw more shit into the story.

```
GT: just laughing and stuff.
GC: H33H33H33!!!!
GC: H4H4H4H4
GT: hehe
GC: 4H4H4H44H4H4H4H4H4H4H4H4
GT: hehehehehe
GC: JOHN
GC: WHY WOULD YOU L4UGH 4T 4 BL1ND G1RL
GT: uh...
GC: YOU H4V3 NO 1D34 HOW MUCH YOU D1SGUST M3
GC: YOUR3 4 TOT4L D1SGR4C3 TO TH3 F13LD OF 3CTOB1OLOGY
GC: 1F W3 3V3R M33T
GC: 1M GO1NG TO CUT YOUR THRO4T
GC: 4ND L1ST3N TO YOU BL33D WH1L3 1 SM3LL YOU D13

-- gallowsCalibrator [GC] ceased trolling ghostyTrickster [GT] --
```

You think it's time to change your chumhandle.

To what, though...

Gotta be something they'll never suspect. What was that thing she said you were a disgrace to? You have kind of a hard time reading shitty leetspeak in spite of your awesome hacker cred.

Here's the origin of John's chumhandle switch. He does it because of some brutal trolling by Terezi. Also, John doesn't know it yet, but he actually likes getting brutally trolled by Terezi.

>PM?: Follow the agent.

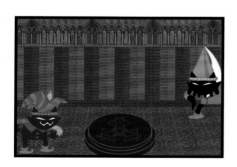 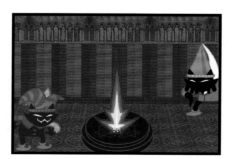 

You have followed the AUTHORITY REGULATOR into enemy territory. It is a risky move and this dark palace makes you very uncomfortable. But it is imperative you press on and recover that parcel.

You have brought along a PARKING CITATION. If confronted, you will say you are only here to deliver payment and leave.

Hey, there she is. What a fun-looking troll. I don't think Terezi had a character design until I drew this panel. A lot of trolls weren't formally designed before the first panel they appeared in. Why waste time sketching concepts when their first appearance panel can serve as the excuse to design them? It's actually more efficient that way. Though I will admit, once it was time to introduce all twelve trolls in Hivebent, I did sketch a bunch of them in advance on paper. There were just too many, and the pacing on Hivebent was flying fast and hot. I had to have all my trolls locked, loaded, and ready to deploy.

You have no idea where you're going.
You are too nervous to ask anyone.

You take a turn somewhere and find an
especially regal looking red carpet.
You wonder where it could possibly lead.

Nice to see the Draconian Dignitary is getting in the spirit of the queen's forced feline-suit themed royal ensemble. He's a real team player, unlike that curmudgeonly piece of shit, Jack Noir.

Here's the Black Queen, all dolled up in her saucy clownwear. She's got her Ring, which has two orbs filled and two orbs empty, per the number of players who have entered the Medium so far. Now we see the extent of the effect prototypings have on the body of the wearer of the Ring and can quickly surmise how garish a carapacian can become once the Ring is fully loaded. Cat bits, tentacles, one arm, one eye, built-in clown hat. Her actual clothing is worn by choice, however. The queen takes this all very seriously. She's a game construct that was built to take things seriously.

The BLACK QUEEN directs you to the office of the ARCHAGENT. He is in charge of most of the tedious paperwork around here.

> Rose, I must leave now.

> This is the last you will hear from me.

It's probably very rare for a mail carrier to pass through the throne room looking for where the parking tickets are supposed to be delivered. Luckily for PM, the queen has no problem whatsoever telling her where to go, so as to dump even more paperwork on her archagent's desk.

125

You return to a more typical mindset. You suddenly feel empowered to make important decisions on your own without supervision. Parental or otherwise.

> Rose: Sip martini thoughtfully.

Such as this one.

Just a tiny sip couldn't hurt...

> Fourth Exile: Suddenly appear.

Welp, looks like she doesn't like alcohol. I guess that's that. Rose will be straight edge for life.

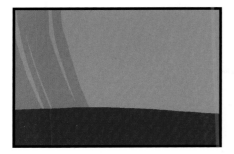

A WINDSWEPT QUESTANT suddenly appears.

This big damn egg is hella high tech. WV's cork station had to blast off with a rocket. PM's apple station had a helicopter propeller and some worms as landing gear.
This egg just teleports around like it's no big deal. And the pilot can teleport in and out of it too. Nothing but the best for Her Majesty.

> PM: Command John to put the carved tablet into a pyxis.

You follow the command telling you to command John to put the carved tablet in the pyxis and type, "John, put the carved tablet into the pyxis."

You successfully do that, and he successfully does that too. Everyone is friendly and cooperative.

What the hell was that???

It almost sounded like a huge egg appeared in the sky and landed, and then someone mysterious teleported out of it.

> PM?: Locate the Archagent.

The player of *Homestuck* commanding a character to type in a command to tell another character what to do is some pretty good shit. But some really next-level good shit is then printing that sequence in a book, and me pointing out how cool it is.

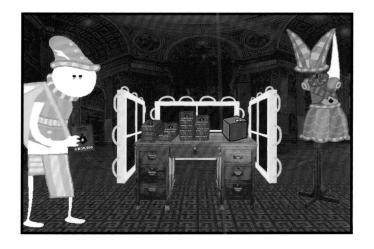
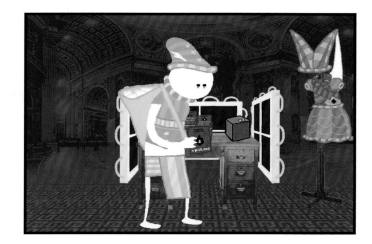

You find the agent's office.
But he is nowhere to be found.

You eye something on the desk there.

> PM?: Grab the box and run!

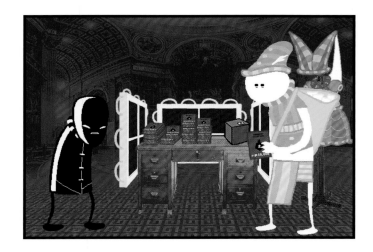

If you act quickly enough maybe you can grab the package and get out of here before CAN I HELP YOU

Jack was probably just in the restroom, taking a break from his crushing paperwork chores. The stacks and stacks of parking tickets on his desk raise about a hundred times more questions than answers pertaining to the traffic patterns of the worlds in this realm. I have zero answers to these questions.

Mr. Noir tells you that ticket had better be notarized and punched in triplicate and presented with the full boondollar penalty plus processing fees, or you are wasting valuable time he could otherwise spend shirking his clerical duties.

Ticket? Oh, this thing. Ha, ha, look at that, you are holding a ticket. How did that get in your hand? It belongs on the desk with the others. No, you are not here to pay a parking ticket.

You explain to the frightening man that you are here to pick up that green parcel.

Jack makes it clear he would rather stab something to death than process the avalanche of paperwork needed to release the confiscated freight. Also any legit courier would have the pickup forms ready to go. In spite of how he's supposed to be dressed now but isn't, he ain't nobody's fool.

Don't worry, PM, it's fine. Jack pulls out a blade of some sort pretty much any time someone comes into his office, or just enters his vicinity in general. It's like saying hello. The fact that you aren't dead already means he likes you.

But perhaps an UNDERSTANDING can be reached.

He gives you a HIT LIST.

Bring him the crowns. He'll give you the box.

> Jack: Examine package.

You get the sense that Jack frequently barters with assassination requests in lieu of accepting forms and fees. (I typed this note, then looked at the next page to see the text literally confirm this. It's a gratifying feeling to observe how often I end up agreeing with myself.)

The PARCEL MISTRESS departs with her mission of double agency. You wonder if she'll actually be so foolish as to attempt to uphold her end of the lopsided bargain. You make a policy of handing out a REGISWORD and a HITLIST to just about everyone who enters your office. But you never think anyone's actually going to GO THROUGH with it.

You wish you could watch. She's a deadwoman.

You wonder why she's so desperate to acquire this package. What could be inside?

> Jack: Open it.

> Dave: Punch some cards.

There's something I've always wondered about this scene. But first, a spoiler: there's a cybernetically enhanced bunny in the box. Okay, that base is covered. What I wonder is, is the bunny "deactivated" right now? Like in sleep mode or something? Or is he just sitting in there with his outlandish arsenal of weapons and cheerfully waving at Jack from inside the box?

You've leeched more than enough grist from John to afford a PUNCH DESIGNIX, which for some reason Jade put in the hallway making it kind of hard to walk through your apartment, but whatever. You also have plenty of grist for messing around with the ALCHEMITER to manufacture some new gear if you want. But you'd like to figure out what the JUMPER BLOCK does first.

Jade keeps dropping a weird assortment of objects for you to captchalogue and punch. You've given up trying to identify any rhyme or reason to the thought process behind it.

> Dave: Put a punched card in a shunt.

You put the punched BLENDER card in a shunt just for the hell of it, and stick it on the jumper pins.

The ALCHEMITER is fitted with the BLENDER UPGRADE.

This upgrade doesn't seem all that useful. Looks like all it does is grind up your totems.

> Dave: Use a punched Gamebro Magazine card.

The jumper block stuff was all about letting you use any conceivable item to upgrade your alchemiter with features of mostly dubious value. Basically it's using alchemy on your alchemiter. And like all alchemy in this story, it's mostly explored by the players in a lot of stupid ways.

The ALCHEMITER is upgraded with a huge metal bust of this awesome bro.
The device has been reduced to an utterly useless heap of shit.
Time to yank out all the shunts and start over.

> Jade: Draw the punch designix.

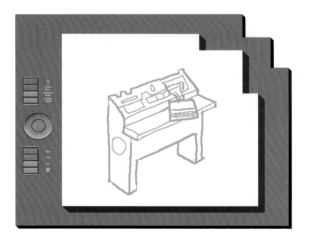

Your inscrutable thought process leads you to draw the PUNCH DESIGNIX on your SCRIBBLEPAD.

Okay, that's it. "Dave: Use a punched GameBro Magazine card" is the last reader command ever used in the story. I will always associate this ridiculous metal bro emerging from the platform with the cessation of all formal input from the readers. I'm not exactly sure why this moment was the tipping point. The readership was already too huge to warrant ongoing command submissions before that. Maybe it was the critical mass of absurdity this particular convergence of ideas represented? I was staring down the barrel of this smug, radical dude here, which was serving no purpose other than to utterly prevent Dave from performing alchemy, and I might have been like: okay, enough. The madness stops here.

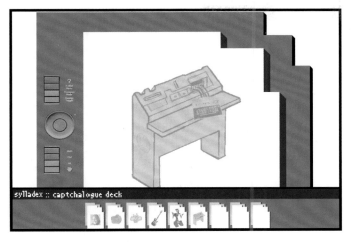 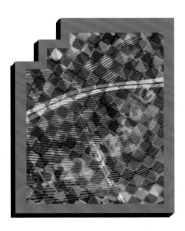

The pad recognizes the drawing, but there is no designix around,
and even if there was, it would obviously be way too big to captchalogue.

Instead, the GHOST IMAGE of the designix is captcha'd, along with its captcha code on the back.

> Jade: Send the code to Dave.

```
GG: dave here punch this code!
GG: L229BxoG
GG: and then put it in the jumper shunty
thing and see what it does
TG: ok
```

> Dave: Punch code and put it in the jumper shunty thing.

I just started making up commands from this point on to move things along, and there was virtually no detriment to doing so, or even any noticeable impact on the way the story progressed. I kept them pretty similar in feel to the commands people tended to submit, while cutting a lot of the bullshit they would throw out there. There was kind of a dumb sentiment among a few people that doing this was somehow "STEALING CONTROL OF THE STORY AWAY FROM THE READER!" I always thought it was silly how some conflated reader-submitted commands with reader control of the story. They were never in control at all. In fact, the commands were sort of a sneaky device to help make that point. Because the author and characters buck the will of the commands so often (e.g., "Get the pumpkin. Wait, what pumpkin? It's gone sucker, nice try."), the device turns out to be a repeated demonstration that the notion readers were exerting their will over the story was always an illusion.

TG: so i guess this is just a built in designix
TG: which is sort of cool i guess
TG: since i wont have to go downstairs and bang the
hallway door into the thing and squeeze through every
time i want to punch a card
TG: because of course you couldnt have just put it
next to the alchemiter in the first place
TG: but then i have to go downstairs anyway to make
totems and get cruxite and stuff
TG: so really who cares
GG: well i think this is only one way to consolidate
all the gizmo features....
GG: hang on ill give you more codes!!!

> Jade: Draw the holopad.

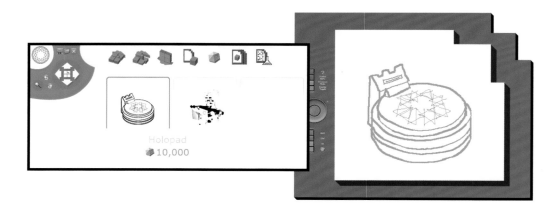

You don't have nearly enough grist to deploy the HOLOPAD, whatever it does.
But maybe you can get it as a freebie upgrade to the alchemiter.

Some of this alchemiter upgrading stuff, while kinda funny unto itself, was still done to serve a practical purpose, mostly for my own convenience and simplicity in ongoing story production. It's much better to have the alchemiter be this centralized source of all alchemy, rather than spreading the process all over the house and making the kids jump through all these hoops—punching cards, carving totems, and all that nonsense. This way, when a kid is near the alchemiter, I could just say (or imply), all right cool, just make some stuff. The expanded alchemy process was fun for a while, but at this point it just doesn't matter anymore.

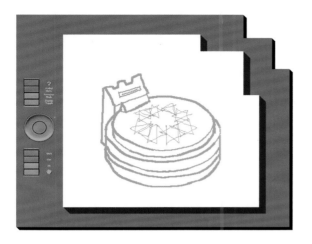 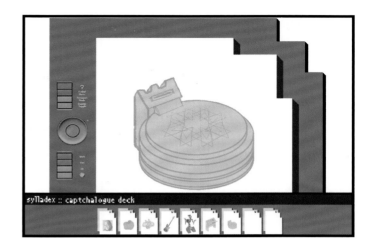

Looks like it worked! You love your scribblepad.

> Dave: Upgrade alchemiter with holopad.

The totem pedestal is converted into a holographic projector. It projects an image of the item the punch code represents.

This seems useful for previewing an item a code will produce, without spending the grist on it. You test it out with the blender card.

But it still renders the alchemiter unusable. At least without further upgrades.

> Jade: Draw the totem lathe.

This is a pretty clever hack by these two to get Dave the holopad. He doesn't have enough grist to make it, but Jade can just draw it to get the code, and then send the code to him. The jumper blocks don't need any grist to upgrade the alchemiter with those items, just a card with the code on it. Watching the kids figure out ways to hack the game is about as important to the story as watching them figure out how the game itself works in the first place. This is because the story is first about the game and the subversion of that game, and then about the narrative and the subversion of that narrative. So, long story short, this is why Dave can now see a completely useless hologram of a blender here.

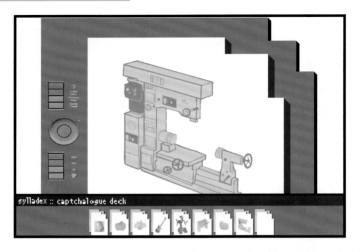

You captcha the lathe ghost image and apply the upgrade.

Now the holopad projects a hologram of the totem that a punch card will create!

This appears to turn the alchemiter into a one stop-shopping hub.
You just punch a card, stick it in, and get your item. Nice!

> Jade: Draw the jumper block.

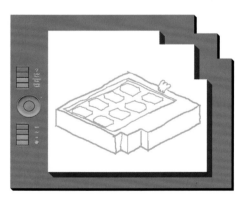
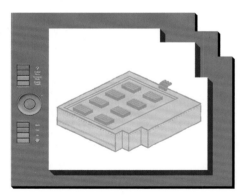

You get the code for the jumper block extension to upgrade the
alchemiter with... uh... the jumper block extension?

Ok that's kind of a crappy drawing but it seemed to work anyway.

> Dave: Upgrade.

We are making progress. The lathe is completely obsolete now. Next we upgrade the alchemiter with the whole jumper block thing, which...it already has? So really, we're just telling the alchemiter to "build this into yourself as a fundamental part of your structure, rather than as an attachment piece." Got it? Listen, I really, really need you to understand all this. It's so important to me.

This is getting a little abstract.

But it appears to economize on space. Now all you have to do is stick a card in a slot to apply an upgrade. Don't have to bother with the shunts anymore.

> Jade: Draw the intellibeam laserstation.

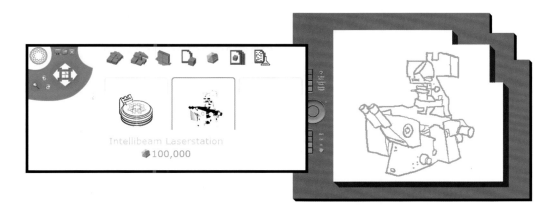

This thing looks kind of complicated.

Think about this for a second. The card Dave just inserted in order to collapse the whole structure like that? That card is still in there. One of those four yellow cards is the one for the jumper block extension. Which means if you take the card out, that huge thing instantly reappears. Try to picture Dave doing that. If he pulled the card out, the jumper block would rocket out of the side of the alchemiter like a huge cash register opening. It would probably launch him off the roof of the building.

139

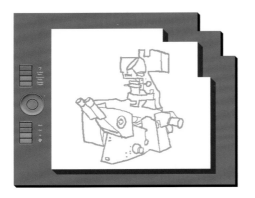

DAMMIT!

> Dave: Captchalogue enlarger.

You grab the ENLARGER from your dismantled photography lab.

> Dave: Upgrade.

The Scribblepad really quite enthusiastically wants to assume you're trying to draw a robot any time you draw something mechanical-looking it can't parse. I think this makes it likely that the Scribblepad is a pretty sophisticated AI, with a whole personality and such. It just really wants you to build it a friend. :(

You apply the ENLARGER UPGRADE.

> Jade: Draw air conditioner on roof.

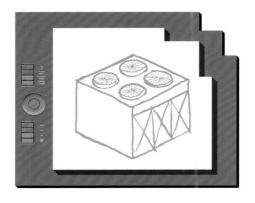

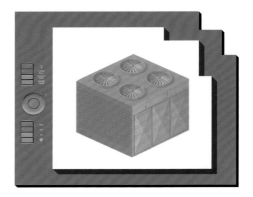

You ghost-captcha the huge air conditioner and give Dave the code to mess around with.

> Dave: Make air conditioner unit.

Finally, Dave's photography hobby pays off. Now he can make things of any size. That's like, REALLY USEFUL! Although making a tiny version of the AC unit like he's doing here admittedly isn't a very useful application of this feature. Anyway, this is pretty much the "final form" of the alchemiter for the rest of the way. It does practically anything you could ever want it to do. Maybe it should be called...the alchemajor??? Hmm, nah.

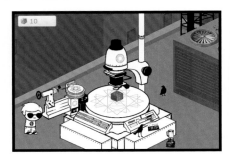 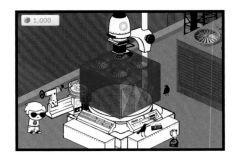 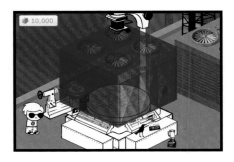

Size of the object you make is now variable. The bigger, the more expensive, as one would expect.

You make a tiny AIR CONDITIONER.

This was totally not a waste of time!

> John: Find the car.

You find your father's car near the base of the rock pillar. It is surrounded by caution tape for some reason. You are reminded to be cautious.

You cautiously inspect the vehicle.
To no one's surprise but yours, the
package and the game are missing.

Someone is bugging you.

John, you aren't being cautious enough. Get the fuck outside the tape. What you're doing is illegal.

```
-- gallowsCalibrator [GC] began trolling ectoBiologist [EB] --
```

GC: JOHN 1TS M3 4G41N
EB: who?
EB: oh, that's right...
EB: the leetspeaking blind one.
EB: go away!
GC: JOHN DONT M4K3 FUN OF MY H4ND1C4P
EB: which one, the blindness or the leetspeak.
GC: 1 4M S3NS1T1VE 4BOUT BOTH
EB: sorry.
GC: YOU C4N M4K3 1T UP TO M3
GC: BY L3TT1NG M3 H3LP YOU
EB: wow, you drive a hard bargain!
EB: but noooooooooooooo.

GC: B3FOR3 YOU K33P TYP1NG MOR3 STUP1D O'S 1N TH4T WORD
GC: JUST L1ST3N 4ND DO WH4T 1 S4Y
GC: YOU KNOW YOUR3 GO1NG TO 3V3NTU4LLY 4NYW4Y
GC: B3C4US3 YOUR3 4 N1C3 GUY 4ND K1ND OF 4 TOT4L W33N13 PUSHOV3R
EB: yeah, well you're a huge...
EB: oh man, whatever, what do you even want.
GC: 1M MOT1V4T3D BY S3LF 1NT3R3ST
GC: TO H3LP YOU 4DV4NC3 MOR3 QU1CKLY
GC: B3C4US3 1V3 GOT YOUR WHOL3 ADV3NTUR3 R1GHT H3R3 1N FRONT OF M3
EB: do you have a braille screen or something?
GC: SHHHHHHHH!
GC: 4NYW4Y TH3 PO1NT 1S
GC: 1TS LONG AND BOR1NG
GC: 4ND YOU COULD ST4ND TO SK1P SOM3 ST3PS
EB: i don't really understand.
EB: so you can "see" my whole future there, right?
EB: by just like, scrolling around on some computer thing that lets you pick what time to talk to me?
EB: how can you be bored by my long boring future, why don't you just scroll around to wherever you want like the other weirdos are doing?
GC: OK 1 C4N DO TH4T
GC: 4ND 1 4M
GC: 1 GU3SS WH4T 1 R34LLY M34N 1S
GC: 1 JUST W4NT TO M3SS W1TH YOU
EB: oh ok, that sounds really great and helpful!
GC: 1 M34N M3SS W1TH TH3 T1M3L1N3

Terezi—after elaborations of a metaphysical nature, a series of insults, and a bunch of sketchy excuses for why she's doing the stuff she's doing—finally just admits that all she really wants to do is mess with John. Here is a woman after my own heart.

```
GC: MY FR13NDS 4LL TH1NK TH4T YOU C4NT R34LLY CH4NG3 4NYTH1NG
GC: TH4T YOUR T1M3L1NE W3'R3 CH4T-HOPP1NG 4ROUND 1S S3T 1N STON3
GC: NO M4TT3R WH4T W3 S4Y OR WH3N W3 S4Y 1T
GC: 4ND TH3YR3 PROB4BLY R1GHT
GC: BUT 1 DONT C4R3
GC: 1 W4NT TO M3SS W1TH 1T 4ND T4ST3 WH4T H4PPENS
GC: >:D
EB: sounds dumb.
EB: but if it means you're going to help me, then go ahead and help me i guess.
GC: L3TS G3T YOU TO TH3 G4T3 F1RST
GC: 1TS NOT F4R
GC: 1 SN1FF3D OUT 4 M4P OF YOUR PL4N3T
EB: whoa, you've got a map?
EB: where'd you get it?
GC: JOHN W3 AR3 SO MUCH B3TT3R TH4N YOU IN 3V3RY R3SP3CT 1TS R1D1CULOUS
EB: can i have it?
GC: 1TS HUG3
GC: 4ND MOSTLY 1RR3L3V4NT
GC: H3R3 L3T M3 DR4W YOU 4 SM4LL S3CT1ON OF 1T
GC: SHOW1NG YOU WH3R3 TO GO
EB: ok.
-- gallowsCalibrator [GC] sent ectoBiologist [EB] the file "GOH3R3JOHN.G1F" --
```

Terezi is horrible at art, in the same way someone would be if they were closing their eyes while trying to draw something. When she draws, faces are disconnected from heads, arms and legs float off somewhere else. We assume it's because she's blind. Except she also clearly has the ability to detect a lot of detail through her sense of taste, to the point of being able to read and such. So it seems odd that she would be so bad at drawing that she wouldn't be able to connect limbs to torsos. It's more likely that she actually *could* draw well if she wanted to, but she either just literally doesn't pay the slightest attention to what she's doing when drawing, or she deliberately draws like this to lay it on thick with her blindness routine and mess with people. Both possibilities seem equally plausible to me.

```
EB: this is the worst crap i have ever seen.
EB: what am i looking at here?
GC: 1TS TH3 B3ST 1 CAN DO
GC: >:[
EB: ok sorry but it's useless.
EB: what's with these colors.
GC: 1 P1CK3D ON3S TH4T SM3LL N1C3
EB: couldn't you just, like...
EB: crop the world map.
EB: i thought you guys were THE BEST.
GC: SHUT UP MY M4P 1S F1N3
GC: LOOK 1TS NOT 3V3N TH4T F4R 4W4Y
GC: 1LL L34D YOU TO 1T
GC: 1TS 4 B1G P1P3
GC: YOU JUMP 1N
GC: TH3 W1ND W1LL T4K3 YOU TO TH3 G4T3
GC: 1TS 4 SHORTCUT
EB: you mean The Breeze?
GC: Y34H WH4T3V3R
GC: L3TS G3T MOV1NG JOHN
GC: 4R3 YOU R34DY TO FUCK UP TH3 T1M3L1N3???
EB: sure.
```

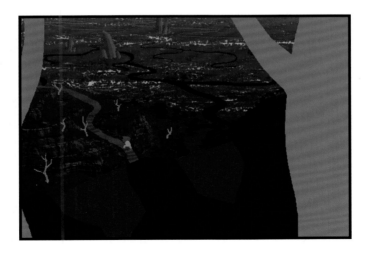

Terezi, sorry, but it really probably isn't the best you can do. I'm just not buying your bullshit anymore.

> Rose: Strife.

The chalk imp is leaving little dusty piles of chalk around wherever he goes. What a slob. At least it's less messy than the oil smears. The chalk could just be vacuumed up. Actually, Rose could go inside right now, pry that bronzed vacuum off its base, and do a little tidying. After she slaughters these fools, obviously.

  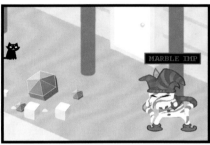

Rose is strangely proficient with this lethal, self-styled form of knit-jitsu she's wielding here. I guess her strifes with Mom have honed her skills. Still, I can't see her pulling off moves like this against her drunk mother, who is superhumanly adroit at parrying attacks with a martini glass. Maybe Rose practiced in her room with a stunt wizard?

147

There is like, a ZERO percent chance Vodka Mutini over there isn't just dying to play with all that wildly lashing yarn.

Believe it or not, this attack presages the moment when Rose does the exact same thing to Guy Fieri as a fifty-something-year-old woman in an alternate universe.

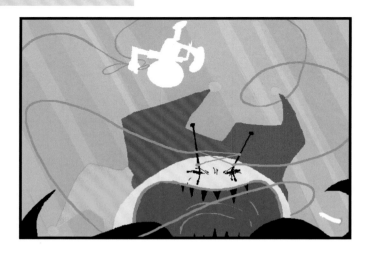
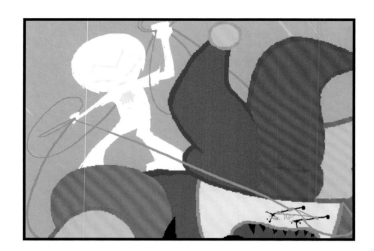

> Rose: Knit the scarf. Ride the ogre.

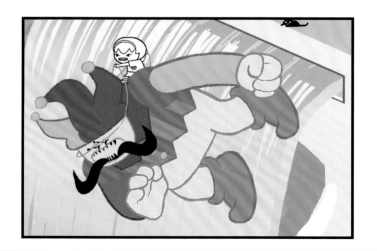

Rose: Execute textbook emergency water landing with hideously maimed ogre.

> Rose: Answer Dave.

I kind of regret not putting another ogre, looking scared, somewhere on the island to help convey the fact that now all ogres in the land are afraid to fuck with Rose. She's made a gruesome example of this one, but really, it's kind of a waste of the message that could have been sent.

TG: im building up your house
TG: by the way why do you live in this weird compound
TG: do you host east european industrial raves
TG: nevermind the point is
TG: im out of grist
TG: so if youre done whipping that ogre like a rented mule
TG: maybe you could convert it into a grist windfall
TT: Right now?
TT: The spoils would sink.
TG: i dont know beach the thing first i guess
TG: unless you were planning on sailing that ogre down the mississippi with a runaway slave
TT: And then what?
TG: what do you mean
TG: you kill it
TG: release a shitload of grist
TG: maybe take one of your needles and puncture the base of its skull
TG: does it even have a skull
TG: or a brain stem
TG: can you find out
TT: That sounds malicious.
TG: what
TG: but you just rigged the thing with an oedipal harness and rode its torso like a log flume ride down a magical rainbow

A gratuitous conversation about how best to murder an unconscious maritime ogre feels like an Extremely Dave/Rose Conversation. It's easy to imagine them having hundreds of conversations like this in the past, of a more hypothetical nature.

TT: That was self defense.
TT: Murdering a wounded behemoth in its sleep strikes me as unseemly.
TG: this is bullshit its an unfeeling monster who gives a fuck
TT: Maybe you could replicate a pillow I could use to smother it.
TT: Make it a clean hit.
TT: I would use one of mine but they've all mysteriously gone missing.
TG: wow fuck ok
TG: you can either kill it for the loot or wait a couple hours for gristtorrent to steal more of johns
TG: but then again ill be pretty busy in a couple hours so make up your mind
TT: Does John know we've been sapping his grist yet?
TG: no but hes still got a ton so screw him
TT: Hold on, someone's messaging me.
TG: yeah me too

> Dave: Answer troll.

-- grimAuxiliatrix [GA] began trolling turntechGodhead [TG] --

GA: You Command The Seer
GA: So You May Have Some Insight Into Her Disposition
TG: who
GA: The One Who Is A Little Snooty
TG: oh yeah sure
TG: i command her alright i am like the pimpmaster hustledaddy of all snippy bookshrews
GA: Thats An Exotic Title
GA: I Thought You Were The Knight
TG: wrong what do you want
GA: Have You Found Her Demeanor To Be Chilly
GA: On A Basis Of Personal Interaction That Hypothetically Extends Beyond The Context Of A Short Lived And Lackluster Trolling Effort
TG: what the hell
GA: I Thought Your Familiarity With Her May Allow You To Furnish Me Insight
GA: She And You Are Familiar Isnt That Right
GA: She Perhaps Even Regards You With Uh
GA: Endearment
TG: you have no idea dude she is so in my grill
TG: like a stray hotdog that rolled down there
TG: and now its too much trouble to fish out with the tongs

I'm not sure how Rose's idea of smothering the ogre with a pillow makes sense, considering he appears to be perfectly capable of surviving facedown in an ocean for an indefinite period of time. This appears to be pretty solid smoking-gun evidence that the underlings don't actually need to breathe.

153

TG: so you just watch it like crack and turn black
GA: Um Is This
GA: A Common Sort Of Practice In Human Courtship
GA: Watching Oblong Meat Products Tumble Into Places They Dont Belong
TG: man wait
TG: whats this about
TG: you have a thing for her dont you
TG: dont deny it bro its obvious
GA: Am I Being Accused Of Falling Prey To The Human Dysfunction Of Amorous Inclination
TG: hahahaha so terrible
TG: what a transparent dodge
TG: all hiding behind your alien shit
TG: just admit it
TG: you want me to help you win her over
GA: I Just Would Like To Gather
GA: Some Means Of Gauging Her Sincerity
TG: ok well its easy
TG: for everything she says take her to mean just the opposite
TG: see not everybody always means literally what they say the way john and jade always do
GA: Maddening
GA: How Do Humans Forge Meaningful Relationships Using Such Communication Patterns
GA: Perhaps It Is The Human Riddle That Is Truly The Ultimate Riddle
TG: oh my flipping christ
TG: ok if you want rose to dig you you got to leave that crap in the shitty scifi novels where it belongs
GA: It Was Not A Sincere Remark
GA: I Have Been Practicing
GA: Your Human Sarcasm
TG: oh ok
TG: that was pretty good
TG: maybe even too deadpan but its a start keep at it
GA: Very Well
GA: I Am Beginning To Feel As Though I Am The Only One Working On Our Friendship
TG: hahaha yes youre on a roll
GA: That Was Sincerity
TG: oh
TG: alright look
TG: if you want to keep her attention you got to pull out all the stops
TG: reverse psychology mind games all sorts of machiavellian bullshit
TG: i mean unless youre really smooth and inherently likeable like me which youre not

GA: Then
GA: Keep Saying The Opposite Things
TG: thats kind of the obtuse alien way of getting it but yeah
TG: be like
TG: an antagonism ninja
TG: like her
TG: i dont know you sort of remind me of her anyway so maybe thats a good thing
TG: it could be a horrible thing though
GA: It Sounds Like
GA: You Are Advising Me To Troll Her Again
GA: Which I Have Tried
GA: It Proved To Be A Fruitless Endeavor
TG: yeah i guess i am
TG: i guess im saying be a less shitty troll
GA: Okay
GA: I Believe I Understand How To Proceed
TG: good luck bro

> Rose: Answer troll.

-- adiosToreador [AT] began trolling tentacleTherapist [TT] --

AT: hIIII, sO,
AT: yOU GET BOSSED AROUND BY THE KNIGHT, oK, gIVEN THAT, i
HAVE A QUESTION,
TT: Who?
AT: oH, tHE ONE WHO'S SUPPOSED TO BE "cool", i THINK,
AT: tHE SUN GLASSES GUY,
TT: Why would someone wear sunglasses while using a computer?
AT: iIII DIDN'T SAY ANYTHING ABOUT A COMPUTER, bUT,
AT: yES, hAAAAAH,
AT: i THOUGHT THE SAME THING ABOUT HOW ASININE THAT IS,
AT: sO, yOU KNOW THAT GUY, uMMM,
TT: I know that anyone committed to such an affectation could only be striving to mask a
severe insecurity complex, and likely harbors a crisis of self-image.
TT: I've been known to lend my charitable attention to such people, but only "bossed
around" by them insofar as the psychiatric professional has cause to humor the demented for
analytical purposes.

This *might* be the only time Tavros and Rose ever talk. They don't have much to say to each other. Luckily for Rose.

TT: Or maybe as a lab chimp commands the zookeeper's interest in its shit by forcing him to duck under its trajectory now and then.
AT: oK, wOW, i DIDN'T UNDERSTAND THOSE THINGS,
AT: bUT, uHH, i MEAN DAVE,
TT: Oh, that guy.
AT: yEAH, oK, gIVEN THAT, i HAVE A QUESTION,
AT: aBOUT HIM,
AT: i WANT TO KNOW ABOUT HIS EMOTIONAL VULNERABILITIES,
AT: aND, uM, wHAT ARE THE TENDER SPOTS THAT ALL THOSE, uHHH,
AT: dEVICES HE EMPLOYS TO CONCEAL THEM, uHH, lIKE ALL THE THINGS HE SAYS HE THINKS ARE FUNNY,
TT: Tender spots?
TT: Your word choices are evocative.
TT: Is your design to couple with this gentleman?
AT: wHOAAAAAAAA, nO, nO, wHOA,
AT: oK, nO, tHAT JUST MADE ME FEEL UPSET TO THINK ABOUT,
AT: i JUST WANT TO REALLY TRY TO BOTHER HIM, iT'S HARD,
TT: If you're trying to get his goat, you should know he only stocks the animal in the first place for ironic purposes.
AT: nO, i'M NOT REALLY INTERESTED IN HIS EARTH GOAT, bUT IF THAT WAS A FIGURE OF SPEECH THEN i GUESS THAT'S OK,
TT: Then we're agreed; you are hellbent upon literally seizing his shrill, bearded livestock.
TT: I'll assist you.
AT: uHH,
TT: If you really want to burn him, I recommend poetry.
AT: wHAT, pOETRY, aS IN LIKE THOSE HUMAN WORD BUNCHES,
TT: Yes. They are the most delicious bunches we have.
TT: I suggest you serve these crisp bunches of honey and verbal annihilation to him as part of a complete breakfast.
AT: oH, aND, wILL THIS BREAKFAST INJURE HIS SHRILL BARN BEAST,
AT: i MEAN THIS FIGURATIVELY, jUST TO BE CLEAR,
TT: A deft cluster-bombing of this sort will leave nothing wriggling from the razed earth.
TT: Except sulfurous tresses while it cracks and turns black.
AT: yOU MEAN, lIKE, tHE SURFACE OF AN OVERCOOKED PROTEIN OBJECT,
TT: Yeah.
TT: I suppose what I'm saying is this.
TT: Drop some hard, peer-reviewed motherfuckin' science on his ass.
TT: Some seriously government funded shit.
TT: It will destroy him.
AT: aAAAAHAHAHAH, yES,
AT: tHIS IS THE IDEA THAT i LIKE,

With all this silly talk of Dave having a goat, one almost forgets that Tavros's good friend literally does have a goat. Or, had. The goat was his father, who abandoned his son. So maybe this whole subject of getting a guy's goat is kind of delicate.

TT: Your obvious cunning with words should depants Strider with such vivid empyrean tempest, a nether-regional sonic boom is certain inevitability.
TT: But even so.
TT: Consider me at your disposal to help craft a comeuppance of such unqualified devastation, the angels will weep pearlstrings of little urban fellows cantillating an unbroken chorus of Oh Snaps.
AT: pLEEEEASE,
AT: i THINK i AM PERFECTLY CAPABLE OF MANUFACTURING THESE ALLEGED "dope" HUMAN RHYMES,
AT: aND STARTING SOME SICK FIRES,
AT: i DON'T NEED YOUR CHARITY, tHAT YOU SAID YOU LEND,
AT: tO, uHHH,
AT: eARTH MONKEYS WHO TOSS AROUND POOP, oR SOMETHING LIKE THAT,
AT: yOU'RE PRETTY SNOOTY,
AT: tHANKS FOR YOUR HELP, bUT I DON'T NEED YOUR HELP,

adiosToreador [AT] blocked tentacleTherapist [TT]

adiosToreador [AT] unblocked tentacleTherapist [TT]

AT: oOPS, sORRY, i DIDN'T MEAN TO BLOCK YOU,
TT: uMMMM,

> Rose: Answer troll.

Rose does appear to be using this brutalized ogre as an actual raft to navigate the waters around her island while offering to compose rap lyrics for this lame troll. Pretty cold-blooded. It's a really bad idea to fuck with a kid who's just about to hit the grimdark phase of her adolescence.

157

-- **grimAuxiliatrix [GA]** began trolling **tentacleTherapist [TT]** --

GA: Your Dark Spectacled Friend Has Advised Me On A More Effective Method For Trolling You
GA: I Think His Contention Is That This Strategy Will Have The Opposite Of The Intended Effect And Precipitate A Sort Of Bond Between Us That Is Established In Mutual Antagonism
GA: What Do You Think About This

TT: I think you're shrewd to have recognized his ploy of sabotage, and you've earned my compliments.
GA: Ah See It Is Working Already
TT: What is?
GA: Ive Listened To His Advice
GA: And Have Resolved To Modify The Approach Slightly
GA: I Know What I Have To Do
GA: What We Have To Do Really
TT: What's that?
GA: Remember The First Time We Spoke
TT: Yes, but you said it wasn't the first time you spoke to me.
TT: We'll graciously omit my embarrassing skepticism however.
GA: The First Time You Spoke To Me Was The Second Time I Spoke To You
TT: This conversation doesn't sound like your first time either.
GA: This Is Your Second Conversation With Me But Is My Seventh With You
TT: And when exactly does your maiden encounter take place?
GA: Thats Next Time
TT: So to clarify.
TT: If the matching of my first with your second is denoted by 1=2, then the sequence would be:
TT: 1=2, 2=7, 3=1, 4=?, ...
GA: Yes And The Rest Of The Sequence Is Simply
GA: 4=3, 5=4, 6=5, 7=6
GA: Unless My Future Self Stowed Another Conversation In Between One Of Those Which Is Entirely Possible
GA: But Urrgh I Dont Want To Think About That
TT: Why is it that when the subject of temporal mechanics is broached your sparing troll intellects etcetera etcetera.
GA: See That Is What I Mean Rose You Are Not As Dumb Of A Girl As I Was Initially Lead To Believe
TT: You mean based on the first impression I am apparently about to make in our next conversation?
GA: Yes
TT: What could I possibly say that will leave such an imprint?

Whoops, here's where it happens. In this overwrought conversation about the temporal order of their future conversations. They fall in love.

GA: That Is Why I Have Contacted You Now
GA: I Will Send You A Copy Our First Conversation Directly From My Chat Log

-- grimAuxiliatrix [GA] sent tentacleTherapist [TT] the file
"ConversationWithAVeryStupidGirl.Txt" --

TT: I guess being forced to cooperate with a stable time loop is the only plausible explanation for my remarks.
GA: Yes And Then I Found It Sort Of Curious That During My Next Conversation With You Your Various Mental Endowments And Wherewithals Were Not As They Seemed
GA: I Suspected The Stratagem Might Be A Counter Trolling Measure But Then Was Not So Sure And Further Examination Grew Warrant
TT: And what if my counter-counter measure is to choose not to transcribe this dialogue accurately in the future-first place?
GA: But See I Have Edited The Copy Already In Ways That Will Remain Secret For Now But You Will Discover Once You Type It
GA: So You Are Destined To Edit It No Matter What And What You Submit Will Be What I Once Read Regardless
GA: !
TT: Unless I decide to copy it word-for-word!
GA: Yes Unless I Lied About Editing It In The First Place
GA: Either Way Through Knowledge Of What You Will Say I Have Precisely Engineered The Nature Of Your Transgression
GA: !!!
TT: So your trolling strategy now is to put idiotic words in my mouth through the machinery of temporal inevitability, and cause me to excruciate over how to subvert the transcription?
GA: Yes
TT: While being perfectly up front about it?
GA: Yes I Suppose Its That Sarcasm All The Time Seems Laborious To Me
TT: I'll admit, it's a more advanced tactic than I gave you credit for.
GA: Yes And The Providence Of This Antagonism Ninja Vice Grip Pinching Your Larynx Has Already Begun To Supply My Purpose With Fruit
GA: The Chilly Frost Shimmering On Our Tree Of Human Friendship Has Begun To Thaw
TT: Mixed metaphor aside, usually ninjas don't announce what they're doing when they're doing it.
TT: Like when stalking an emperor to assassinate him.
TT: Or befriend him.
TT: But that's fine.
TT: I guess the only pointless question we haven't exhausted is, why?
TT: Why the convoluted artifice?
GA: Dave Raised Insight Into The Human Psychology Of Friendship Development

All I have to say on this page is, I like the idea of a ninja stalking an emperor just to become his friend. Rose says a funny thing there.

GA: By Allotting You Your Side Of The Conversation I Have You At The Disadvantage In Your View And You Will Seek To Reclaim Higher Ground
GA: In Successive Conversations
GA: 4=3 And 5=4 And Such
GA: Your Demeanor Will Be Terse If Not Saturated With Disdain And It Will Cause Me To Be Confused And Question Your Motivation
GA: But Now I Know Your Motivation Because I Am Supplying It Here And Now
GA: They Will Be Simple Acts Of Friendly Human Retaliation
TT: So you're not only rigging the first impression I make on you, but orchestrating my revenge for the rigging as well?
GA: Yes
GA: It Seems Friendship For Some Humans Is A Basic Aggregation Of Shallow And Insincere Hostilities
TT: That's an interesting take on it.
TT: But now I know for sure Dave isn't behind this plan.
TT: It's too complicated.
GA: I Dont Understand
GA: Who Better To Coordinate Such Events Than The Knight Of Time
TT: You're awfully quick to his defense.
TT: Are you sure you don't have a thing for him?
TT: It's ok, bro. You can admit it.
GA: I'm Hopping To 8=8
GA: Ideally You Will Have Long Since Discarded This Train Of Thought
TT: Ok.
TT: I'm going to talk to my dead cat.

Kanaya seems pretty pleased with herself about all this. And why shouldn't she be? This "scheme" she's hatching, whatever it is, is a pretty clever if preposterously overcomplicated way of hitting on someone, probably without even realizing that's what she's trying to do. But then again, she wasn't the one who came up with this plan, was she? I was. So maybe she's not so smart after all. Food for thought!

> Dave: Answer troll.

```
-- adiosToreador [AT] began trolling turntechGodhead [TG] --

AT: oKAYYYY, mY BROMO SAPIEN,
AT: r U READY,
AT: tO GET STRAIGHT IN, FLAT DOWN, BROAD SIDE, SCHOOL FED UP THE BONE BULGE,
AT: bY A DOPE SMACKED, TRINKED OUT, SMOTHER FUDGING,
AT: tROLLLLLLLLLLLLLLLLLL,
TG: dont care
AT: oK, lET ME,
AT: oRGANIZE MY NOTES HERE,
AT: oKAYYY,
AT: (tURN ON SOME STRICT BEATS MAYBE, iT WILL HELP TO LISTEN TO THEM WHILE i DESTROY YOU,)
AT: wHEN THE POLICE MAN BUSTS ME, aND POPS THE TRUNK,
AT: hE'S ALL SUPRISED TO FIND I'M TOTING SICK BILLY,
AT: wHOSE,
AT: gOAT IS THAT, hE ASKS, wHILE HE STOPS TO THUNK
AT: aBOUT IT, aND i'S JUST SAY IT'S DAVE'S, yOU SILLY
AT: gOOSE,
AT: bUT THE MAN SAYS, gOOSE! wHERE, lET ME SEE YOUR HANDS,
AT: aND i SAY SHIT SORRY, i DIDN'T KNOW IT WAS HONKTRABAND,
AT: wOW, oK,
AT: i AM GETTING OFF THE POINT, wHICH WAS,
```

Probably the worst and most cruel injustice Dave faces in this story is how people keep interrupting him when he's drawing his great comics. Tavros, back the fuck off. An artist is at work.

161

AT: lIKE THE COP i MENTIONED, bUT INSTEAD OF YOUR BADGE,
AT: aND YOUR GUN, IT'S YOUR ASS THAT YOU HANDED IN,
AT: (aND THEN GOT HANDED BACK TO YOU,)
AT: cAUSE THAT'S HOW HUMANS GET SERVED,
AT: aND GUYS LIKE YOU DESERVE TO UNDERSTAND THAT iT'S,
AT: a CIRCLE AND HORNS IN YOUR BUTT THAT GOT BRANDED IN,
AT: (uMM, bEFORE i GAVE YOUR ASS BACK TO YOU, i DID THAT, iS WHAT i MEAN,)
AT: bUT i MEAN, gETTING BACK TO THE POINT, oR MAYBE TWO ACTUALLY,
AT: tHE FIRST IS YOU SUCK, aND THE SECOND IS HOW i SMACKEDYOUFULLY,
AT: (oH YEAH, tHAT RHYME WAS SO ILLLLLLLLL,)
AT: bUT NO, jUST JOKING, lET'S SEE, hOW CAN i PUT THIS TACTFULLULLY,
AT: i MEAN THE POINTS ON THE HORNS ON MY HEAD,
AT: cOMING AT YOU THROUGH TRAFFIC,
AT: aIMED AT THE TARGET ON YOUR SHIRT THAT IS RED,
AT: wE'RE ABOUT TO GET MAD HORNOGRAPHIC,
AT: (i MEAN SORT OF LIKE A GRAPHIC CRIME SCENE, nOT LIKE,)
AT: (aNYTHING SEXUAL,)
AT: (eRR, wHOAAAAA,)
AT: (nEVERMIND,)
AT: oK, gETTING BACK TO THE ACTUAL, tACTICAL, vERNACULAR SMACKCICLE,
AT: i'M FORCING YOU TO BE LICKING, (aND lIKING,)
AT: gRAB MY HORNS AND START KICKING, lIKE YOU'RE RIDING A VIKING,
AT: cAUSE i'M YOUR BULLY, aND YOU'RE NOT IN CHARGE,
AT: yOU THINK YOU'RE IN CHARGE BUT YOU'RE NOT IN CHARGE,
AT: i'M IN CHARGE, cAUSE i'M CHARGING IN,
AT: yOUR CHINASHOP,
AT: bREAKING, uH, yOUR PLATES AND STUFF, WHICH i DON'T REALLY KNOW,
AT: wHAT THE PLATES ARE SUPPOSED TO REPRESENT, bUT,
AT: (fUCK,)
AT: iT'S JUST THAT YOU THINK YOU ARE THE COCK OF THE WALK'S HOT SHIT
AT: bUT WHEN IN FACT YOU ARE NOT, mORE LIKE YOU ARE,
AT: sOMETHING THAT RHYMES WITH THE COCK OF THE WALK'S HOT SHIT,
AT: bUT IS SO MUCH WORSE THAN THE COCK'S SHIT,
AT: sO, gIVEN THAT, lET ME BE THE FIRST,
AT: tO SAY YOU ACT LIKE YOU'RE GOLD FROM PROSPIT,
AT: wHEN YOU'RE REALLY COLD SHIT FLUSHED FROM DERSE,

162   It's good to see that this time Dave has the discipline to ignore Tavros and focus on his art. It's not unreasonable to assume Dave doesn't read a single word of this.

YOU JUST STARTED SOME

SICK FIRES, BRO

> John: Take shortcut.

At this moment in time, it was not yet a canon fact that Tavros is in a wheelchair. That fact was fanonized into canon later, by me, as a "boon" to the speculators and fan comic artists out there. I think this speculation may have been fueled by the fact that we can't see his legs (even though for now, you can't really see any of the trolls' legs when they're at their computer stations). But even though it became a part of his profile later, and even if you could just peek under that counter there right now, you still wouldn't see a wheelchair. Because at this point in time he has his robot legs. So in summation, this whole issue is kind of stupid.

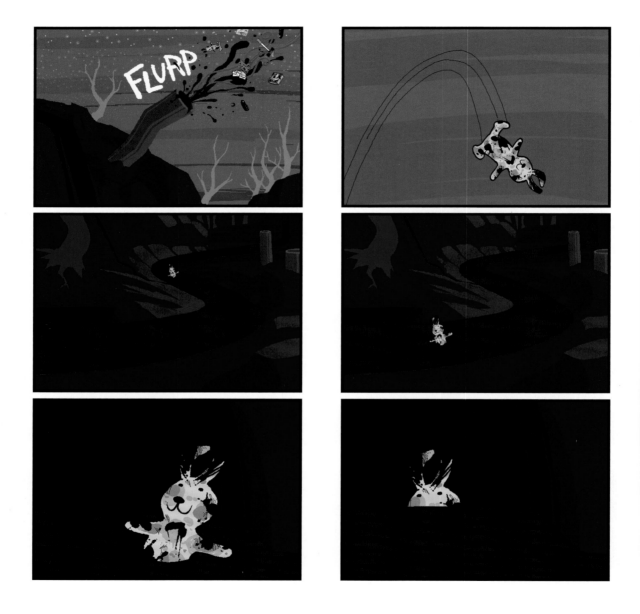

Good thing Terezi's "map" sent John through this filthy oil pipe. I'm sure that shortcut was completely necessary.

> John: Reunite with your loving wife and daughter.

> John: Give dear sweet Casey the bunny.

This is the final emotional scene in *Con Air*. In the movie it's initiated by Nic Cage scooping the dirty bunny out of the gutter at the last minute before it goes down the drain, just like John does here. Which is probably what gave him the idea to reenact this scene with a couple of salamanders for no good reason. *Homestuck*'s repeated references to this film have caused just about every member of the fandom to watch this fairly bad movie multiple times as a matter of ritual. I don't think anyone even thinks of it as a normal movie from the '90s anymore. It's just a *Homestuck* movie now. *Homestuck* basically owns it.

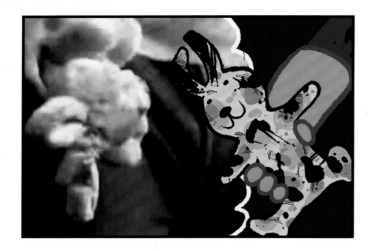

I got a present for you, Casey.
It's a little dirty.
A LITTLE ROUGH AROUND THE EDGES
JUST LIKE YOUR DEAR OLD EX CON DAD
WITH A HEART OF GOLD

> John: Surrender to overwhelming emotions.

> John: Answer CG.

John gets pretty worked up about this movie. He loves his shitty movies on such a pure, sincere level. I was thinking about this the other day, how I used to watch unbelievably shitty movies all the time. And while we recognize bad movies are bad technically, sometimes we bond with them irrationally, like John does. In the old days—say, the '90s and earlier, before there was quite so much media to consume, and before sites like Rotten Tomatoes warned you about awful movies in no uncertain terms—you really had no choice but to consume almost everything out there and see how you felt about it. So you were exposed to a lot more bad stuff than you tend to be these days. Which sort of forced you to deal with the bad things, think about them critically, and consider what you actually liked about them in spite of the badness. You were more likely to feel some sense of fondness for the bad stuff out there, because it was part of such a limited overall palette of media, and it was more likely to help shape your experience and memories.

-- carcinoGeneticist [CG] began trolling ectoBiologist [EB] --

CG: JOHN WHAT THE WET BAG OF HUMAN HORSE SHIT TO THE FACE DO YOU THINK YOU'RE DOING.
CG: OH MY LORD.
CG: NO WONDER YOU LOSERS ALL FUCK UP THIS GAME SO BAD.
EB: what?
EB: i am just acting out a scene from an awesome movie and having some fun, what's wrong with that?
CG: WHAT KIND OF CRAPPY EARTH MOVIE IS THIS.
CG: STUPID RABBIT ASSHOLE SCREWS THE POOCH?
EB: no, it's about these criminals on a runaway plane, and they've got to be stopped by nick cage and john cusack together as a team.
CG: OH.
CG: OK, THAT ACTUALLY SOUNDS PRETTY GOOD I GUESS.
EB: it is sweet, so sweet, you would probably like it.
CG: I'VE HEARD OF JOHN CUSACK I THINK.
CG: WASN'T HE IN SERENDIPITY?
CG: THAT WAS PRETTY GREAT FOR A HUMAN FLICK.
EB: hahaha, oh man, that sucked so bad!
CG: OK I DON'T SEE HOW WE'RE SUPPOSED TO BE BECOMING FRIENDS IF YOU RECOIL FROM MY OLIVE BRANCH LIKE I'M WIGGLING A GNARLED TREE MONSTER'S DICK IN YOUR DIRECTION.
EB: don't you have alien movies from your alien planet?
CG: YEAH OF COURSE, WE HAVE TONS OF MOVIES AND THEY ARE INFINITELY SUPERIOR TO YOUR PRIMITIVE CINEMATIC NEANDERTHRASHINGS.
EB: ok, so what is a really good one?
CG: YOU'LL PROBABLY LAUGH IF I TELL YOU THE NAME OF ONE.
EB: well, i already laughed when you said the name of one of ours, so who cares?
CG: OK FINE.
CG: ONE THAT IS AMAZING AND IS A CLASSIC IS...
CG: WHEREIN NUMEROUS VIGILANTES CONFRONT PERIL; ONE OF THEM BETRAYS THE OTHERS; (BUT IT TURNS OUT TO BE PART OF THE PLAN ALL ALONG);
CG: SEVERAL ATTRACTIVE FEMALE LEADS PROVOKE ROMANTIC TENSION; FOUR MAJOR CHARACTERS WEAR UNUSUAL HATS; ONE HOLDS PLOT-CRITICAL SECRET;
CG: 47 ON-SCREEN EXPLOSIONS, ONE RESULTING IN DEMISE OF KEY-ADVERSARY; 6 to 20 LINES THAT COULD BE CONSTRUED AS HUMOROUS;
EB: wait...
EB: this is the title?
CG: IT GOES ON.
CG: THEY TEND TO BE MORE LITERAL AND INFORMATIVE THAN YOUR TITLES.
EB: how do you even say them in casual conversation?
CG: WELL WE DON'T OBVIOUSLY.

I think this is the first indication that Karkat is into romantic comedies. What an incredibly good character trait for him to have. Also, trolls have all the same celebrities that humans do, which is probably the dumbest idea I'll ever be responsible for in my entire life. Fortunately for everyone, I intuitively recognize the need to counterbalance my extraordinary genius with occasional feats of staggering stupidity.

CG: IT'S LIKE SOMEONE SAYS, HEY GUYS WHY DON'T WE GO SEE A MOVIE, AND THEN EVERYONE JUST ENDS UP THERE
CG: WATCHING IT.
CG: NOT SAYING IT, THAT'S DUMB.
CG: JOHN, TRY TO THINK OUTSIDE YOUR MINUSCULE CULTURAL BUBBLE FOR A CHANGE.
EB: ok, i just think it's still cumbersome and completely illogical.
CG: YEAH THAT'S WHAT HAPPENS WHEN YOU START RUNNING OUT OF MOVIE TITLES AFTER RACKING UP THOUSANDS OF YEARS OF FILM HISTORY.
CG: YOU KNOW I THINK YOUR CIVILIZATION JUST DIDN'T MATURE ENOUGH OR SOMETHING.
CG: BEFORE LETTING THIS EARTH ARABIAN YOU CALL A GENIE OUT OF THE BOTTLE.
CG: MUST EXPLAIN WHY IT SPROUTED SUCH A MISERABLE CROP OF PLAYERS.
CG: INSTEAD OF BASICALLY GODS LIKE US.
EB: well, i've got one of your godly players helping me now, so we can't be in such bad shape.
CG: WHAT ARE YOU TALKING ABOUT.
EB: GC gave me a map.
EB: and showed me a shortcut.
CG: WHAT THE HELL IS SHE DOING.
CG: THIS ISN'T WHAT WE TALKED ABOUT DOING AT ALL.
CG: HOLD ON LET ME ASK HER ABOUT THIS...
EB: ok.
CG: OK...
CG: NOW SHES JUST OVER THERE GIGGLING AT ME LIKE AN IMBECILE.
CG: WHAT ARE YOU TWO UP TO, WHY ARE YOU IN CAHOOTS NOW?
EB: umm...
CG: OW FUCK!!!
CG: OK SHE JUST WALKED OVER AND PUNCHED ME.
CG: AND SAID IT WAS FROM YOU.
EB: uh, sorry i guess?
CG: I TOLD HER TO STOP THESE SHENANIGANS...
CG: BUT IT SEEMS LIKE WHATEVER SHE WAS DOING WITH YOU SHE ALREADY DID A WHILE AGO.
CG: FROM MY PERSPECTIVE AT LEAST.
EB: i don't know why you guys are doing this to yourselves.
EB: all this time jackassery, it's giving me a headache.
CG: OK IF YOU TALK TO HER AGAIN WHEN SHE TRIES HATCHING MORE PLANS GIVE HER A MESSAGE INTO THE PAST FOR ME.
EB: ok.
CG: TELL HER TO POLISH MY HEAVING BONE BULGE AND SET A TABLE FOR FUCKING TWO ON IT.
CG: ITS FOR OUR CANDLE LIGHT HATE DATE.
EB: i like how you guys have basically resorted to trolling each other, through us.
CG: FUCK YOU.
EB: oh, did you talk to jade yet?

A "candle light hate date"? At this point, it sounds like he's just talking smack with some funny terms he's making up on the spot, like the sassy boy he is. But this, of course, is a real idea on Alternia. I can't wait to talk about Troll Romance here in the laugh gutter of these books. Alas, we must have patience.

CG: JADE, WHAT WHY WOULD I WANT TO TALK TO HER?
EB: ummm, that's what you said you wanted to do last time you talked to me, i dunno.
CG: OH DAMMIT.
CG: ARE YOU SURE?
EB: yeah, you told me dude.
EB: want me to paste the conversation?
CG: NO NO, GOD NO, I HATE IT WHEN WE START GOING DOWN THAT ROAD.
CG: OK THIS IS GOING TO REQUIRE FURTHER INVESTIGATION.
CG: I'VE GOT TO GO.
EB: ok.
EB: but next time you talk to me, you might want to tell me to calm down first so i don't just block you.
EB: back then i won't really want to hear from you.
CG: OK, I'LL DO THAT.
EB: later.

> John: Answer GC.

-- gallowsCalibrator [GC] began trolling ectoBiologist [EB] --

GC: H3H3H3H3H3
GC: JOHN STOP HUGG1NG THOS3 S4L4M4ND3RS 4ND B31NG SO STUPIDLY 4DOR4BLE
GC: W3 4R3 ON 4 STR1CT CH3AT1NG T1M3T4BL3 H3R3
GC: W41T WHO 4R3 YOU T4LK1NG TO NOW
GC: 1S 1T ON3 OF US
GC: 1S 1T M3???

By the end of Act 4, or maybe 5, it's going to become clear that virtually all of these conversations are entirely propped up by self-supporting logic like, "Dude, I'm saying this stuff now because earlier you or someone else said that's what I was going to be saying later!" It's like, you know those guys who are supreme masters of balancing random objects on each other and can create a big sculpture of chairs or something, where the only reason the structure is stable is because the chairs are all interlocking in this impossibly perfect way so they're all holding each other up, like some sort of miracle? It's like that, but with stupid conversations among cranky teens instead of chairs, and also a lot of absurd plot shit.

EB: it was carcino.
GC: H4H4H4H4H4
GC: 1 B3T H3 1S CONFUS3D 4ND GRUMPY
EB: yeah, sorta.
EB: he has no idea what you're doing.
GC: 1 H34R H1M OV3R TH3R3 B4NG1NG ON THOS3 K3YS
GC: 1 TH1NK TH1S WHOL3 TH1NG 1S JUST 4 W4Y TO V3NT SOM3 FRUSTR4T1ON
GC: H3 H4S NO PURPOS3 Y3T
GC: NOT L1K3 YOU 4ND M3 JOHN >:D
EB: oh, he said to give you a message...
GC: OH >:?
EB: he wants you to touch his bone lump or something.
GC: WH4T!!!
EB: and that he's pretty much basically in love with you.
GC: W41T
GC: D1D H3 4CTU4LLY S4Y TH4T
GC: 1N CONF1D3NC3
EB: yeah, i dunno, pretty much.
GC: C4N YOU COPY 3X4CTLY WH4T H3 S41D
EB: ohhh no, we're not going down that road!
EB: besides, it was a private conversation among private gentlemen colleagues.
EB: oh, also you're going to punch him.
GC: 1 4M
GC: WH3N
EB: i guess in your future.
EB: but in your pretty soon future i think.
EB: it's when he says stuff to you and then you laugh at him.
GC: BUT 1M 4LW4YS L4UGH1NG 4T H1M
GC: HOW W1LL 1 KNOW?????
EB: also he says you said it's from me.
GC: FROM YOU
GC: DO YOU W4NT M3 TO PUNCH H1M JOHN
EB: pffff, i don't care!
EB: i'm just the timey-wimey messenger here.
GC: 1M SUR3 M4NY H1GHLY JUST1F1ABL3 4ND W3LL D3S3RV3D PUNCH3S W1LL B3 THROWN 1N DU3 T1M3
GC: BUT L3TS ST1CK TO TH3 G4M3PL4N FOR NOW
GC: JOHN T4K3 4 LOOK 4T WH3R3 TH3 SHORTCUT TOOK YOU
GC: TURN 4ROUND >:]

> John: Turn around.

This really is some fantastic trolling by John. Ruffling the feathers of Karezi's oft-fraught teenmance. Saying it was a private conversation among private gentlemen colleagues was a nice touch too. He makes it sound like they had some real heart-to-heart bro talk, when that's not even close to what happened. This is probably driving Terezi nuts.

Here's Typheus's palace. It's a pretty nice palace design, considering it almost certainly took me five or ten minutes to draw it, with no revisions or fixes whatsoever. If you couldn't guess by looking at it, this is the top part of a huge pipe organ that goes all the way down to the center of the planet. The piano part of the organ is in the core, but it can't be played until all that oil is cleared away...*somehow*. Terezi's leading John into this palace right now for *reasons*, but we suuure won't be seeing the interior for a while. Certain problems need to be present before the execution of this task can serve as a solution to anything.

```
EB: oh, wow.
EB: what's that?
GC: 1TS YOUR D3N1Z3NS P4L4C3
EB: my denizen?
GC: 3V3RY PL4N3T H4S 4 D3N1Z3N
GC: TH4T L1V3S D33P UND3RGROUND
GC: SL33P1NG
GC: 4ND GU4RD1NG 4 HUG3 GR1ST HO4RD
EB: ok...
GC: TH3 W4Y DOWN TO 1TS L41R 1S THROUGH TH3 P4L4C3
EB: so you want me to go down there and kill him?
EB: won't that be, uh, kinda hard?
GC: H4H4H4H4H4H4
GC: ORD1N4R1LY YOUD H4V3 4BSOLUT3LY NO CH4NC3
GC: 4T YOUR M34G3R L3V3L
GC: BUT YOU H4V3 4N 4DV4NT4G3
EB: oh?
GC: USU4LLY HOW 1TS SUPPOS3D TO GO 1S
GC: OV3R TH3 COURS3 OF YOUR QU3ST
GC: YOU W1LL W4K3 TH3 D3N1Z3N
GC: 4ND TH3N F1N4LLY YOU GO THROUGH TH3 S3V3NTH G4T3
GC: WH1CH 1S TH3 ONLY W4Y 1NTO TH3 P4L4C3
GC: TH3N YOU GO DOWN 4ND F1GHT TH3 D3N1Z3N
GC: 4ND K1LL 1T
GC: R3L3AS1NG TH3 HO4RD
EB: so what's my advantage?
GC: YOU WONT BOTH3R W4K1NG 1T
GC: W3 W1LL SK1P R1GHT TO TH3 S3V3NTH G4T3
GC: F1ND 1TS L41R
GC: 4ND K1LL 1T 1N 1TS SL33P
EB: um, ok.
EB: what's the point of releasing the grist hoard?
EB: is it just so i can make tons more sweet loot?
GC: H3H3 NO W4Y
GC: TH3 HO4RD CONT41NS SO MUCH MOR3 GR1ST TH4N YOU COULD 3V3R US3 1N 4N 4LCH3M1T3R
GC: 1 M34N YOU COULD 1 GU3SS
GC: BUT TH4TS NOT TH3 PO1NT
GC: 1TS FOR TH3 ULT1M4T3 4LCH3MY
EB: what's the ultimate alchemy?
GC: 1TS NOTH1NG FOR YOU TO WORRY 4BOUT NOW
GC: S33 TH4T G4T3 OV3R BY TH3 BROK3N BR1DG3
GC: GO CH3CK 1T OUT
EB: alright.
```

I don't remember what people thought the Ultimate Alchemy was referring to before it was revealed at the end of Hivebent, but there are only so many things it could refer to. After all, the word "ultimate" is a pretty big deal. Then again, ultimate Frisbee doesn't strike me as much to write home about. Just some guys getting a bit carried away with a Frisbee is all. Kind of diminishes the concept of ultimateness for everyone else, when you think about it.

> John: Examine gate.

EB: so this is the seventh gate?
EB: that'll take me into the palace and
down to the sleeping denizen?
GC: NOP3 >:]
GC: TH1S 1S JUST 4 S1MPL3 R3TURN NOD3
GC: TH3R3 4R3 LOTS OF TH3S3 4ROUND
GC: JUST HOP 1N
GC: DONT WORRY 1LL G3T YOU TO TH3 G4T3
SOON 4FT3R TH4T

> John: Hop in.

> WV, AR: Prepare gift for the WQ.

John: Breathe huge sigh of relief that no imps stole your bunny's certificate of authenticity while you were gone.

> Meanwhile, in a long discarded memory...

WV sure is quick to discard his passionate anti-royalty convictions the moment a hot queen strolls into the picture.

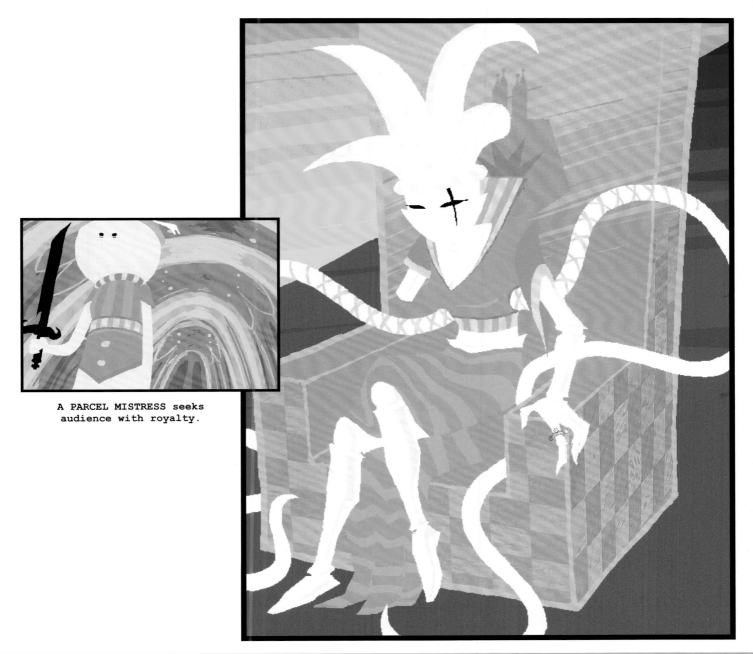

A PARCEL MISTRESS seeks
audience with royalty.

Pausing here to reflect on the fact that the White Queen is inclined to dress somewhat more modestly than the Black Queen. They both uphold their solemn duty to wear clowny things, but only one of them takes it up a notch in the sluttiness department. My best guess as to why is that, as far as we know, the White Queen doesn't have a White Jack she likes to torment in ways that combine clear sexual undertones with constant belittlement.

A flurry of disquieting happenstance is related to the ADORED SOVEREIGN.
With no other options, her counsel is all that is left to be sought.

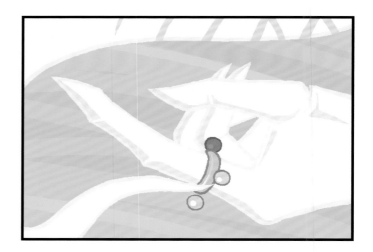

Of course she's not going to kill her beloved queen. What a ridiculous thought. The queen knows what to do. She probably saw this all coming and had a plan ready. She's unbelievably wise, obviously. That's what anthropomorphized chess pieces do. They think in terms of chess play, many moves ahead. The better the piece, the smarter they are.

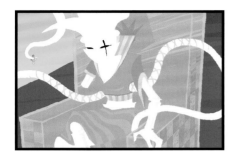

Abdication is never ideal. But in the face
of inevitable conquest, conceding ground can
supply the only remaining advantage.

The final hope for victory lies in patience
and planning.

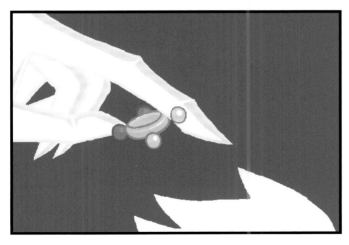

The WHITE KING of course can be found on the
BATTLEFIELD. His CROWN may be retrieved there.

The RING must be designated for protection. He
will supply further instruction on this matter.

Pretty slick move, the queen dangling the ring she just took off on a tentacle that's about to disappear, just above a missing hand that's about to appear, which will catch the ring when it falls. I wouldn't have to explain this if the image were animated. But then again, if the image were animated, you wouldn't get the privilege of reading me talk about it. Everything is a trade-off, you see.

The royal duty has been accepted.

And in time, fullfilled.

No one is more flabbergasted by PM's coronation than Serenity. She just did NOT see that coming.

> Rose: Consult with Jaspersprite.

JASPERSPRITE: Meow.

The heavenly pink turtle shells elicit, in my opinion, an *intense* craving to see Mario bop them one by one. Mario isn't in *Homestuck*, unfortunately. But I do believe he is mentioned in at least one conversation later.

ROSE: Is that all you have to say?
JASPERSPRITE: Purr purr purr.
ROSE: I thought you were supposed to be more helpful after your resurrection.
ROSE: Like a ghostly spirit guide. Wise, if frustratingly cryptic.
JASPERSPRITE: Purrrrrrrrrr.
ROSE: Actually, cryptic behavior would be welcome at this point.
ROSE: This is just inane.
JASPERSPRITE: :3
ROSE: Should I report to the others that my Kernelsprite is a Lolcat?
ROSE: Maybe Dave can take some screen captures and overlay some poorly spelled captions.
ROSE: Assuming he hasn't already.
JASPERSPRITE: Meow.
ROSE: What are you doing there, by the way?
JASPERSPRITE: Im fishing!
ROSE: Oh. So you can talk.
JASPERSPRITE: But sadly there are no fish i think.
JASPERSPRITE: They were all eaten by the Denizen!
ROSE: Who?
JASPERSPRITE: It ate everything in the ocean and got so full that it took a long nap.
JASPERSPRITE: No there is surely not a single living thing left!
JASPERSPRITE: Which is too bad because im pretty hungry.
ROSE: I think there might be some tuna in the cabinets.
JASPERSPRITE: Oh good idea i will look there!
JASPERSPRITE: Purr purr.
ROSE: Jaspers, the message you gave me years ago before you disappeared...
ROSE: What did you mean?
JASPERSPRITE: Meow.

Lolcats seem like a really dated reference now. I barely even remember what they were. Pictures of cats? Jesus Christ, who cares.

```
ROSE: Sigh...
JASPERSPRITE: :3
ROSE: I don't understand.
ROSE: Is there some meaning to these responses, or are you just being obstinate?
JASPERSPRITE: You will understand when you wake up!
ROSE: Am I asleep?
JASPERSPRITE: Yes!
JASPERSPRITE: Rose im just a cat and i dont know much but i know that youre important and
also you are what some people around here call the Seer of Light.
JASPERSPRITE: And you dont know what that means but you will see its all tied together!
JASPERSPRITE: All the life in the ocean and all the shiny rain and the songs in your head and
the letters they make.
JASPERSPRITE: A beam of light i think is like a drop of rain or a long piece of yarn that
dances around when you play with it and make it look enticing!
JASPERSPRITE: And the way that it shakes is the same as what makes notes in a song!
JASPERSPRITE: And a song i think can be written down as letters.
JASPERSPRITE: So if you play the right song and it makes all the right letters then those
letters could be all the letters that make life possible.
JASPERSPRITE: So all you have to do is wake up and learn to play the rain!
JASPERSPRITE: Does that make sense rose sorry i disappeared for so long.
ROSE: Sort of.
ROSE: It sounds like you aren't exactly in complete command of this information yourself, so
I won't press you on it for now.
ROSE: You're a pretty good cat, Jaspers. I missed you.
JASPERSPRITE: Purr purr purrrrrrr.
```

> Rose: Pester Jade.

```
TT: I spoke with Jaspers.
TT: I didn't understand what he told me.
TT: He said I'll understand once I "wake up".
TT: For some reason this made me think of you.
GG: hehehe......
GG: yeah i bet hes right!
TT: We wouldn't happen to be talking about awakening in a
sort of breezy, philosophical sense, would we?
TT: Is my dead cat concerned with my enlightenment? Should I
prepare to shed this coil of ignorance and suffering?
GG: wow no i dont think so...
```

Jaspers sure is a simple cat, but now he's wired to know all about the lore of the land and to provide helpful exposition in his cute and friendly feline manner. Here he describes the nature of Light. Not the physical phenomenon, but the aspect. There's a lot to Light, even more than is conveyed here. (Such as luck stuff. See: the Serkets.) It's about information, which is what DNA is. There's important DNA data trapped in Rose's head, which Jaspers mysteriously is the key to releasing, and which is also relevant to the "play the rain" quest Jaspers seems so excited about. But of course Rose is a rebellious miscreant, so her quest really isn't going to matter much at all, except as a hypothetical cool mythoquest that she tells to go fuck itself repeatedly. This is a topic I guess we are going to have to keep revisiting as we talk about Rose over the whole story. If we want to understand Rose, there will be no avoiding this, sorry.

GG: hes being a bit more literal than that!
GG: what did he say?
TT: I doubt I could reproduce the statements with fidelity.
TT: It was like listening to a five year-old describe a dream.
TT: The content manages to take a back seat to the simple heartwarming spectacle of the moment.
GG: :)
GG: well what he meant was.....
GG: that you have a dream self
GG: who is supposed to wake up whenever your real self goes to sleep
GG: we all do! all four of us i mean
GG: but see your dream self still stays asleep when you go to sleep
GG: because you havent woken up yet!
TT: I think I get it.
TT: I take it your "dream self" is wide awake when you sleep?
GG: yes
TT: And would I be out of line in additionally presuming this has been the case for many years, at least as long as I've known you?
GG: no you would not be out of line!
GG: in fact im asleep now
TT: That was to be my next wild presumption.
GG: :p
TT: So when I wake up, can I look forward to being able to message people in my sleep too?
GG: no only i can do that!
GG: because of my robot
TT: Oh, right.
TT: I forgot about your robot.
TT: My short term recall seems to eschew the profoundly ridiculous.
GG: you guys can probably make your own i guess......
GG: but you need to wake up first for it to matter and maybe by the time that happens you might not even need them!!!
TT: I'm not sure if necessity is a concept I'd associate with such a contraption even under some of the more obscure scenarios imaginable.
TT: But good to know I guess.
TT: Here's another question, which I'm sure will look stupid once I've finished typing it.
TT: If my dream self is asleep, does that mean she's dreaming, and if she is, who's dreaming the dream, her or me?
GG: um.......
GG: ok well i dont really know how to answer the second part but yeah shes dreaming!
GG: shes most likely lying in your bed troubled and restless
GG: about things burdening her
GG: which is to say you!!!!!

Oh, a Jade/Rose chat. Let's enjoy this rarity. They finally have The Talk about dream selves, which is just as beneficial for the reader as it is for them. Rose gets at some spooky stuff with that last question. The truth is—as we start to infer later from some fucked-up events concerning Jade's dream self—that a dream self is actually a pretty distinct version of yourself. A separate person from your waking self, yet one whose mind is fully inhabited by your waking self's mind when you fall asleep and "wake up" as the dream self on Prospit or Derse, in the course of which the dream self is sort of "displaced" temporarily. Also, you can take over the dream self permanently if your waking self dies and is resurrected with a kiss, in which case the dream self that was inhabiting the dream body just dies. The dream self can also die independently of the waking self and then be resurrected as a totally separate person via prototyping (like Jadesprite). Long story short, Rose is right to be asking hard-hitting questions about this already. It's a complete morass of pseudospiritual quackery and existential dread.

GG: things about who you really are and what your purpose is
GG: but you cant start figuring those things out yet because youre not awake because youre not ready yet
GG: thats why you have such terrible dreams all the time rose!
TT: Ok. How do I wake up?
GG: im sure it would help to start piecing together the clues to nudge your subconscious
GG: or maybe face some things you havent faced yet?
GG: i dunno! its for you to find out
GG: maybe the stuff you wrote on your walls can give you a clue?
TT: What stuff?
GG: the....
GG: er
GG: didnt dave tell you?
TT: Tell me what?
GG: ._.
TT: Are you saying he said I defaced the walls of my room?
TT: While not appearing to be cognizant of the scrawlings?
TT: Like John?
TT: I really hope that's not what you're saying.
TT: It might freak me out.
GG: he said he was going to tell you <_<;
TT: Hold on.

> Rose: Pester Dave.

TT: Strider.
TT: I need you to do me a favor.
TT: Can you take a capture of my bedroom and send me the file?
TT: For no reason in particular?

The kids all write stuff on their walls that's invisible to them. Or their subconscious is blocking them from seeing it or something. They are troubled by the visions of their unwoken dream selves, who force them to sleepwalk and scrawl things on their walls. What must their guardians think? Oh right, John's dad saw a bunch of gross clown graffiti on John's walls and assumed it meant John loved clowns, thus spurring Dad to get really into clowns himself to support his son's interest. What a dad. When Rose's mom saw her daughter's graffiti, she probably just thought something like, "I am currently too inebriated to show any concern about this. Anyway, time to continue getting hammered and admire my wizards some more."

TT: He's not answering.
GG: yeah hes pretty tied up right now!
TT: Can you hassle him via Sburb and tell him to talk to me?
TT: Bop him on the head with a puppet or something?
GG: noooooooooooooooooo

GG: he made me promise not to bug him while im asleep!
TT: Can you do it anyway?
GG: but he will find a way to be clever and make me punch myself in the face again :(
TT: Did he tell you what I wrote on the walls?
TT: Wait.
TT: What?

184

Dream Jade is being very positive and encouraging to John so he can fight his restless sleep-demons and wake up. I bet they're going to have a great time when he finally wakes up. Dream Jade will give him a hug, and they will probably laugh and play, flying through the clouds of Skaia. Dream Jade will definitely be alive when he wakes up, so they can do all that stuff. Mark it down.

> John: Await further instruction.

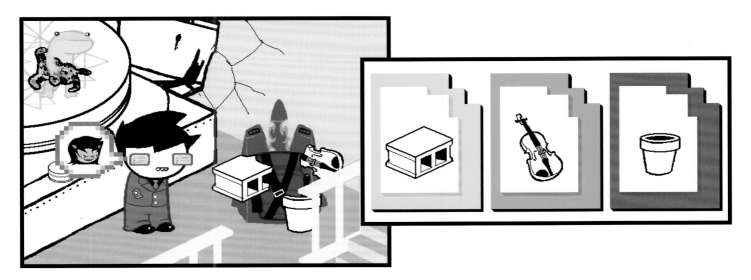

Dave is working really hard to retrieve that egg. But what exactly does he think he's going to do with it once he gets it? Sit on it? It's not improbable that he's thinking about exactly this issue right now, as he climbs. It's also not improbable that he's thinking, "what am i going to do sit on it? yeah maybe ill just sit on it. what else are you supposed to do to hatch an egg."

```
GC: JOHN S33 TH4T B1G P13C3 OF JUNK TH3R3
EB: the rocket pack?
GC: Y34H C4PTCH4LOGU3 TH4T 4ND S3ND M3 TH3 COD3
GC: 1 GOT TH3 COD3S FOR 4LL TH3 OTH3R 34RTH CR4P STUCK 1NS1D3 1T FROM YOUR FR13NDS
GC: FROM D1FF3R3NT T1M3S
GC: WH3N TH3Y W3R3 F33L1NG COOP3R4T1V3
GC: 1 C4N M4K3 1T WORK FOR YOU >:]
EB: ok...
EB: but you can't just "subtract" object codes from other codes!
EB: it's like, mathematically, um...
EB: ambiguous.
EB: like just reverse AND/OR'ing the flower pot alone could make hundreds of possibilities.
EB: subtracting all three could be millions!
GC: Y34H W3LL 1M NOT S4Y1NG 1M 4NYWH3R3 N34R 4S HUG3 OF 4 DORK 4S YOU
GC: OR TH4T 1 UND3RST4ND 4NY OF TH4T
GC: COMPUT3R COD3S T4ST3 TO M3 L1K3
GC: LOTS OF T1NY N33DL3S 4ND B4TT3R13S
EB: wow, what?
GC: 1M G1V1NG 4LL TH3S3 COD3S TO OUR H4CK3R GUY
EB: oh man, you have a hacker??
EB: i bet he is THE BEST!!!!
EB: hackers are always the best.
GC: H4H4H4H4H4
GC: W3LL H3 SUR3 TH1NKS H3 1S
EB: who is it?
EB: have i talked to him?
GC: NO H3 S4YS H3 DO3SNT W4NT TO T4LK TO 4NY OF YOU 3V3R
GC: B3C4US3 H3 H4T3S YOU
GC: BUT H3 W1LL DO TH1S
GC: B3C4US3 H3 WONT B3 4BL3 TO R3S1ST TH3 CH4LL3NG3
EB: uh, ok.
EB: brb then.
```

> John: Captchalogue rocket pack.

John seems really excited to hear about Sollux. Too bad Sollux is so antisocial and will never talk to John about anything. Maybe they would have become great friends? They meet a lot later but don't really care about each other at all then. By that point they have more important things than programming to concern themselves with. Like how many times each of them has died.

```
EB: ok here...
EB: dskjhsdk
GC: TH4NKS
GC: W41T
GC: THOS3 K1ND4 S33M L1K3 R4NDOM K3Y M4SH1NGS
GC: 4R3 YOU M3SS1NG W1TH M3 JOHN >:?
EB: um, no.
EB: they sort of are random.
EB: but it's the right code, i promise!
GC: OH
GC: OK B3 B4CK IN L3SS TH4N ON3 S3COND
GC: PCHOOOOO
```

```
EB: hello?
GC: WH4T
EB: it thought you said you'd be back
in less than a second?
GC: 1 W4S
GC: 1 G4V3 YOU TH3 COD3
GC: 1TS PCHOOOOO
GC: 1T TOOK 4 WH1L3 FOR H1M TO F1GUR3
OUT
GC: BUT 1 G4V3 IT TO YOU 1NST4NTLY FROM
YOUR P3RSP3CT1V3
GC: WHY WOULD 1 M4K3 YOU W41T???
```

There's a nice unspoken beat here where John takes a moment to angrily hammer some cheeky imps into grist, without making it a big enough deal to mention, or even interrupt his conversation at all. He truly is developing the spirit of a warrior.

```
GC: TH4T WOULD B3 SO 1NCONS1D3R4T3 >:[
EB: oh...
EB: i just thought that was just you going off to get the code...
EB: and making like this rockety noise or something, i dunno.
EB: because you're kind of goofy.
GC: W3LL YOUR3 K1ND OF
GC: W3LCOM3
GC: YOU UNGR4T3FUL 34RTH HORS3S NO1SY BUTTHOL3!!!
EB: oh gosh, i'm sooooo sorry!
EB: this is just a stupid code, i'm sorry.
EB: are you sure it's right, it seems kind of...
EB: obvious.
GC: H3 W4S CONV1NC3D TH1S 1S TH3 R1GHT COD3 4ND H4D SOM3 UNFL4TT3R1NG TH1NGS TO S4Y 4BOUT TH3
1NT3LLIG3NC3 OF YOUR SP3C13S FOR NOT B31NG 4BL3 TO F1GUR3 1T OUT
GC: WH1CH 1 W1LL K33P TO MYS3LF B3C4US3 UNL1K3 YOU 1 4CTU4LLY H4V3 SOM3 FUCK1NG M4NN3RS
EB: bluuuh, oh man, i got so served, bluuuuuuuuuh!
GC: 1 4M UNF4Z3D BY YOUR HUM4N BLUHS
GC: 4NYW4Y 1F 1T W4S SO OBV1OUS WHY D1DNT YOU GU3SS TH3 COD3?????
EB: well you see, the explanation is perfectly simple and scientific.
EB: it was because shut up.
EB: shut up is why.
GC: >:D
EB: i guess i'll make this rocket now.
EB: and see if this dumbass code actually does the trick.
GC: OK JOHN
GC: ONC3 YOU M4K3 1T 1M SUR3 3V3N YOU 4ND YOUR UND3RD3V3LOP3D BON3 NOOK W1LL B3 4BL3 TO
F1GUR3 OUT WH4T TO DO
GC: T4LK TO YOU ON TH3 OTH3R S1D3 >:]

-- gallowsCalibrator [GC] ceased trolling ectoBiologist [EB] --
```

> John: Make rocket pack.

A tip from me to you: try to keep "ungrateful earth horse's noisy butthole" in your back pocket as a sick own, for the next time someone doesn't appreciate something you do for them.

188

> John: Answer Dave.

```
-- turntechGodhead [TG] began pestering ectoBiologist [EB] --

TG: ok im in
EB: in where?
TG: the medium
EB: oh, already?
TG: what do you mean already shit took 4 goddamn hours
EB: huh, i guess time flew by while i was doing other stuff.
EB: how did it go?
EB: with you and jade i guess?
TG: i dont want to talk about it
TG: imagine the worst day of my life
TG: just stood up and clinked a glass like it was about to give a speech
TG: then took a shit in my dinner and passed out with its pants down
EB: ew dog! ewwww!
TG: yeah
EB: so nasty! gross dude!!!
TG: stfu
TG: what are you doing
EB: i'm in a rocket pack and i am about to blast off into space.
TG: ok
EB: it should be sweet.
```

Some tricky nonchronological stuff is happening again. From John's POV, we're skipping ahead to when Dave is already in the Medium. He was climbing the radio tower to get the egg just a few pages ago, so what happened? Dave makes it sound really bad, but we know this boy has a flair for melodrama, so who knows. Revealing what happened and how it happened, and the circumstances under which these facts are revealed, is the point the narrative is now marching toward. I had been stitching all this together in a fast-and-loose ad hoc manner, but at this point I felt like I had to start making some pacing adjustments to keep things more interesting. HS got so deep into the granular details of basic game activity, like kids trading codes to remove flower pots from a rocket, that at a certain point I had to dispense with the baby steps and start taking some big strides to move things along. We're about to see a lot of that, as Terezi kicks off her scheme here. With this intriguing little time skip, we've barely seen anything yet. The story's about to go bananas.

189

```
TG: i need some advice
TG: my kernelsprite which was this brainless feathery asshole with a sword in it
TG: turned into this bigger like ghostly feathery asshole
TG: with a sword in it
TG: it seems to want me to prototype it again
TG: not sure what to do
EB: hmm...
EB: have you asked rose?
TG: shes asleep for some reason
EB: wow, really?
TG: yeah i saw her there
TG: all tuckered out
TG: like she got smacked in the face with a pillow case full of the snooze wizards beard
dander
TG: cause obviously its fuckin prime time for swiping some shuteye about now
TG: like a few hours into her magic stupid quest
TG: anyway what do you think
EB: i don't really know, i mean...
EB: it's supposed to be like your ghostly spirit guide or something.
EB: unless you have the remains of a wise old dead grandparent lying around, i'm not sure
what to tell you!
TG: ok fine but
TG: it seems to be suggesting something here
TG: and
TG: i guess im kinda weirded out by its suggestion
EB: i don't know, just do what it says!
EB: it knows stuff about the game, so it probably knows better than i do...
EB: i gotta go!
EB: gonna blast off to the seventh gate.
EB: and, uh, win this game i guess.
TG: ok well it definitely sounds like youre fucking something up over there
TG: but alright later
EB: later.
```

> John: Captchalogue Casey.

Yes, John is about to fuck something up over there. And yes, the bird is suggesting something weird to prototype with. We learn later through implication that Dave was being urged to prototype the sprite with Cal. Why? I don't know why the bird would want that. But I do know that the doll is chock-full of some rather Troubled Souls, who have a way of influencing others in unfortunate ways.

This is absolutely no place for children. You take dear, sweet CASEY into protective custody.

> John: Blast off.

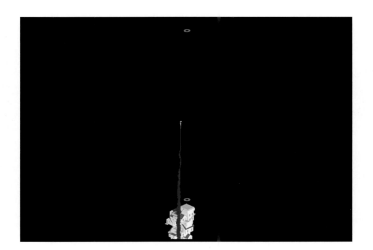
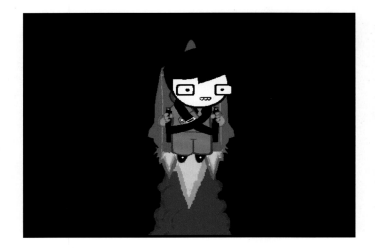

PCHOOOOO

It's incredibly important that John takes Casey with him. First, the fated journey of the rabbit must continue. Second, Casey must continue on her/his journey toward becoming the legendary necromancer and ultimate savior of the final epic battle, Viceroy Bubbles Von Salamancer. Think I'm bullshitting you about this? I would never do that. How dare you.

192

This is the face of a boy who is extremely determined to do something stupid. Sayonara, John. This is the last time we will see this exact instance of you alive. We'll catch up with him again thousands of pages later, sure. When he's a ghost. And then even later on, that ghost will die too. I guess this is technically the first time someone dies in the story? (I'm not counting the Felt. Don't worry about those guys.) It's an offscreen death, but it was a sad and shocking one for folks to reckon with nonetheless. Bear in mind that when this was happening, nobody had the slightest idea what I was up to here until it all played out later. Maybe I went insane? That was always a legitimate possibility, which I think kept things exciting in this story for many years.

> [S] Dave: Accelerate.

GATE 5

As you watch this animation load, the "GATE 5" up there is really ominous. The Fifth Gate? What happened to...the first four?

Land of Heat and Clockwork

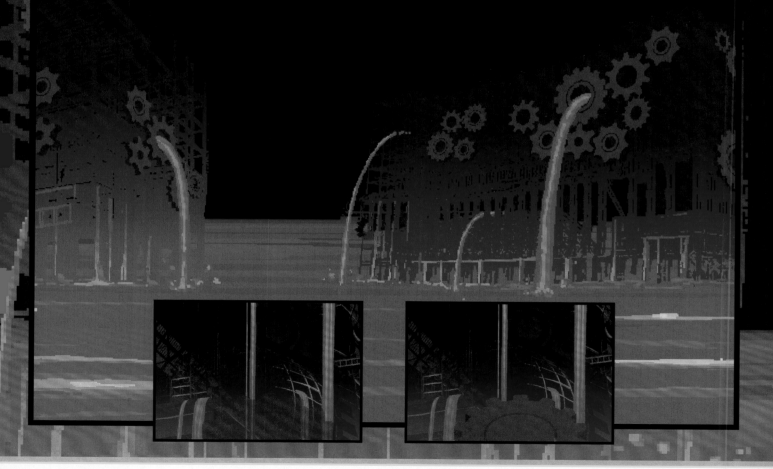

You wouldn't guess it just going by the scenery, but LOHAC is the bustling financial capital of the Medium. There is a thriving stock exchange here, run by energetic, greedy lizards.

194

s animation was pretty sick at the time. Lots of action, cool music. Neat time tricks by Dave. It's an absolutely massive time skip that left everyone overwhelmed by implications. Dave has already been here for months, battling monsters, hopping around gears. He's made a stylish new suit too, I guess to foster a certain Secret Agent chic. He's like the James Bond of horsing around with weaponized time travel, is the message being conveyed here.

Just as the monsters on LOWAS and LOLAR have oil and chalk themes, these ones on LOHAC are amber-themed and yield grist accordingly. I touched on this a while back, but the "planetary pollutant" in a world full of clockwork would be a substance that could gum up the clockwork and make it tick slowly or grind to a halt. That would be a sticky, hardening substance like amber. The quest here on this planet, if done by the book, would involve clearing the land of its sticky pollutants so the gears could tick freely, which probably would wake up the denizen, and so on and so on...

196

But here's the first glimpse of why so often in this story the by-the-book quest falls into the background as something trivial, like a sidebar of mythos-color that's mainly of academic interest and not plot importance. It's because there's always bigger fish to fry. Something more imminently concerning or threatening, like having to survive for months in this hellhole while two of your friends are dead.

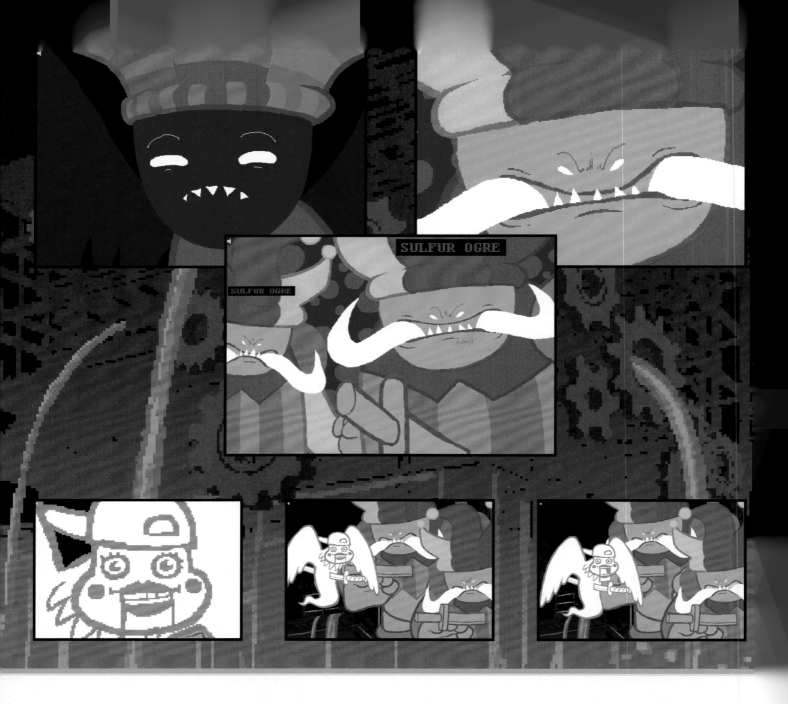

He did it. He prototyped the crowsprite with Cal. He knew it was a bad idea. But he did it anyway. The cursed journey of Davesprite begins with one unspeakable folly. So tragic.

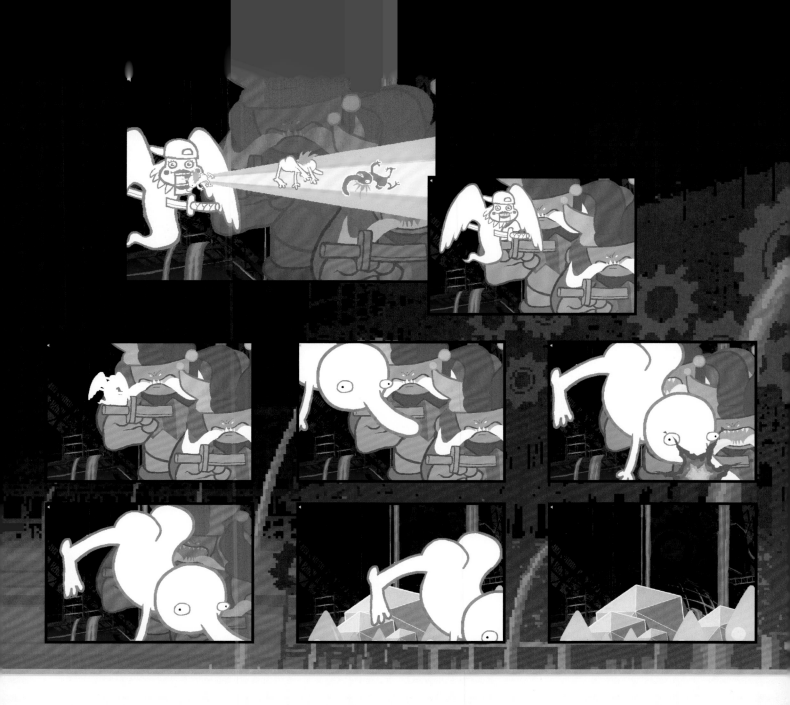

Say what you will about Calsprite. He's a formidable combatant. That huge puppet-ass attack? Absolutely devastating.

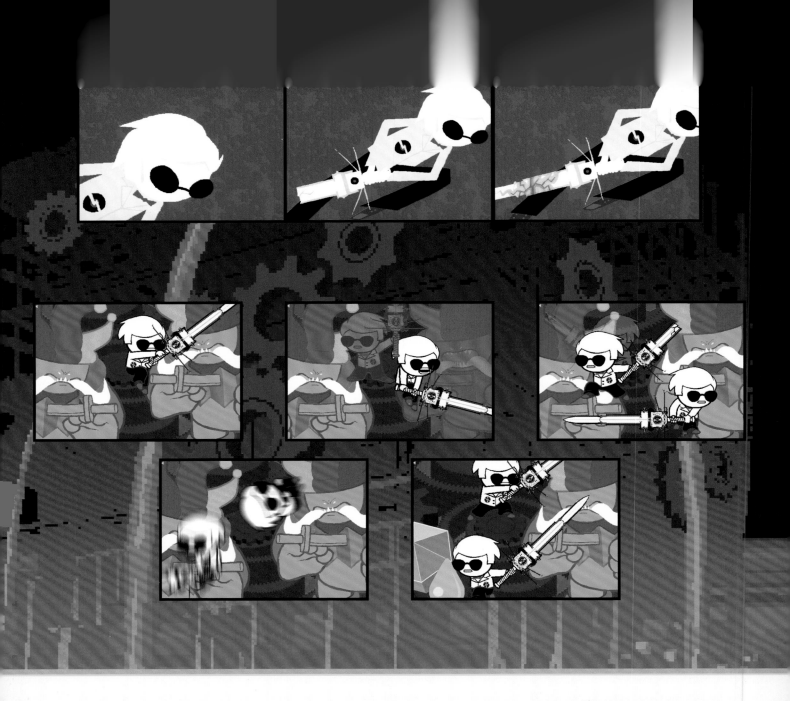

This sword concept is pretty cool. Caledscratch, as the weapon is named, is a broken sword, which Dave can wield thanks to his ½bladekind specibus. But it has a built-in time travel mechanism that allows it to cycle through previous states in its history, including back to a period of time when it was not yet broken. So it can extend and contract at Dave's will. A bit like a lightsaber, maybe? If you could turn on a lightsaber only halfway, I guess.

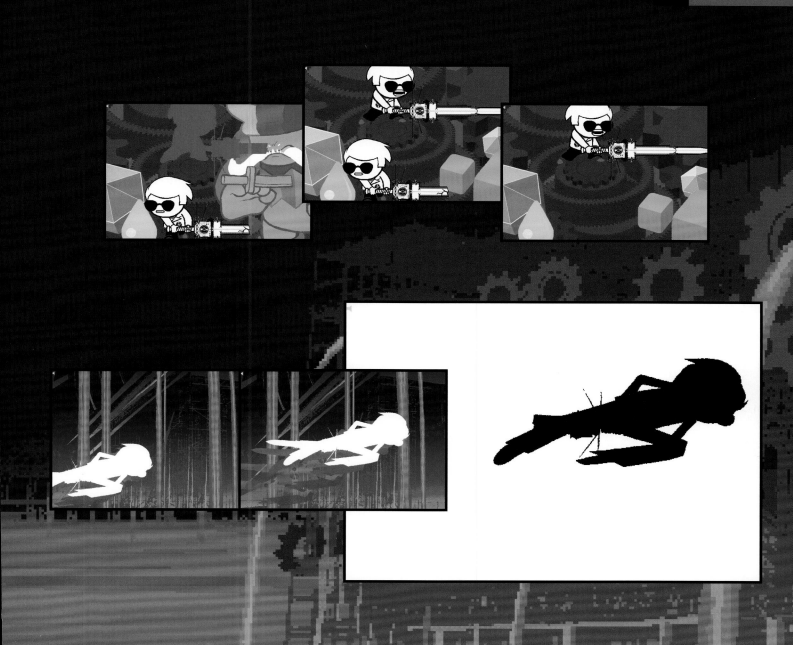

Hard to do it justice here on the page, but Dave is doing all these cool time-attack tricks. Hopping forward and backward in time, but only by a little to keep the maneuvers simple. Each time he does, he's creating a little stable time loop he has to account for. Good practice for a Knight of Time.

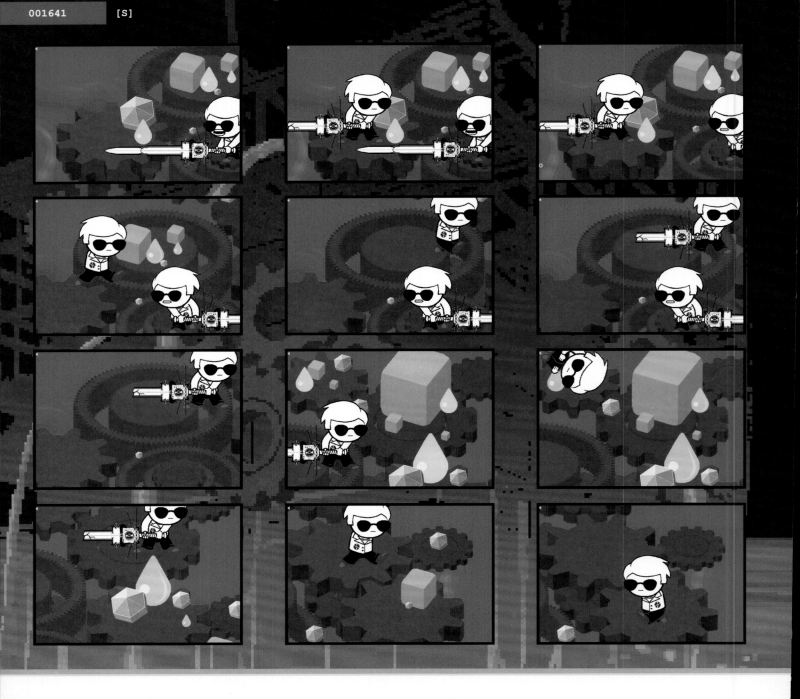

Starting now, Dave gets into the habit of casually encountering himself a lot. It's kind of his thing. Some kind of charactery thing about his character that he has to deal with, think about, and learn from. What? Referring to it as a charactery thing about him isn't highbrow enough for you? Why don't you go back to book school for lame nerds, you dork.

He made some TURNTABLES offscreen over the last few months. They let him time travel. I'm not sure what he used to make them, other than his record players from home. Looks like some sort of mystical gear component he probably plundered from the local industrial ruins. He probably went on a lot of exciting but lonely adventures on this planet we'll never get to see or hear about.

203

Getting some good mileage out of this animation as far as book page count goes. Listen, I worked hard on these. I'll be damned if I let too many precious screengrabs slip through the cracks. Not on my watch!!!! Enjoy them. Every last one. That completely white panel there? /kisses fingers like a chef/ Perfection.

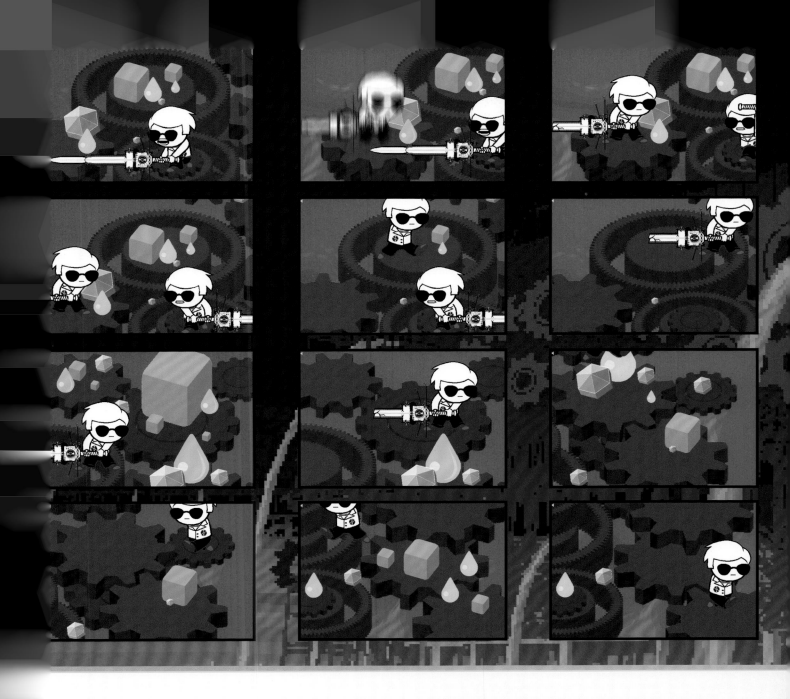

...ose block-type grists are sulphur. I wonder how many huge sulphur cubes have fallen into the lava over the course of his Knight of Time berserker fits? They're kind of ...e giant, stinky bouillon cubes falling into a huge vat of boiling broth. It probably absolutely reeks on LOHAC when Dave goes on a rampage.

205

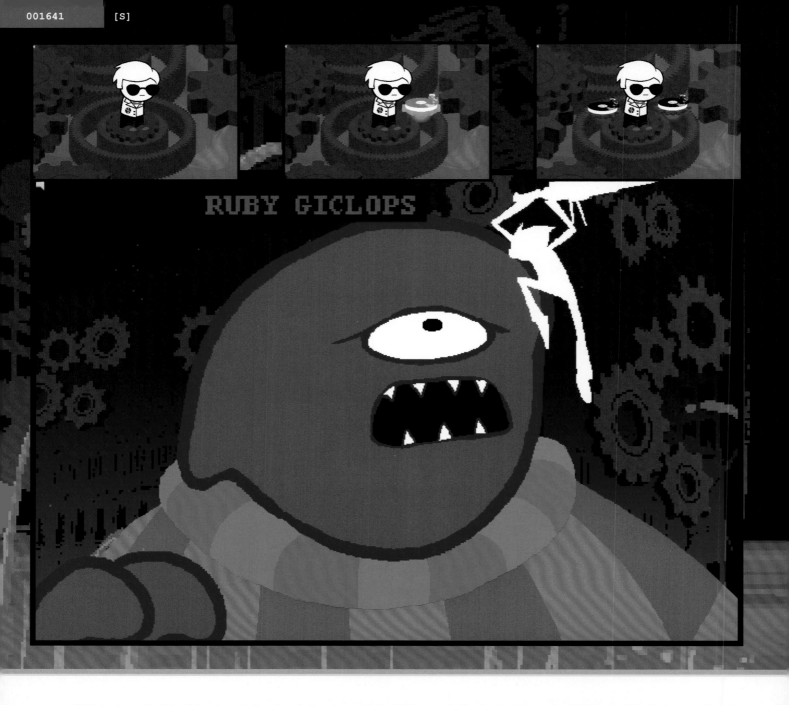

Right about now, the Ruby Giclops is wondering where it all went wrong in his life. It was probably when he, for some inexplicable reason, decided to swim through an ocean of lava to go mess with this boy in a suit going nuts with a sword.

> Dave: Consult with Calsprite.

You can tell Dave is probably overloaded with grist he doesn't particularly need by now. He carves up that giclops, and it starts raining huge rubies everywhere. But he doesn't seem to care at all about harvesting them. Instead, he takes a moment to yell at his puppet.

```
CALSPRITE: HAA HAA HEE HEE HOO HOO
DAVE: shut up
CALSPRITE: HOO HOO HAA HAA HEE HEE
CALSPRITE: HEE HEE HAA HAA HOO HOO
DAVE: no
DAVE: just
DAVE: god damn it
CALSPRITE: HEE HEE HEE HEE HAA HAA
CALSPRITE: HEE HEE HOO HOO HEE HEE
DAVE: please
DAVE: just once
DAVE: shut the hell up
CALSPRITE: HOO HOO HAA HEE HEE HOO
CALSPRITE: HOO HOO HEE HAA HEE HAA
CALSPRITE: HAA HAA HAA HAA HAA HAA
DAVE: shut up
CALSPRITE: HEE HEE HEE HAA HAA HAA
CALSPRITE: HOO HOO HOO HEE HEE HEE
DAVE: shut
CALSPRITE: HAA HAA HEE HEE HOO HOO
DAVE: the
CALSPRITE: HAA HAA HEE HEE HOO HOO
DAVE: fuck
CALSPRITE: HAA HAA HEE HEE HOO HOO
DAVE: up
```

```
CALSPRITE:
```

> Dave: Pester Rose.

Seems pretty clear this is all Calsprite's ever had to say. Poor Dave didn't even have a decent spiritual guide to help him through this troubling dark timeline. Guess that means he had to figure a lot of things out for himself. Hopefully Jaspers wasn't quite this useless.

-- turntechGodhead [TG] began pestering tentacleTherapist [TT] --

TG: thats it i cant take it anymore
TG: it was such a huge mistake prototyping seppucrow with this useless mindnumbing jackass
TG: im going back
TT: Already?
TG: what do you mean already shit took 4 goddamn months
TG: or something
TG: i dont know im kind of losing track of how long its been with all this time hopping
TT: It just sounds like you're making a rash decision based on temporary aggravation with a laughing puppet.
TT: I thought we planned to progress as far as we could before you went back.
TT: To gather information, and avoid repeating mistakes.
TG: what else is there to know
TG: we lost
TG: cant finish the game with a dead heir and witch
TT: We don't know Jade is dead for sure.
TG: yeah well she had a big fucking meteor bearing down on her and we never heard from her again
TG: or the trolls for that matter
TG: after they tricked john into skipping way ahead and getting his ass handed to him by the denizen
TG: i guess once they managed to sabotage us they were done with us
TG: and since john died he couldnt get jade in on time so whether shes alive or not shes as good as dead from our perspective
TG: only thing left to do is change all that

It's been seven years and Apple STILL hasn't released the iShades. Get with the program, guys.

```
TT: Are you sure you're ready?
TT: You'll remember the plan we discussed?
TG: theres not much to remember
TG: i go back and tell john not to be an idiot and get trolled like such a gullible stooge
TG: i dont know what he was thinking
TG: even we couldnt kill one of those things yet
TG: with our higher levels and all our sick gear
TT: It still seems hasty to me.
TT: Maybe I'm just not as comfortable with time travel as you.
TG: nah itll be fine dont worry
TT: After you go, what do you think will happen to me?
TT: Will I just cease to exist?
TG: i dont know
TG: i mean your whole timeline will
TG: maybe
TT: Maybe?
TT: Is there a chance it'll continue to exist, and I'll just be here alone forever?
TT: I'm not sure which outcome is more unsettling.
TG: the thing with time travel is
TG: you cant overthink it
TG: just roll with it and see what happens
TG: and above all try not to do anything retarded
TT: What do you think I should do?
TG: try going to sleep
TG: our dream selves kind of operate outside the normal time continuum i think
TG: so if part of you from this timelines going to persist thats probably the way to make
it happen
TT: Ok.
TG: and hey you might even be able to help your past dream self wake up sooner without all
that fuss you went through
TT: I think the true purpose of this game is to see how many qualifiers we can get to
precede the word "self" and still understand what we're talking about.
TG: the true purpose is to make a sprite that doesnt make me want to flog myself raw with my
own brain stem
TG: anything else is gravy
TT: If my past self can wake up sooner, maybe I'll be the one to visit you first this time.
TT: I'll fly by and remind you you're already awake and don't know it.
TG: yeah thatd be cool i guess
TG: im gonna go now
TT: Good luck.
```

> Dave: Reverse.

It's time to reflect on the fact that, at this point, Dave and Rose haven't learned that they are brother and sister yet. Four months is a long time. Did something happen between them? I guess we'll never know. (Something happened between them.)

Re: their conversation on the previous page, they're touching on what happens to Doomed Rose's consciousness when Dave goes back and alters the timeline, implying there could be some persistence between this version of her and the version from the offshoot timeline he will create. They are just speculating here, but it's a not-inaccurate conception of how paradox space works, and of the tenuous partitions between the minds and memories of many alternate selves. Ordinarily those partitions are strong, and individuals have discrete solo identities with no recollection of alt-self experiences. But there are ways that those partitions can break down, become porous, or result in multiple selves merging altogether. The story explores this idea from a lot of different angles right up until the end. "What is the self?" is a real, long-running thematic riddle for you to chew on. If you haven't started already, you should probably start chewing now.

-- turntechGodhead [TG] began pestering ectoBiologist [EB] --

TG: ok im in
EB: in where?
TG: the medium
EB: oh, already?
TG: what do you mean already shit took 4 goddamn hours
EB: huh, i guess time flew by while i was doing other stuff.
EB: how did it go?
EB: with you and jade i guess?
TG: i dont want to talk about it
TG: imagine the worst day of my life
TG: just stood up and clinked a glass like it was about to give a speech
TG: then took a shit in my dinner and passed out with its pants down
EB: ew dog! ewwww!
TG: yeah
EB: so nasty! gross dude!!!
TG: stfu
TG: what are you doing
EB: i'm in a rocket pack and i am about to blast off into space.
TG: ok
EB: it should be sweet.
TG: i need some advice
TG: my kernelsprite which was this brainless feathery asshole with a sword in it
TG: turned into this bigger like ghostly feathery asshole
TG: with a sword in it
TG: it seems to want me to prototype it again
TG: not sure what to do

We read this already, guys. Come on.

EB: hmm...
EB: have you asked rose?
TG: shes asleep for some reason
EB: wow, really?
TG: yeah i saw her there
TG: all tuckered out
TG: like she got smacked in the face with a pillow case full of the snooze wizards beard dander
TG: cause obviously its fuckin prime time for swiping some shuteye about now
TG: like a few hours into her magic stupid quest
TG: anyway what do you think
EB: i don't really know, i mean...
EB: it's supposed to be like your ghostly spirit guide or something.
EB: unless you have the remains of a wise old dead grandparent lying around, i'm not sure what to tell you!
TG: ok fine but
TG: it seems to be suggesting something here
TG: and
TG: i guess im kinda weirded out by its suggestion
EB: i don't know, just do what it says!
EB: it knows stuff about the game, so it probably knows better than i do...
EB: i gotta go!
EB: gonna blast off to the seventh gate.
EB: and, uh, win this game i guess.
TG: ok well it definitely sounds like youre fucking something up over there
TG: but alright later
EB: later.

TG: WAIT
EB: what?
TG: dont go yet
TG: somethings up
EB: ugh...

Rereading this entire conversation almost makes it feel like *we're* the ones time traveling here, amirite?! Hehehe.

```
TG: ok its me from the future
EB: huh?
TG: its me
TG: i just appeared
TG: from the future
TG: wearing a rad suit
TG: he says dont go
TG: or youre gonna die
EB: pfffff.
EB: lame.
EB: what kind of gullible stooge do you think i am?
```

```
TG: he says i dunno gullible enough
to trust a leetspeaking troll who
wants you dead and strap on a
rocket pack cause she said to
EB: this is like some terrible
april fools prank.
EB: but 13 days too late.
EB: remember, you are talking to
the pranking MASTER.
```

Dave is talking about his future self showing up using the same tone as he would when telling his bro to hang on while he goes and answers the door because his pizza is here. His brand is airtight.

TG: ok that was probably the dumbest thing you ever said just now
EB: **if future you is real, then why don't you let me talk to him.**
TG: do you hear what youre saying oh my god
TG: this guy is me if i get him to talk to you youre just talking to me again jesus it proves nothing
EB: **hold on, someone else is bugging me.**

-- **turntechGodhead** [TG] **began pestering ectoBiologist** [EB] --

TG: john stop being a tool and unbuckle yourself from that piece of shit
TG: if our friendship means anything youll listen to me and past dave
TG: this is future dave by the way
EB: **hahaha!**
EB: **wow, you're really pulling out all the stops for this stunt!**
EB: **using your phone and computer at the same time to message me.**
EB: **you're kind of going through a lot of trouble actually, i don't know why you're bothering with this.**
TG: yeah exactly why would i bother
TG: this sort of cornball horseshit is your cup of tea not mine
TG: dont make me track you down through time and stop you in person
EB: **you can't track down through time WHAT YOU CAN'T CATCH!**
EB: **pchooooooo!**
TG: oh god did you just blast off
EB: **no...**
EB: **but that would have been sweet if i did just then.**
TG: ok well just dont ok
TG: im turning this timeline over to past dave
TG: and helping you all stay alive and do this thing the right way this time
TG: just stay on the goddamn ground for fucks sake
EB: **ok, i guess...**

Here is the first big test of friendship between these two solid, lifelong pals. Do they have another one after this brief crisis of brosmanship? I guess there's also the time Terezi and Vriska use them both as pawns against each other during their bouts of Scourge Sister warfare. Maybe some other times too, I guess. You know how you could find out? Just read the damn story. To be perfectly honest, I'm not sure why you even need me down here. Just kidding, these notes are why you bought the book, and I know you're hanging on each and every word I write down here. I'm here all night, folks.

DAVE: hey
DAVESPRITE: sup

Absolutely iconic *Homestuck* conversation here. Arguably one of the best I ever wrote. Some real baby shoes shit going on. Now excuse me while I go do an exceptionally flamboyant endzone dance on Hemingway's grave. On a less self-congratulatory note, it was really nice of Davesprite to dump his entire sylladex in a neat pile in front of Dave before prototyping himself. We just saw all that sick equipment. It would have been such a shame if Real Dave never got to use any of it.

The face John is making seems to betray his true feelings about what he is currently doing. Duh, look at me, I'm John Egdumb, and I'm not listening to my best buddy's dire warnings, duhhhh. That's what's happening here. He really should turn around. I hope and pray that he does.

> Rose: Pester Dave.

```
TT: Strider.
TT: I need you to do me a favor.
TT: Can you take a capture of my bedroom and send me the file?
TT: For no reason in particular?

TT: He's not answering.
GG: yeah hes pretty tied up right now!
TT: Can you hassle him via Sburb and tell him to talk to me?
TT: Bop him on the head with a puppet or something?
GG: noooooooooooooooooooo
GG: he made me promise not to bug him while im asleep!
TT: Can you do it anyway?
GG: but he will find a way to be clever and make me punch myself in the face again :(
TT: Did he tell you what I wrote on the walls?
TT: Wait.
TT: What?
```

> Rose: Prepare for nap.

Well, now we know why Dave wasn't answering. Jade of course failed to mention that Dave is busy talking to his bird self from the future. Maybe she felt that was too much info to dump on Rose all at once? Or maybe she's just being deliberately obtuse, as usual.

You bundle up your knittings into a cozy nest. You aren't all that tired though. It's hard to imagine falling asleep without the luxury of Harley's narcolepsy.

> Future Dream Rose: Cease to exist.

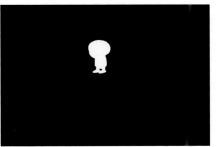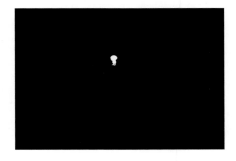

> [S] ==>

Look how big future Mutini is. What a cute detail. So good. /Goes back to Hemingway's grave and dances some more./

> Davesprite: Troll GC.

```
-- turntechGodhead [TG] began
trolling gallowsCalibrator [GC] --

TG: dont talk to john anymore hes an
impressionable doofus
TG: your plan didnt work
TG: i mean it did
TG: but then suddenly it didnt
TG: so you might as well quit trying
```

Doomed Dave going back in time accomplished three very important things: it created Davesprite, it prevented John from getting killed, and apparently it also triggered Rose's dream self to wake up. All of these events are essential to the continuation of the alpha timeline. Which begins to suggest how complicated paradox space can get. Alpha timeline outcomes can depend entirely on the impact of events from doomed timelines, by way of time travelers going back in time, and effectively sacrificing themselves, to bring about necessary results. Later, Aradia takes this to an extreme with her lethal bot-splurge.

GC: YOU SM3LL L1K3 OR4NG3 CR34MS1CL3S
TG: what
TG: youre aliens do you even have orange creamsicles
GC: OF COURS3 WH4T K1ND OF 4WFUL C1V1L1Z4T1ON WOULDNT 1NV3NT OR4NG3 CR34MS1CL3S
GC: NOT ON3 1D W4NT 4NYTH1NG TO DO W1TH
TG: ok pretty far fetched but whatever
TG: no more hijinks from you cause ill make sure they wont work
GC: W3LL OBV10USLY 1 KN3W 1T W4SNT GO1NG TO WORK
GC: MY FR13NDS H4V3 B33N T4LK1NG TO JOHN FROM TH3 FUTUR3
GC: YOUR FUTUR3
GC: WH3R3 H3S NOT D34D
GC: SO TH3R3 W4S NO W4Y WH4T 1 D1D W4S GO1NG TO K1LL H1M
GC: 1 JUST W4NT3D TO M3SS W1TH H1M 4ND STUFF
TG: i dont think youre following
TG: you DID kill him sort of
TG: then i went back in time to stop him
GC: Y34H 1 G3USS3D TH3R3 W4S 4 CH4NC3 SOM3TH1NG L1K3 TH4T M1GHT H4PP3N
TG: alright but
TG: did you guess that by trolling john to his grave
TG: and making me splinter us off into an alt timeline
TG: that you were basically complicit in making our timeline go the way it was supposed to go all along
TG: where future me is now helping dave and we just keep playing
TG: and our actions ultimately lead to the trouble youre all in now
TG: thus leading you all to troll us incompetently
GC: OH
GC: NO >:[
GC: 1 D1DNT TH1NK OF TH4T
TG: yeah
TG: see
TG: none of you ever thinks anything through
TG: whos in charge of timeline management there
TG: i gotta give him the business
GC: SH3 DO3SNT W4NT TO T4LK TO 4NY OF YOU
GC: 4ND H4S M1SG1V1NGS 4BOUT TH1S WHOL3 TH1NG
GC: NOT 4LL OF US 4R3 TH4T 3NTHUS1AST1C 4BOUT TROLL1NG YOU GUYS
GC: 4ND TH3 ON3S WHO 4R3 SORT OF SUCK 4T 1T >:|
TG: well at least you got john to off himself so i guess youre not totally incompetent like the others
TG: like that awful rapper

This isn't actually the first time Dave's ever talked to Terezi. He had a conversation with her quite some time ago, where he thought she was six years old and was characteristically dismissive of her solicitations. So she didn't exactly accomplish nothing here, as Davesprite suggests. She managed the feat of getting him to take her seriously. In fact, she's why he has to be a bird forever now. That ain't nothing.

GC: SO JOHN 4CTU4LLY D1D WH4T 1 S41D?
TG: yeah
TG: im telling you
TG: huge pushover
TG: he will do what you say
TG: unless it happens to be for his own good
TG: then all a sudden hes a tough nut to crack go figure
GC: NOW 1 F33L K1ND4 B4D
GC: 4R3 YOU SUR3 1 C4NT T4LK TO H1M
GC: 3V3N 1F 1TS JUST TO 4POLOG1Z3
GC: WOULD TH4T B3 OK W1TH YOU S1R BR4V3 KN1GHT >:?
TG: yeah thats fine i guess
TG: no more coy bullshit antics though
TG: not even like
TG: an idiotic angry winking emote
GC: OR WH4T
GC: YOUR3 GO1NG TO HUNT M3 DOWN THROUGH T1M3 OOOOOH OH NO
GC: >;]
TG: yeah
GC: YOU DO R34L1Z3 1M W4Y H1GH3R ON MY 3CH3L4DD3R TH4N YOU
GC: 3V3N 1F YOU 4R3 FROM TH3 FUTUR3
GC: 4R3 YOU SUR3 YOU W4NT TO G3T YOUR CLOCK3D CL34N3D BY 4 BL1ND CH1CK
TG: ok even if thats true
TG: i just merged with an impaled orange goddamn bird and now i got all these crazy powers
GC: UGH
GC: S3LF PROTOTYP1NG SO DUMB
GC: TH1S 1S WHY YOU 4LL SCR3W UP SO B4D
GC: 4LW4YS B3ND1NG TH3 RUL3S L1K3 TH4T
GC: OH W3LL C4NT STOP YOU NOW SO M1GHT 4S W3LL DROP 1T
GC: H3Y D4V3
TG: what
GC: 1V3 B33N R3S34RCH1NG SOM3 OF YOUR 34RTH SO4P OP3R4S
GC: 1S TH1S YOU
TG: oh jegus fuck no
TG: why would that breathtaking douche remind you
of me at all
GC: BUT H3 H4S 4 F13RY P3RSON4L1TY
GC: SORT OF BR4SH 4ND 1MP3TUOUS
GC: 4ND 1N YOUR F4C3
GC: L1K3 F1R3 1TS3LF >:D
TG: now i know youre bullshitting me
TG: do i seem like the kind of guy whod accept a magic ring from whoopi goldberg

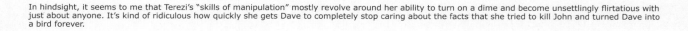

In hindsight, it seems to me that Terezi's "skills of manipulation" mostly revolve around her ability to turn on a dime and become unsettlingly flirtatious with just about anyone. It's kind of ridiculous how quickly she gets Dave to completely stop caring about the facts that she tried to kill John and turned Dave into a bird forever.

TG: to awaken some egregious homofantasy for a ripped blue dudes mammoth eco friendly bulge
TG: that guys an asshole and needs to be sealed in a dufflebag and whipped something ungodly with a bamboo chute
GC: WHOS WHOOP1 GOLDB3RG
TG: who cares
GC: OK 1 M4D3 SOM3 MOD1F1C4T1ONS
GC: TH1S 1S SO YOU D4V3 COM3 ON 4DM1T 1T
TG: ahahahahaha
TG: ok yeah that is pretty much fucking spot on
TG: youre actually a pretty good troll
TG: as long as you dont bug john i guess thats all there is to say on the matter
GC: TH4NKS D4V3
GC: TO B3 F41R
GC: 1M SUR3 3V3RY ON3 OF US W1SH3S W3 THOUGHT OF FUTUR3 S3LF PROTOTYP1NG F1RST
GC: SO
GC: YOUR3 NOT R34LLY 4LL TH4T T3RR1BL3 >;]

> Davesprite: Chill with Dave.

DAVE: who were you talking to
DAVESPRITE: just telling a troll to step off
DAVE: ok cool
DAVE: so now that youre a sprite
DAVE: do you know everything about the game
DAVESPRITE: well i knew a lot anyway
DAVESPRITE: cause im from the future
DAVESPRITE: but yeah i know more stuff now

No, Dave. Awakening some "egregious homofantasy"... No. There's no way that's ever going to happen.

DAVESPRITE: like things meant specifically for sprites to clue players in on
DAVESPRITE: but packaged in these like
DAVESPRITE: i guess riddles
DAVESPRITE: im supposed to be cagey about it
DAVESPRITE: but i dont really feel like it
DAVESPRITE: ask me anything go ahead ill give you a straight answer
DAVE: alright
DAVE: here goes
DAVE: why are we so fucking awesome
DAVESPRITE: thats the best fucking question anybody ever asked
DAVE: yeah
DAVE: so is everything cool with this john business
DAVE: is he gonna be ok
DAVESPRITE: thats up to him
DAVESPRITE: if he decides to wise up and listen to us
DAVESPRITE: if not then we just bail everyone out yet again
DAVE: ok
DAVESPRITE: all that gear you picked up should let you breeze through the first couple gates
DAVESPRITE: even at a low level
DAVESPRITE: later youll unlock the ability to bring your sprite down with you
DAVESPRITE: and well take care of shit together
DAVESPRITE: til then i guess just mess around and let jade build up or whatever
DAVESPRITE: ill go kill some time
DAVESPRITE: maybe draw some comics
DAVE: like what
DAVESPRITE: i dont know
DAVESPRITE: whats the last one you did
DAVE: i was in the middle of the nancho party arc
DAVESPRITE: oh yeah
DAVESPRITE: i gave up on that half way through
DAVE: yeah that was sorta the plan
DAVE: making a ten part story about nachos was always a bullshit idea
DAVESPRITE: lets do some brainstorming later
DAVESPRITE: blow everyones minds
DAVE: yeah sure

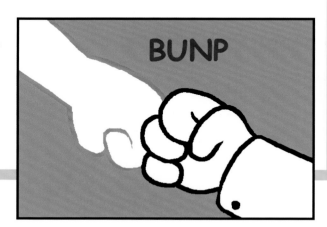

> Meanwhile, hundreds of pages ago...

224

Davesprite's answer to Dave's question also happens to be, word for word, the last line of dialogue in the entire story. And while the words are the same color, they aren't spoken by the same guy. Who could it be? Chances are, you probably already know. Why is it repeated at that moment? Let's just say that at this point in time, we are establishing these lines as a symbolic exchange between two cool guys who have decided to trust each other so absolutely that no particularly important questions need to be asked, nor do informative answers need to be provided.

You open the package. There is something suspicious inside.

Something suspiciously dirty and smelly.

It is a STUFFED BUNNY. Much like the one held hostage briefly by Malkovich's Cyrus "The Virus" while taunting hard-luck protagonist Cameron Poe. And strikingly similar to the one scooped up from the soot of a burning Vegas strip by Cage's Poe and offered to his daughter, a gesture symbolic of a tattered exterior surrounding a heart of gold. Poe wasn't much to look at. But he was a good man.

But no, it is not merely LIKE that bunny. According to this NOTE OF AUTHENTICITY, it is the VERY SAME BUNNY.

This is so awesome.

Included is a note from your best bro Dave.

> so hey

It's this page again. How gratuitous. No, wait! It's important to see it again, to set up the scene. A Fun Conceit during these earlier acts, when we're getting to know these four main characters and their relationships with each other, is that seeing the actual text of their birthday notes to each other is always saved for moments when it seems necessary to reveal some particular aspect of their friendships. John at this juncture needs a little reminder that Dave is his good friend. And according to me, I suppose, so do we.

225

so hey

since its your bday i had to get you back for the sick memorabilia you got me so i
got you this godawful thing and now i just know youre standing there flipping your
shit over it so youre welcome.

its the actual gross bunny in the movie so that means nick cage actually grubbed it
up with his clownish no talent fingers. i would suggest you put it somewhere and
display it ironically but i know youre dead serious about this ridiculous shit so
youll probably sleep with the damn thing and nibble its ear and stuff.

but the weird thing is thats whats cool about you. youre this naive guy like
pinocchio tumbled ass backwards off the turnip truck and started liking ghostbusters.
then the fairy godmother kissed your nose or some shit and you turned out to be not
made of wood and also pretty cool to talk to. one day your gooberish ways are gonna
land you in a jam and i know im going to have to get you off the hook but its cool i
got your back bro.

then we'll meet and hug bump and get each others filthy wife beaters that much
filthier so yeah

peace dawg

tg

Here's a fact about me you may not know. I actually own the original *Con Air* bunny. I bought it in 2013, I think, for around $1,000. It was a lavish expenditure I guess, but it seemed worth it, just so I could be sure the bunny would be protected forever, stuffed somewhere carelessly in my closet. It also came with a certificate of authenticity, just like John's did. I had to buy it for myself, because I don't have any friends good enough to buy something like that for me. None of us do. Well, except for John.

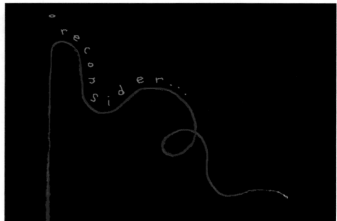

> John: Get pestered by Dave.

Only the recollection of Dave's bunny-gifting-tier friendship could cajole this dumb, stubborn nerd into r e c o n s i d e r i n g his silly suicide mission. Look at the expression on his face when he finally remembers. I spent probably an hour carefully rendering that face, to perfectly convey his "My god, what am I doing?" epiphany.

227

TG: did you blast off like a spazzy douche yet or what
EB: yeah, of course!
EB: there was no way i wasn't trying out this sweet ride.
TG: god dammit what do i have to do to make you believe me
TG: fist bump my future self til i got bloody knuckles and write you an even sappier bday note in my own blood
TG: on a back to the future poster
EB: relax, i'm not going through the gate!
EB: i am just flying around, and having a good time in the sky.
TG: oh ok
TG: so you believe me then
TG: about future me
TG: and like
TG: him turning into a floating sword bird
EB: um...
EB: ok, i don't know anything about that...
EB: but it doesn't matter!
EB: you're my best bro, and if you say not to go then i won't go.
EB: hey, can you hold on?
EB: i'm getting trolled again.
TG: oh man and if weve just concluded anything its that talking to those dbags should be priority number one so yeah go right ahead
EB: ok, brb.

> John: Get trolled by CG.

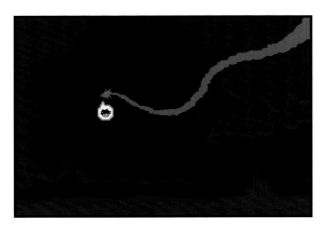

CG: I KEEP SCROLLING BACKWARDS THROUGH YOUR ADVENTURE.
CG: TRYING TO PIECE TOGETHER HOW YOU BOTCH THIS UP SO BADLY.
CG: AND I KEEP FINDING THESE STRIKING POCKETS OF FOOLISHNESS.
CG: LIKE WHAT YOU'RE DOING NOW.
CG: RIDING YOUR LITTLE RED ROCKET.
CG: LIKE YOU ARE A FRESHLY HATCHED HUMAN LARVA AND THIS IS JUST ALL A BIG SCHOOLHIVE RUMPUS RESPITE.

The first four lines Karkat says here literally sound like they could be a disgruntled *Homestuck* fan talking smack to me as they scan backwards through the story. Which sounds like a funny thing for me to say—and it is—but it's also not that remarkable, since at any given moment *Homestuck* is full of surrogates for various factions of the readership. Basically, any character who is viewing the actions of other characters on a screen can be seen as a consumer of that story through some form of in-canon digital media. Whether they type in character commands like the exiles, or use Trollian to skip around the "archive" in a nonlinear way like the trolls do, for the sake of "adventure analysis" or to heap scorn on those involved, every narrative-viewing character is temporarily filling the role of the *Homestuck* reader from a certain angle. Later, cherubs become the ultimate distillation of this idea.

EB: humans aren't hatched as larvae dummy.
EB: we don't hatch at all.
EB: we are born as these like little pink monkeys called babies.
CG: BULLSHIT.
CG: THAT'S NOT WHAT YOU JUST TOLD ME.
EB: what did i say?
CG: I'LL PASTE WHAT YOU SAID.
EB: i thought you didn't like going down that road?
EB: copy-pasting future/past conversations...
CG: WHY WOULD I HAVE A PROBLEM WITH THAT.
EB: i dunno, that's what you just told me.
CG: WHATEVER, LOOK:
CG: EB: this is really weird...
CG: CG: WHAT'S SO WEIRD ABOUT IT.
CG: EB: well, normally humans hatch...
CG: EB: from like these slimy pods.
CG: EB: then we wriggle out as a little pink larva.
CG: CG: OH REALLY.
CG: CG: HUH, MAYBE WE HAVE MORE IN COMMON THAN I THOUGHT.
EB: hahaha!
EB: i was punking you dude!
EB: or at least i will be in our next conversation.
EB: thanks for the great prank idea.
CG: ARGH.
CG: WHY WOULD YOU TRICK ME ABOUT THAT, WHAT IS EVEN THE POINT.
EB: i don't know, it was just a friendly prank.
EB: don't you ever play pranks?
EB: i mean, of course you do, one of you just tried to prank me good.
CG: WHAT, WHO.
EB: pffffff, you'll find out.
CG: WELL FINE.
CG: I GUESS YOU GOT ME BACK, SORT OF.
CG: FOR MY TROLLING, EVEN THOUGH YOU HAVEN'T EVEN READ MY WORST TROLLING EFFORTS YET.
CG: BECAUSE THEY HAPPEN IN YOUR FUTURE.
CG: AND EVEN THEN YOU DIDN'T EVEN MIND MUCH, ALMOST LIKE YOU WERE DELIGHTED TO HEAR IT.
CG: KIND OF PERVERSE REALLY, WHAT'S WRONG WITH YOU?
EB: well, we're friends by then, aren't we?
EB: or sort of like, uh, reverse anti-mutual friends.
CG: WHAT THE HELL DOES THAT EVEN MEAN.
EB: look, you're going to have to face it at some point...
EB: that you're learning the meaning of this human emotion called friendship.
CG: IS FRIENDSHIP REALLY AN EMOTION?

There's something kind of eerie about these stable time loops when it comes to the absurd, bitchy conversations the characters have with each other. There is literally no discernible origin to this prank John is playing. It's pasted to him from the future, he thinks it's a great prank, and he decides to play the prank in the future because of it, exactly as typed here. And yet, the whole exchange appears to be perfectly in character and in full alignment with their personalities. So entire exchanges between two individuals can be totally without origin, yet still sound exactly like them. This opens up a whole bunch of creepy possibilities. Ghosts or afterimages of their personalities seemingly can emerge from pure void in a convincing way, like bodiless simulacra. Echoing time loop mimic-wraiths, intruding on their conversations. All right, that's enough creepypasta for one night. Pleasant dreams!

EB: yes, absolutely.
CG: I GUESS IT'S HARD TO SEE HOW WE BECOME FRIENDS.
CG: THIS IS SO FRUSTRATING.
CG: EVERY TIME I GO FURTHER BACK INTO YOUR PAST AND TALK TO YOU, YOU SAY STUFF THAT PERTAINS TO MY IMMEDIATE FUTURE.
CG: AND THEN YOU WON'T EXPLAIN TO ME WHAT'S GOING ON, BECAUSE IT'S ALREADY OLD NEWS FOR YOU.
EB: dude, you've been doing the same exact thing!!!
CG: I'VE DONE NO SUCH THING.
CG: I'VE BEEN EXCEPTIONALLY INFORMATIVE AND HELPFUL.
CG: IF JUSTIFIABLY ACRIMONIOUS.
EB: you never answer my questions, though.
EB: how am i supposed to know what's going on, or what you're alluding to?
CG: THIS GAME IS KIND OF A GAME OF A MILLION GUIDES.
CG: EVERYWHERE YOU TURN THERE'S ANOTHER WAY TO FIGURE OUT WHAT'S GOING ON, SO PLEASE, GO SECRETE ME AN EARTH RIVER THROUGH YOUR STRANGE HUMAN TEAR DUCTS.
CG: YOU'VE GOT SPRITES, EXILES, GUARDIANS, CONSORTS...
CG: TIME HOPPING FUTURE SELVES, MYSTICAL DREAM ORACLE DOPPELGANGERS...
CG: AND IF THAT WASN'T ENOUGH, YOUR PARTICULAR GROUP OF PLAYERS IS LUCKY ENOUGH TO HAVE US TO GIVE YOU THE SCOOP ON STUFF.
CG: THROUGH A SORT OF SUBVERSION OF THE WHOLE DAMN THING.
CG: EVEN THOUGH WE HATE YOU.
CG: AND EVEN THOUGH THE FACT THAT WE HATE YOU
CG: IS AN IMMUTABLE FACT AS UNALTERABLE AS THIS WRITHING KNOTTED HELL OF A TIMELINE CHOKING US ALL TO DEATH
CG: IT DOES NOT MEAN WE HAVE ANY REASON TO WITHHOLD ANY INFORMATION FROM YOU
CG: OR DISH IT OUT THROUGH CRYPTOBAFFLING MIND FUDDLERY.
CG: SO GO AHEAD, ASK ME ANYTHING.
EB: ok...
EB: what's the point of the game.
CG: ASK SOMETHING ELSE.
CG: ALREADY TOLD YOU THAT.
CG: IT WAS THIS WHOLE BIG CONVERSATION WE HAD.
EB: augh!
EB: fine.
EB: where are you now?
CG: IN THE MEDIUM.
CG: A SEPARATE SESSION FROM YOURS.
EB: no no, i know that!
EB: you already told me.
CG: I DID?
EB: yes, in your future.
CG: DAMMIT.

One of the most passive-aggressive things the trolls do is saying stuff like "YOUR STRANGE HUMAN TEAR DUCTS," as if the concept of crying is foreign to them, and really, as if they aren't all bawling their asses off constantly like a bunch of shitty babies.

```
EB: what i mean is...
EB: are you in your house right now, or in one of your magical lands, or what?
EB: just curious cause you can see me, but i can't see or know anything about you!
CG: WE'RE HIDING IN THE VEIL.
CG: WHAT'S LEFT OF IT.
EB: what's that?
CG: IT'S A HUGE BELT OF METEORS
CG: ORBITING WAY OUTSIDE SKAIA, BEYOND THE ORBIT OF THE PLANETS
CG: DIVIDING THE MEDIUM FROM THE FURTHEST RING
CG: WHERE DERSE ORBITS.
EB: derse?
CG: THE DARK PLANET.
CG: PROSPIT'S THE LIGHT ONE NEAR SKAIA.
EB: well jeez, how am i supposed to know any of this??
CG: YOU'D PROBABLY FIND OUT SOONER OR LATER FROM YOUR DUMB GRANDMA.
CG: BUT BY FUSING WITH THE SPRITE SHE HAS TO WITHHOLD STUFF AND BE MYSTERIOUS AND ALL.
CG: TO MAKE YOUR ADVENTURE SEEM MORE "MAAAAAGICAL!!!!"
CG: IT'S INFURIATING.
EB: ok, so the veil is a bunch of meteors...
EB: what do you mean "what's left of it"?
CG: OK, THERE COMES A TIME WHEN BLACK INEVITABLY BEATS WHITE
CG: ON THE BATTLEFIELD IN THE CENTER OF SKAIA
CG: THE WHITE KING IS CAPTURED OR KILLED OR SOMETHING
CG: THAT'S WHEN THE RECKONING STARTS.
EB: ok...
CG: THE RULERS OF DERSE
CG: THE BLACK KING AND QUEEN
CG: GET THE POWER TO SEND THE VEIL TOWARD SKAIA
CG: TO DESTROY IT
CG: THAT KIND OF STARTS YOUR BIG "COUNTDOWN"
CG: WHEN SHIT GETS SERIOUS.
EB: so then it's up to us to save it?
CG: YEAH, YOU HAVE THAT LONG TO KILL THE BLACK QUEEN AND KING
CG: AND SKAIA ITSELF SORT OF BUYS YOU SOME TIME
CG: BY ACTIVATING ITS DEFENSE PORTALS
CG: TO CATCH SOME OF THE METEORS
CG: THE THREAT GETS BIGGER THE LONGER YOU TAKE THOUGH
CG: SMALLER METEORS COME FIRST AND THEY GET PROGRESSIVELY BIGGER AND BIGGER
CG: AND THERE'S ONLY SO MUCH OF THEM SKAIA CAN ABSORB FOR YOU.
EB: ok, but it sounds like we've got plenty of time before that happens, right?
CG: THAT'S JUST IT.
CG: YOU DON'T.
```

If I were really, really on the ball here this far in advance of crafting certain points of troll lore, instead of calling her "YOUR DUMB GRANDMA," I might have said "YOUR DUMB RESURRECTED ANCESTOR" instead. That's surely how Karkat would have parsed the concept of a human's dead grandmother he'd never met before. There was no such thing as troll ancestors at the point when I was writing this, though. Even the hemospectrum concept hadn't been fleshed out yet. Sorry, nerds.

```
CG: ORDINARILY YOU WOULD BUT
CG: YOUR RECKONING STARTS MUCH SOONER
CG: BECAUSE OF SOME DUMB THINGS YOU'VE DONE
CG: YOU COMPLETELY BLEW IT ALREADY AND YOU HAVE NO CHANCE OF WINNING ANYMORE
CG: WHICH ORDINARILY WOULD BE FINE
CG: JUST ANOTHER BUNCH OF LOSERS TO FAIL AT THIS GAME
CG: IT'S WHAT YOU DO LATER THAT CAUSES SO MUCH MORE TROUBLE THAN THAT
CG: AND NOW WE HAVE TO DEAL WITH IT TOO.
EB: oh no...
EB: what is it?
CG: ALREADY TOLD YOU.
CG: IT'S INEVITABLE AND COMPLETELY POINTLESS TO TALK ABOUT ANYWAY.
EB: yeah, well...
EB: maybe you're wrong!
EB: maybe there's something we can still do to stop it, if you just help us?
CG: I'M NOT WRONG, IT'S ALL RIGHT HERE IN FRONT OF ME, YOU FUCK UP ROYALLY, END OF STORY.
EB: ok, we'll see about that, mr. sourbulge.
EB: hey, aren't you kind of uncomfortable sitting on a meteor?
EB: are you all huddled in a crater or something?
CG: NO, THERE'S ALL KINDS OF CRAZY SHIT IN THE VEIL.
CG: A LOT OF THESE METEORS ARE KIND OF LIKE...
CG: BIG SEEDS.
EB: seeds?
EB: um...
EB: well, what kind of crazy shit is there?
CG: STUFF LIKE...
CG: BUILDINGS
CG: FACILITIES
CG: LIKE LABS AND STUFF.
EB: weird.
CG: YEAH, THE VEIL IS KIND OF LIKE NEUTRAL GROUND FOR THE KINGDOMS, LIKE OUR PLANETS.
CG: SOME PLACES ARE USED TO GENETICALLY ENGINEER SOLDIERS AND AGENTS FOR THE TWO SIDES.
CG: USING GENETIC MATERIAL FROM THE EXOTIC MENAGERIE OF CHESS PIECES ON THE BATTLEFIELD.
CG: TO HELP FUEL THE WAR AND KEEP RAISING THE STAKES.
EB: wow, i don't think i'm following this.
CG: YEAH NO SHIT!
CG: BUT YOU'LL FIND OUT WHEN YOU GET THERE
CG: SINCE YOU WERE IN THE VEIL WHEN WE LAST TALKED.
CG: ANYWAY THAT'S MORE THAN ENOUGH INFO FOR YOU TO THINK ABOUT AND BE LESS STUPID IN TIME
FOR CONVERSATIONS WE'VE ALREADY HAD.
CG: I'M OUT OF HERE.
EB: ok, but wait...
```

From my perspective, the great thing about this stupid backwards conversation was that any time someone wanted to know the answer to an obvious question, like "What's the point of the game?", and I didn't think it was time to reveal that info yet, I could just have this jerk say "I ALREADY TOLD YOU THAT" and justifiably be reluctant to repeat himself. But he *would* indulge in other details of lesser importance, like the material here about the Veil. He hasn't mentioned that yet, so he can take some time to cover it now. It's a totally organic and logical way of concealing critical story information so that it flows in an order of least critical to most critical.

```
EB: can you give a message to GC for me?
EB: tell her nice try.
CG: WHAT
CG: WHY WOULD I GIVE HER A MESSAGE FOR YOU
CG: DO IT YOURSELF, I'M NOT A RELAY SERVICE.
EB: oh, well i thought you'd be cool with it since you asked me to give her a message for
you last time.
EB: but whatever.
CG: I FIND THAT HIGHLY IMPLAUSIBLE.
CG: I'M NOT FALLING FOR ANY MORE OF YOUR HUMAN PRANKS.
CG: "NICE TRY" JOHN
CG: HAHAHAHAHAHAHA.

-- carcinoGeneticist [CG] ceased trolling ectoBiologist [EB] --
```

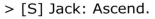

> [S] Jack: Ascend.

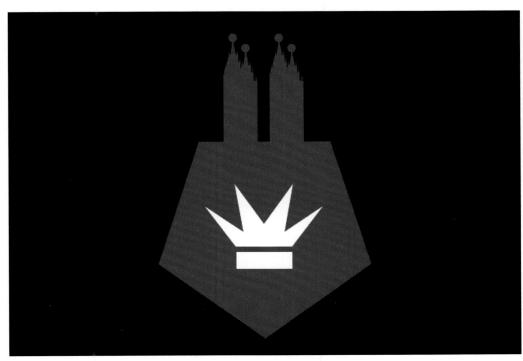

[S] Jack: Ascend, if memory serves, was posted exactly one year from *Homestuck*'s start date. What an absurd amount of content I produced in that year, especially when you consider the animation stuff. Good thing I slowed down after that, right? No, I kept doing the exact same thing for the next several years. Yikes, sounds bad... So about this animation. I think this one marks the start of *Homestuck*'s trend thereafter of dropping exceptionally violent, high-octane, game-changing animations out of nowhere. There are so many like this from here on, right up to the end of Act 5. Only then does the number sort of taper off. But from this point on I just sorta started shoveling more and more red meat into the story's maw. This stretch is where I was starting to get a feel for this type of sensationalistic storytelling content as something I'd later code (mostly for my own internal purposes) as "meat," in the meat/candy binary of storycraft theory. I really shouldn't talk about this yet, though. It's too soon.

233

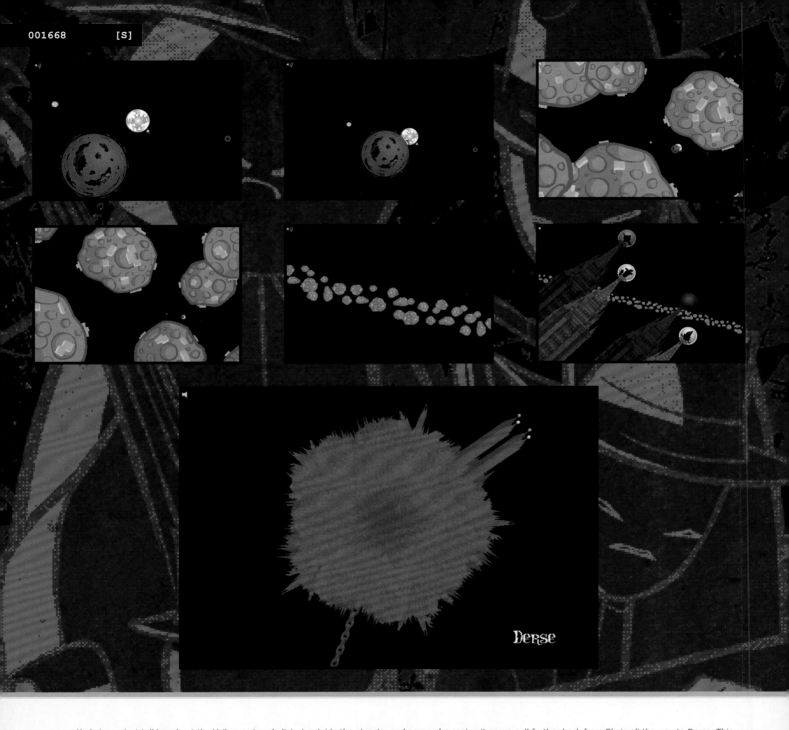

Derse

Karkat was just talking about the Veil, a meteor belt just outside the planets, and now we're seeing it as we pull further back from Skaia all the way to Derse. This sequence provides a visual perspective on the full cosmology of the session, which we haven't had until now.

Jack is so pissed at his queen. These two getting testy with each other is built into their relationship across all sessions. No matter what the specific situation, she's probably always finding ways to needle him. Dress code, paperwork, it doesn't matter. This is programmed into them as game constructs to guarantee that there will always be friction between them, which allows for more interesting variations in how any given game of *Sburb* can play out. There's always a powder keg of mutiny waiting to go off, and depending on the actions of the heroes, there are many, many ways this can play out over a session. We see one way right here, in this animation, and another in the troll session, with totally different results. But what remains constant is Jack's inclination to betray his queen.

235

Here's the first time we see the queen after the crow/sword prototyping. She's now got a sword through the chest and wings, in addition to the other nonsense. The schematics for the final villain (only of this session, mind you) are coming closer to completion.

It looks like the queen catches Jack...spying on her? He's lustily spying on her as she approaches his office in order to force him to wear a demeaning garment, probably also in a lusty manner. These two. SMH.

Wearing six pink garters on each tentacle really is one of the most risqué fashion choices imaginable.

The music is pretty quick-paced and jaunty here. It really emphasizes how Jack's dancing around, throwing a little tantrum over being ordered to dress up. You're totally missing out.

Even though it lasts only about a second or two, this dress-up montage is kind of incredible when you think about what it implies. They're actually spending...hours, maybe?...trying out different clothes that Jack might like better. Think of what this means, and of all the actual conversations that have to take place between them to facilitate this. It shows the queen is actually willing to exercise some lenience and let Jack's taste determine the garb, so long as it's sufficiently clown-princess themed. Jack also displays a surprising degree of patience in trying on so many variations. It also suggests that somewhere the queen has an entire wardrobe of this stuff ready to go.

Continuing from the previous note, this scene also puts into context how unreasonable Jack's final tantrum is. He just finally SNAPS! But Jack, if you were going to fly into a murderous rage over this kinky little dress-up game, why did you bother putting up with it for so long in the first place?

This brief interlude in the animation shows that Rose's dream self has finally woken up, due to her future doomed self going to sleep and "ceasing to exist." She has inherited some hazy memories from that version of her self, or if not all her memories per se, at least some of her perceptual faculty. Now she can see the graffiti she wrote on her walls, which previously was invisible to her due to some psychological block.

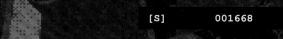

This is the secret Jaspers once whispered to her, which was simply, "Meow." This word didn't really tell Rose's younger self anything informative so much as it unlocked information already in her brain, which was an important genetic sequence. She uses the letters of MEOW in place of the usual letters for genetic codes, GCAT. This gene sequence is an important part of the full code that's later used to genetically engineer.....(drumroll).....an omnipotent dog.

243

Here we also take a peek at what the guardians are up to. Looks like they're wandering the planets, being generally badass. Nice to know. A lot of times the songs I was animating around were a little long. So if the key purpose of an animation, like "Jack usurps queen in murderous fit," wasn't quite enough material to fit the length of a song, I would look for little ways of padding out the action like this.

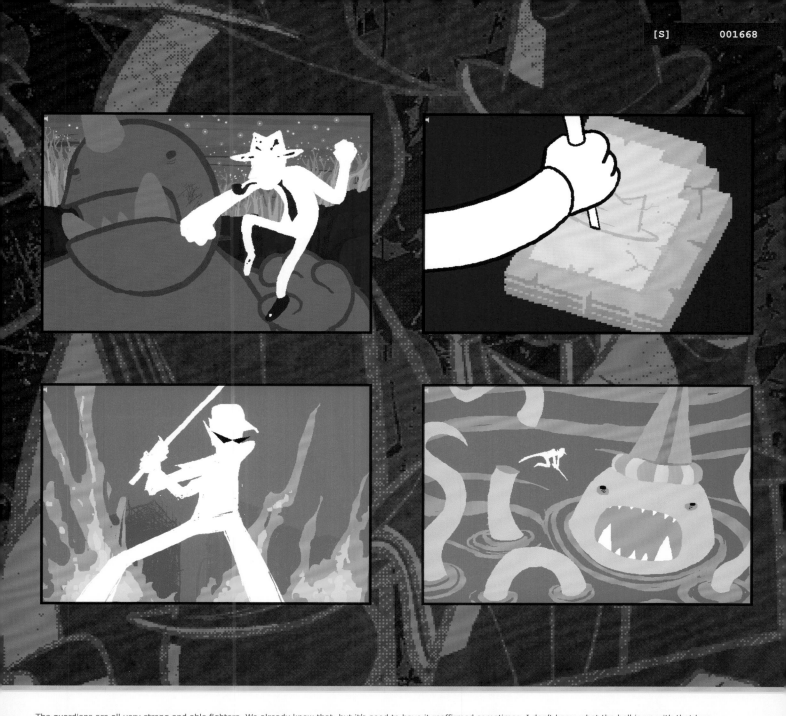

The guardians are all very strong and able fighters. We already knew that, but it's good to have it reaffirmed sometimes. I don't know what the hell is up with that lava octopus wearing a princess hat. That's the only time we see anything like that. I liked to promote the impression that the underling population is actually really diverse. Maybe you could play ten sessions of *Sburb* and never really catalogue them all. Also, this makes me wonder if that princess hat is fireproof, or if the octopus just takes great care to never fully submerge in the lava?

Jack, just use your safe word. There is absolutely no reason to reach for the bunny box and murder this sexy queen.

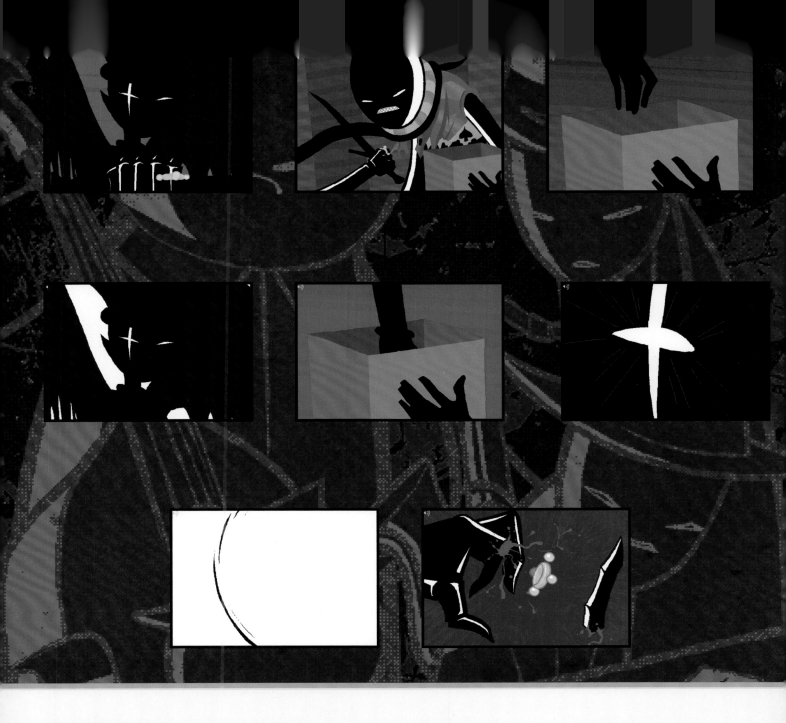

Goddamn it. What did I just say.

Okay, I keep referring to the fact that there is a lethal bunny in that box, which really is completely ruining the mystery of it. I am FUCKING sorry. At this point, even though it's clear that whatever Jade and her pen pal put in that box possesses extreme destructive power, we still have no idea what it is. It's an ongoing mystery, right up until we finally see what's inside, when the culmination of this fairly long-running gag reveals it's the same damn bunny at different stages of its history inside every birthday box. Just thought I'd note that all here, that we still don't know what's in the box, but it's not worth getting hung up on because something much more dramatic is happening... Look!

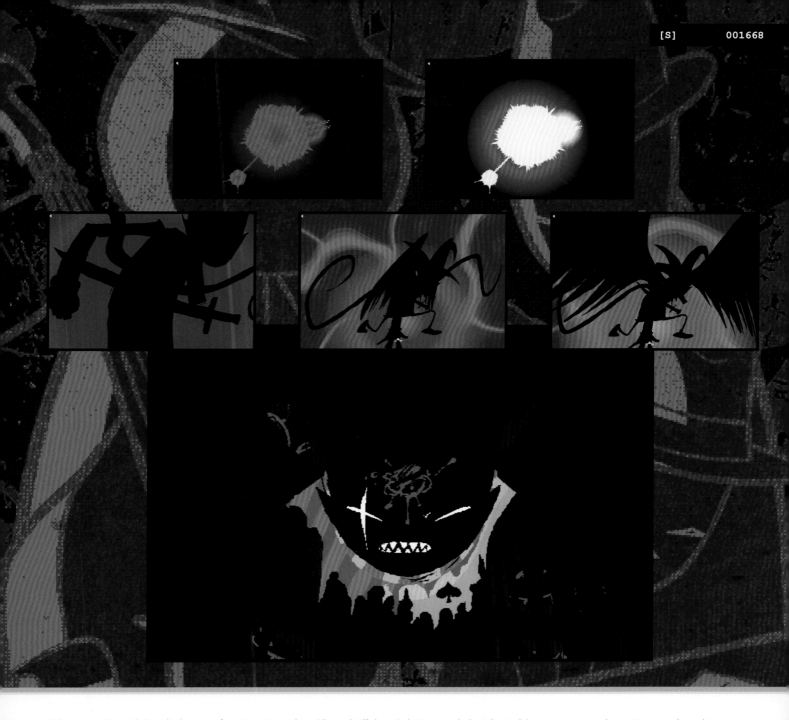

Jack's mutiny, along with his ridiculous transformation, is complete. What a devil's bargain he just struck. In order to claim supreme power, he must agree to have the absurd attire he so vehemently resisted actually become physically inseparable from himself. Yet the choice he has made is clear. Power prevails over dignity. That said, being forced to look like a clown in exchange for this boon isn't exactly going to keep him in a good mood.

END OF YEAR 1
4/13/2009 — 4/13/2010

> Locate fourth wall.

Because this animation went up on 4/13, it almost formally locked *Homestuck* into Magic Date Syndrome thereafter. There were always huge expectations revolving around what might occur on some key date in HS numerical lore—which, to be fair, was always being fueled by the fact that I kept putting significant moments on those key dates. For example, something significant happened on just about every 4/13 after this, right up until the final page, which was posted on 4/13 of Year Seven.

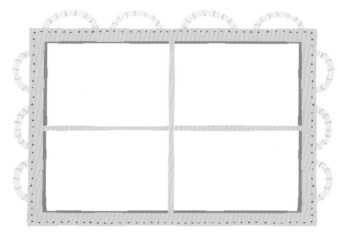

> Activate.

What?

Oh hell no. This is always such
a terrible idea. Leave me alone.

> AH: Engage in highly indulgent self-
insertion into story.

> AH: Examine wall.

You really wish your side of
the wall had an off switch.

Which is to say, I really wish my
side of the wall had an off switch.

> AH: Forget it. Go back to work.

Ok. You're just going to ask me to
recap Homestuck though. I don't know why
you'd want to sit there and watch me type.

This is going to be pretty long.

> AH: Recap first year of Homestuck.

There are those orange fingers again. We saw them back when I was introducing Jack. So even though I made it a whole year before putting myself in the story, you know I clearly *intended* to do so in some way, at some point. It's important to seed these things, so when I pull bullshit stunts like this, at least you think to yourself, oh okay, he *carefully planned* this bullshit stunt. For a significant period of time, he was incredibly determined to foist this exact idiotic charade on us, and that's what makes it seem okay for some reason. Brilliant, even? Yeah, that's what you think, admit it. But also note that the orange fingers (and the guy attached to them) reappear right after Jack's ascension, and when we first saw them they were typing Jack's name. I'll repeat this: villainy, and the extent to which a character can be considered villainous, is directly tied to how close they are to the surface of the story's metabubble—that is, how closely they are associated with the general awareness and acknowledgement that this is, in fact, a story they exist inside of. Jack, by his proximity to me here, establishes himself as such a character, but this is only a start. There are others much higher up the metaladder than he, but it's important to establish a baseline here, before the idea really means anything.

252

Homestuck began on April 13th, 2009, the 13th birthday of our chief protagonist and future boy-skylark, John Egbert. Three days prior was supposed to be the day he received the Sburb Beta in the mail, but it was running late. It showed up later that afternoon, and after overcoming a variety of domestic adversities, he retrieved the game, along with a birthday package from his internet friend, Dave Strider.

John soon established a game connection with another friend, Rose Lalonde, who'd spent the day badgering him about playing with her, after unsuccessfully attempting to convince Dave to play. Upon connecting, Rose was able to manipulate John's environment, move his furniture around via cursor, and restructure the shape of his room. John was unable to do this to Rose's environment however. He'd installed the client copy of the beta, and required the server copy for that.

The server copy was trapped in his dad's car, along with a birthday package from another friend, Jade Harley. Jade messaged John inquiring about the package. As of this moment, neither her package nor the server copy has been recovered by John. Rose had also prepared a package for John, but had not mailed it yet. It still sits in her room. Dave's package contained the authentic stuffed bunny from Con Air.

In addition to allowing Rose to control John's environment, Sburb provided an array of devices Rose deployed throughout John's house. These devices used together provided a system by which the players could manufacture any item using the code on that item's captchalogue card, if they gathered enough grist to pay for it. Later, they would learn to combine item codes to master the art of punch card alchemy, whereby items could be fused together in purpose and design.

One device on being activated began a countdown, and released an entity called a kernelsprite. The countdown ticked down to the moment John's house would be struck by a meteor, destroying his neighborhood. To escape this demise, John had to use the devices to manufacture a special item that looked like a blue apple, and take a bite of it, in order to transport his entire house just before impact to the safety of a mysterious dark realm, where his house would situate itself atop a tall rock column high above a blanket of clouds. This realm is called the Medium. Before he entered the Medium though, John and Rose prototyped his kernelsprite with the large harlequin doll his dad got him for his birthday, transforming the sprite to bear its likeness, including the way the doll was disfigured via earlier hijinks. It had a slashed eye and one arm, and so too did the sprite. When John entered the Medium, the sprite's kernel hatched, thus imbuing all the enemies John and his friends would face with properties of the sprite. The lesser adversaries John faced first, Shale Imps, all wore harlequin garbs. They became more powerful and more radically mutated with each successive pre-Medium prototyping.

After entering the Medium, John's dad was kidnapped by imps. While John was looking for him, he accidentally prototyped the sprite with his grandmother's ashes, transforming it again. This prototyping had no effect on the enemies, since he was already in the Medium, and the kernel had already hatched. Instead, only the sprite was affected, and it took on the appearance, personality, and memories of his grandmother, becoming Nannasprite, a game-supplied albeit customized guide for John. She explained aspects of the game, about Skaia residing at the center of the Medium, beyond seven gates floating directly above his house, and about an eternal/timeless war fought there between dark and light, one that light was always destined to lose.

Rose, who'd been having frequent internet connection issues, lost her connection as she tried to lift John's car to retrieve the game and the package. The car fell into the abyss below. A storm caused her house to lose power along with its wireless internet connection. Her laptop was able to run on battery power for a time, while she tapped into the wireless signal from the laboratory next door. When her laptop ran out of power, she had to overcome more family strife (and endure a gift pony in the process), go outside in the rain, and plug it into the small generator outside the mausoleum of her dead cat, Jaspers. She continued her session with John inside the mausoleum, while the meteor-sparked forest fire surrounding her house grew more intense. From the house, Rose's mom opened a secret passage in the mausoleum to help her escape. The passage lead to the lab next door, where Rose found a stable, portable source of power and internet for her computer. She also found a terminal projecting the impact times and locations for the millions of meteors presently bombarding the planet, along with all the other live sessions of other players around the world. She also found a little girl's room, a mutant kitten she named Vodka Mutini, and a cloning machine operating through the science of ectobiology. Its terminal was locked on to her cat Jaspers at whatever point in his life the user specified. She attempted to apparify Jaspers from a moment in her early childhood, before he whispered a secret to her. But doing so would have caused a paradox, so it apparified (paradoxified) a pile of slime instead. The machine used the slime to create a fetal paradox clone of Jaspers in a glass tube. On the monitor, Jaspers then told young Rose the secret, then vanished, only to show up dead weeks later and put in the mausoleum for years until the present. Rose left the laboratory moments before it was destroyed by a meteor impact. She transportalized back to her mom's room, proceeded to her room to wait for Dave to connect with her and rescue her from the next imminent impact. Dave was charged with acquiring his bro's copy of the game to help Rose. Earlier he had lost his copy of the game to a mishap involving a crow. It saw in his window, seized the game, and Dave accidentally impaled it with a sword, sending the crow and the game out the window onto a landing far below his apartment. He searched his bro's room unable to find it, was briefly shadowed by Lil Cal, and then found a note beckoning him to meet on the roof for a confrontation. Dave and his bro dueled on the roof extensively, and Dave was thoroughly bested. Upon defeating Dave, his bro dropped the copies of the game, and flew off in his rocket board into the sky. Dave used the copies to connect with Rose, and quickly deployed the devices while her house was on fire, surrounded by flaming tornadoes, and minutes away from being destroyed by a meteor. Rose prototyped her kernelsprite with Jaspers, specifically to understand the meaning of the secret he whispered to her years ago. She was advised to do this by Jade, who told her about the game in the first place. Dave then prototyped the kernelsprite again with the tentacled princess doll given to Rose on her birthday by her mom. Both of these prototypings would have an effect on the enemies once Rose entered the Medium and the kernel hatched. Rose used the alchemiter to create the special item - for her, a purple wine bottle - which she needed to break to enter. She eventually did, transporting her house just before the meteor collided. The meteor left a crater. Over time, at the site of impact, a large, white structure that looked like a wine bottle grew there, and the crater filled up with sand as the climate of the post-apocalyptic Earth gradually changed. The "rock" of that bottle was a large metal cylinder with an interior much like an advanced science station, with a variety of devices and monitors inside. 413 years after the meteor impact, the Wayward Vagabond walked through the desert and discovered this station. Inside, he found canned rations, a firefly he named Serenity, an appearifier, and four monitors hooked up to a keyboard. On one of the monitors was John, after he'd entered the Medium. WV could type commands to John directly, much as the readers of this story could type commands for the characters to follow.

Hey look, it's a bunch of bullshit we don't need to read. Okay, moving on.

253

He picked up Jade's package to John, removed what was inside, and used it to slice her ring finger off. He then killed the Black Queen, put on the ring, and donned the full upgrade supplied by the three prototypings.

He then became Jackspers Noirlecrow, which is a name I just made up now.

And then after that you started watching me type in this ridiculous study I photoshopped for myself with my cool horse painting propped up in the background.

> AH: I didn't read any of that. Do something less boring.

> MSPA Reader: Shut the hell up.

> AH: Retrieve arm from background.

Huh? Oh.

Cal, please. Not now.

> AH: Why don't you keep drawing Homestuck or something.

Oh, but I don't merely draw Homestuck...

(Type "==>", I am about to make a joke.)

> Ok. ==>

A fan made that Cal doll for me. I think I still have it, probably stuffed deep somewhere in the same closet where the *Con Air* bunny is. It's about as cursed an item as you'll ever find. I should probably burn it.

I CONJURE THIS INTREPID FANTASYSCAPE WITH TEARS BLED FROM THE WISDOM-WEARY EYES OF FIFTY THOUSAND IMAGINARY MAGICIANS. I PULL HEAVY DRAGS FROM THE BRUMES OF INSPIRATION WITH ENCHANTED BELLOWS MARAUDED FROM A GUILD OF CHURLISH MYTHICAL DWARVES. VAST BULBOUS RIDDLESPIDERS PUSH THE SILKEN STRANDS OF PURE WHIMSY THROUGH HIDEOUS ABDOMINAL SPINNERETS AND IT IS THAT WITH WHICH I WEAVE THIS AUDACIOUS COCOON OF EXQUISITE LIES. AND WHEN IT HATCHES A GREAT MOTH OF TITILLATION WILL AWAKEN AND ROAR AND BEAT ITS WINGS, AND THE POWDER SETTLING DOWN WILL ARREST THE HUMORS OF AN ENORMOUS TERRIBLE OLD BEGGAR, RELAXING THE VULTUROUS LEATHERY VICEGRIP HE'S FIXED AROUND YOUR CAPTIVE MIND.

> AH: This is stupid. Stop being a wiseass and get drawing.

I think this rant speaks for itself. I stand by every word of it to this day. EVERY. WORD. That said, here's some more stuff to say. AH, the character, as the cartoon avatar for The Creator, has a sort of arc, I guess you could call it. There are many facets to the psychological profile of the creative individual. One of them is this preposterously megalomaniacal, self-absorbed, power-drunk persona which, arguably, is often the motivating force behind an individual's desire to create certain things in the first place. A being supremely enamored of art's ability to let them conjure anything out of thin air, manipulate people's emotions in any direction on a whim, and to revel in this whole process as some sort of innate celebration of their ingenuity. In this grand farce called *Homestuck*, we introduce the AH author-god in this way to set him on a path to reveal different qualities of the creative psyche. More to the point, he is set upon a long-term trajectory from being the supreme goofball-savant in absolute command of his craft to gradually becoming a victim of the forces it unleashes as he was the original architect of their unleashing.

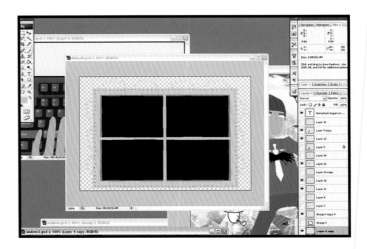

Alright. It won't be that exciting to watch though.

I'll pull up Photoshop again. Here's the file I was using for the fourth wall.

What do you want me to draw?

> AH: Can you show us what's going on with John again?

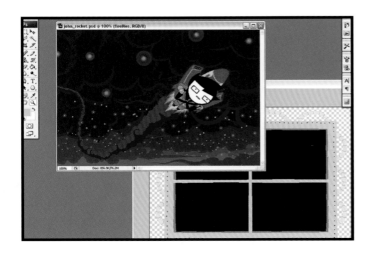

Sure.

How about if I drag the content from one of the John files under the fourth wall layer, so we can make a more graceful transition out of this ludicrous, highly disruptive self-insertion arc?

> AH: That sounds like a good idea.

I didn't actually work in a lavish blue study with my horse painting on the mantle. That's Andrew Carnegie's study, tinted blue. This fake thing I was doing in his study is probably better than any real thing he did in it. He probably never even went in there. I doubt he was any good with Photoshop, for that matter.

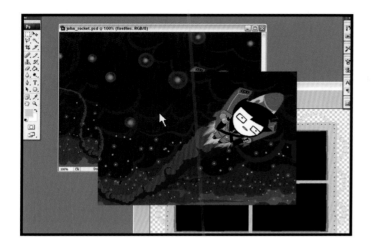

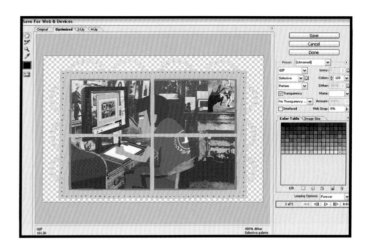

Oh! And then you can type something like "Switch wall's view to show us what's going on with John."

Here, I'll prepare the GIF file for that. It'll just take a few seconds.

Go ahead. Say that.

> Switch wall's view to show us what's going on with John.

You decide that's entirely enough of that. If this website becomes any more self-aware in a playfully self-deprecating yet weirdly self-aggrandizing manner, you're going to go drown a bag of puppies in a sewer.

This scene works better if you can actually see the Fourth Wall switch shots from me to John. It's a good transition idea. This entire AH sequence is a great transition, actually—if you have a soft spot for dumbass nonsense. If you don't, you're probably a bad person? We just saw this fire sequence of Jack ascending, which gave us heart palpitations. Cutting to John is a little too abrupt, we need some horseshit to grease the wheels. Like a mini-intermission, unlabeled as such. I guess I could have labeled it, but I didn't have the brilliant idea of putting 500 intermissions into HS yet. That masterstroke comes in Act 6, when we all start spiraling downward into hell together for eternity.

> John: Answer GC.

-- gallowsCalibrator [GC] sent ectoBiologist [EB] the file "LOW4SM4P.FL4" --

EB: what's this?
GC: 1T'S YOUR WORLD M4P
GC: W1TH YOUR S3COND G4T3 L4B3L3D
GC: SO YOU C4N GO TH3R3
EB: oh man, let me drop everything and go there, because i'm in such a huge hurry to take more of your advice!
GC: JOHN PL34S3
GC: G1V3 M3 ON3 OF YOUR HUM4N BR34KS
GC: 1 F33L 4WFUL 4BOUT K1LL1NG YOU
GC: 3V3N THOUGH T3CH1N1C4LLY YOU N3V3R 3V3N D13D SO 1 DONT KNOW WH4T YOUR3 B1TCH1NG 4BOUT >:[
EB: yeah, well, dave said i did, and i believe him!
GC: TH4T 1S B3C4US3 H3 4ND YOU 4R3 B3ST PUP4 P4LS FOUR LYF3
GC: C4NT 1 B3 YOUR P4L TOO JOHN???
EB: i don't know, i thought you were ok for a while, but now you are kind of giving me the creeps!
GC: J3GUS JOHN
EB: what?
GC: 1 4M 1NVOK1NG TH3 N4M3 OF YOUR 34RTH J3GUS
GC: TO 3XPR3SS FRUSTR4T1ON
EB: you mean my earth jesus?

I think what John actually means here is: first she threatened to slit his throat, which gave him the creeps, then for some stupid reason he thought she was okay for a while, but then she tried to kill him, which started giving him the creeps all over again. But it's fine, he's going to start thinking she's okay again. He's an easygoing guy.

```
GC: 1 DONT KNOW
GC: DO 1
EB: do you have a troll jegus?
GC: JOHN
GC: W3 H4V3 TH3 B3ST TROLL J3GUS
GC: YOU DONT 3V3N KNOW
EB: wow, really?
EB: or is this a joke?
GC: 1TS 4 JOK3
GC: 1M NOT R34LLY SUR3 WH4T 4 J3GUS 1S >:?
EB: well...
EB: neither do i, i guess.
EB: it's pretty much not anything.
GC: JOHN
GC: W1LL YOU PL34S3 FOLLOW TH3 M4P?????
GC: L3T M3 34RN YOUR TRUST
GC: 1F YOU DONT L1K3 WH4TS ON TH3 OTH3R S1D3 OF TH3 G4T3
GC: YOU C4N JUST TURN 4ROUND!
EB: um...
EB: ok.
EB: i'll take a look.
```

> John: Open map.

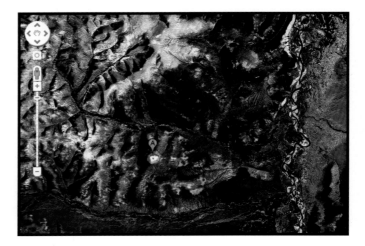

Yes, they absolutely do have a Troll Jegus. He wears a really, really tall pair of pants.

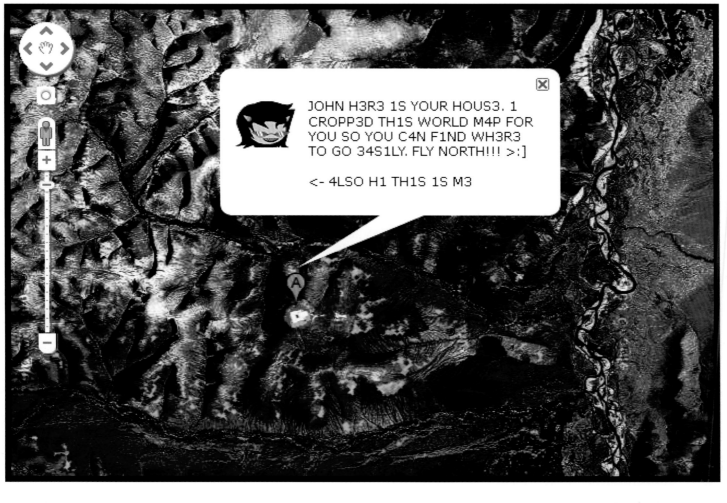

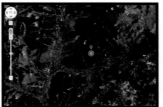
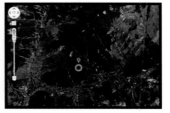

Google LOWAS is a great mini-application that simulates the functionality of Google Maps, letting you scroll around and zoom in and out of some overhead shots of LOWAS that I made. Things like this are what make such a strong case for HS still being available to consume in its native digital format. Also, how the hell did Terezi crop the world map for him? I think what she means is: I was the one who cropped the world map, so I didn't have to create thousands of square miles worth of this damn blue terrain.

> John: Proceed to the second gate.

Another nice thing about the interactivity here is that it lets the reader navigate the map to find the gate themselves. They don't *have* to in order to advance the story, but what kind of clown wouldn't bother with that? Some weak, speed-reading fool, I suppose.

> John: Enter.

GATE 2

1%

You spend the next twenty minutes staring at this image before you realize it's not a Flash file.

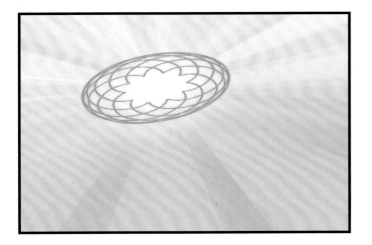

262

One wonders how long it would've taken the kids to make progress through their session if the trolls weren't coaching/messing with them? How long would it have taken for John to find the gate to Rose's house like this? Days, weeks? The more you learn about the game, the more you start to infer that its natural cadence involves a lot of time going by. Months, maybe even years for some people. It really makes the characters work for certain things, and thus makes them appreciate finally getting to meet up with their long-distance friends when they get to the right gate. Assuming said friends aren't asleep when they get there.

> John: Get up.

This is the first time a Breath player riding a rocket through a gate crashes into the bedroom of a sleeping Light player. Will it be the last time? That is left up to the speculation of the reader.

Despite the pandemonium of your entrance, Rose is still sound asleep. She must be really tuckered out!

It looks like this little guy is awake and ready for action though. He is adorable. You decide to name him Dr. Meowgon Spengler.

> John: Answer Dave.

```
-- turntechGodhead [TG] began pestering
ectoBiologist [EB] --

TG: wow ok
TG: youre a little early
TG: but thats fine i guess
TG: also you suck at rockets
EB: ARGH!
TG: what
EB: she tricked me again.
TG: who
EB: GC.
```

The *Homestuck* Kid Policy is, never let a good pet go rudely un-renamed, or ideally, unstolen either.

EB: she told me how to get to the 2nd gate.
EB: so i went through, but it took me to rose's house instead.
EB: another prank!
TG: dude you did go through the second gate
TG: i mean i dont know why you would listen to her again
TG: kind of moronic but thats a whole other issue
TG: she didnt trick you this time
EB: oh...
EB: then, i don't really get this.
TG: what were you expecting
TG: this is how it works
TG: the progression of gates is like this whole round robin thing
TG: cycling through each planet
TG: gate 2 on your planet leads to gate 2 on roses
TG: then you build up to gate 3 above her house which leads somewhere else on her planet
TG: you look for gate 4 somewhere there
TG: which leads to gate 4 above my house
TG: and so on
EB: wow, ok.
TG: ordinarily rose would have already gone through her gate 1
TG: but shes sleeping pretty hard obviously
TG: and ordinarily you wouldnt have gone through gate 2 until her house was built up
TG: so you wouldnt fall to your death
TG: but you got your cheat rocket so thats fine
TG: see we all got to coordinate on this thing
EB: ok...
EB: how do you know all this?
TG: fuck
TG: come on dude
EB: oh yeah...
EB: you're the orange dave.
EB: hey no offense, but do you think i could talk to the real dave for a second?
TG: god dammit
TG: i am the real dave
TG: you know the one who saved your life
TG: im more real actually cause ive been through some heavy shit already hopping around on red hot gears and i-beams for like a year
TG: and grinding shit out for your ungrateful ass
TG: here look check out this code from the future not that you deserve it WIin189Q
TG: youre fucking welcome
EB: wow, calm down!
EB: i'm sorry, that's not really what i meant...

Davesprite, now the exposition birdboy, helps us understand how gate logic works. They are the means of interplanetary travel. So now, as a student of *Sburb*, you finally know these planetary quests aren't insular, solitary events where the player never leaves their planet or meets their friends. They're huge, planet-hopping schemes requiring hella teamwork. Also, here we begin the chronicles of Real Dave vs. Bird Dave, and what the meaning of someone's "real self" even is. It's a sore subject, and John is routinely insensitive about it to his bro. John probably flashes a lot of "real self privilege" throughout the story because he's one of the only characters who remains the original version of himself all the way until the end. It's a nice perk of being the designated protagonist.

EB: i mean, of course you're a real dave, but what i mean is...
EB: the dave from my time is also my friend, and i guess he's in the same boat i'm in, not knowing stuff and all.
EB: and i'd feel bad keeping him out of the loop!

-- turntechGodhead [TG] began pestering ectoBiologist [EB] --

TG: yo
EB: oh, hey.
EB: i think i pissed off your future self.
TG: what did you do
EB: i said he wasn't the real dave.
TG: ahahahahaha
EB: i think i might have really hurt his feelings though!
TG: pff
TG: dont worry about it
EB: why not?
TG: cause i wouldnt give a shit
TG: and hes me
EB: ok.
EB: i'm in rose's room by the way.
TG: what
TG: really
EB: yeah, but she's asleep!
TG: ok
TG: dont go anywhere
TG: im coming down to the computer
EB: ok.

TG: dave is here he wants to use the computer
TG: probably to help you scope out roses room and snoop and stuff
TG: i mean thats what i would have done
TG: if you were alive
TG: so im gonna go
TG: use these flappy ghost wings and tear shit up in space or something
EB: sure!
EB: hey dave...
TG: what
EB: in case i forgot to say so before...
EB: thanks for saving my life!
TG: yeah

-- turntechGodhead [TG] ceased pestering ectoBiologist [EB] --

The "cause i wouldnt give a shit" line is such a flagrant and obvious lie. It's disproven in many conversations, including the one immediately preceding this one. Also, I like how John, instead of saying, "That doesn't sound true, it sounds like bird-you is actually very sensitive about it," just says "ok" and changes the subject. Teens are kind of a bunch of dicks?

> John: Snoop.

```
TG: ok i dont know what youre doing here
TG: but i think we can both agree that youve got to rummage through as much of her shit as
possible before she wakes up
EB: man, i don't know how i feel about that!
EB: i don't really like the idea of capering around her room while she's asleep, it feels
weird.
EB: i'm going to wake her up.
TG: dude no come on
TG: shes out like a light anyway
TG: it was some like weird future thing that happened that made her sleep
EB: a future thing?
TG: yeah
TG: shit doesnt get more clear than that
EB: well, yeah, she won't wake up.
EB: so i guess so.
EB: but i'm not snooping!!!
TG: fine dont
TG: but here just do this one thing
TG: see those two notebooks on the floor behind you
EB: yeah.
EB: they look sorta like journals.
EB: i don't think i should read those!
TG: you dont have to read them im not telling you to
TG: what kind of prying tool do you take me for
TG: just pick them up
TG: you know like tidy up a bit since you made a royal fucking dump of her room just now
EB: uh, ok.
```

> John: Pick up books.

267

```
TG: now i need you to do something else
TG: this is important
TG: like for important game reasons and stuff
TG: take the card the books are on
TG: flip it over
EB: umm...
TG: so you can see the code
EB: wait a minute!
EB: i see what you're trying to do.
EB: i won't tell you the code for rose's books!
TG: dude you dont have to tell me the code
TG: just flip it over and let me know if theres a code there thats all
EB: ok...
EB: i guess.
EB: yeah there's a code.
TG: alright cool
TG: you can ditch the books now if you want
TG: maybe put them back on the floor
TG: so rose doesnt think you were snooping
TG: seriously youve got some grubby fingers bro why dont you mind your own business there
TG: what is even with you
EB: HAHA DAVE,
EB: I THINK ALL THIS LAUGHING MADE ME POOP IN MY PANTS TOO HARD.
TG: isnt that your birthday package there
EB: oh, yeah, i think it might be.
```

Dave just wants to read Rose's diary. That's all that's happening here. Nothing else. Then he accuses John of being nosy. Could this be his worst shittyboy moment in the story? It's probably in the running.

```
TG: maybe you should look at it
TG: i dont think it counts as snooping since its technically yours
EB: yeah, maybe.
EB: i wonder if she finished...
EB: she was so tight lipped about the damn thing! i am really curious.
```

> Dave: Zoom in.

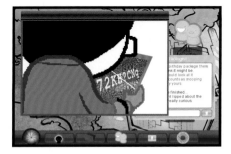

Would Rose be this happy to do Dave the favor of waking his dream self up if she knew he was working this hard to clown on his best buddy to steal her diary?

It's not totally clear here why Dave's dream self appears to be already awake while his real self is also awake. I think we must infer that his dream self is in some sort of "waking trance" where he's technically awake but too preoccupied by certain things to be considered fully awake. (Preoccupied, for instance, by Dream Cal, who has been haunting his dreams for most of his life.) One thing that *is* clear, though, is the fact that throwing a ball of magic dream yarn at Dream Dave's head will snap him out of it.

270

It's kind of bothering me that he's using that *GameBro* magazine as a mousepad but only like...halfway? He keeps rubbing the mouse right over the edge of the magazine. It's really aggravating.

271

> John: Check Rose's bookshelf.

You eye your birthday package again curiously.
It's awfully tempting to peek inside, but you
feel guilty about it for some reason, even though
it's yours anyway.

You suppose a perusal of her bookshelf would
be harmless enough. Just a bunch of books. The
knowledge within is meant for everybody.

Dave pesters you with the message, "TG:
afdsjjjjjjjjjvffffffffffffffffffffffffffffffffff"
which you decide not to bother dignifying with a
whole pesterlog ordeal because it's probably just
him being a truculent jackass again so screw him.

> John: Look at a book.

By now we understand that there are patterns of hidden graffiti on the kids' walls that reveal their deep psychological mysteries and problems. So surely Dave
has some really disturbing and crazy stuff on his walls we couldn't see before, right? But without any fanfare at all, it's casually revealed here that he's just been
subconsciously scrawling awful *Sweet Bro and Hella Jeff* murals in his sleep. Kinda no big deal. But then again, this is more telling than it may seem, since *SBaHJ*
has the distinction of being the symbolic language of his subconscious. It reveals hidden meanings and forecasts certain things about the story in some frustratingly
dumb and obtuse ways. Dave (or more accurately, me) making *SBaHJ* comics is like rolling your eyes back in your head and speaking in a really moronic form of
Bad Webcomic Tongues about the deepest meanings of *Homestuck*.

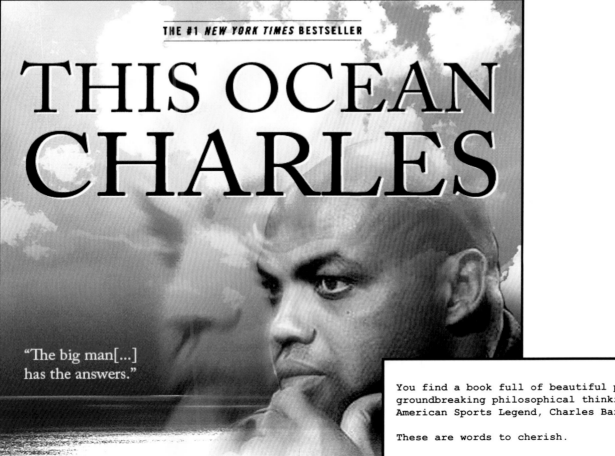

THE #1 *NEW YORK TIMES* BESTSELLER

THIS OCEAN
CHARLES

"The big man[...]
has the answers."

CHARLES BARKLEY

You find a book full of beautiful poetry and
groundbreaking philosophical thinking by
American Sports Legend, Charles Barkley.

These are words to cherish.

This is a man to treasure.

> John: Take book.

The completely inexplicable "quote the wrong guy for wise, famous sayings" gag repeated a few times early in the story is made a little (only a little) less inexplicable with stuff like this. There are two absurd, immutable rules that govern the presence of celebrities in *Homestuck*. One is, Alternia has all the same celebrities we do, but they're trolls for some reason. The second is, all celebrities in real life also exist on Earth in HS, but none of them quite have the same biographies. Barkley here is a philosopher poet in addition to being a basketball legend. Ben Stiller is responsible for seditious underground anti-fascist propaganda. Guy Fieri and the Insane Clown Posse... Well, let's just leave it there for now.

You captchalogue Rose's autographed copy of THIS OCEAN CHARLES. Jewels of wisdom like this don't just fall into your lap every day, and shouldn't be parted with lightly.

You doubt she'll mind if you borrow her book. She's always trying to get you to read her weird books anyway.

> John: Oh, just open the package already.

You can't take it anymore.
You're going to see what's inside.

> John,

You know. I'm beginning to think. MAYBE. It could just be the same friggin' bunny in every box. It's a hunch. How did this happen? **[S] Descend** has a lot of answers to all this porous-plot time baloney, including a lot of answers to questions we already forgot about. Like how did Dave actually enter the Medium? Oh, right. That was a thing we didn't see. We *will* see it, though.

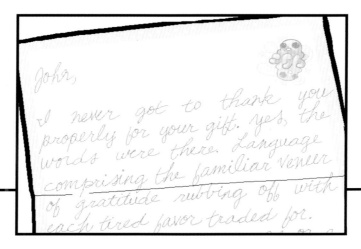

John,

I never got to thank you properly for your gift. Yes, the words were there. Language comprising the familiar veneer of gratitude rubbing off with each tired favor traded for. A God bless to a sneeze or a few pennies cradled in a receipt. Perhaps it's the deplorable romantic in me, but I thought your present, and your friendship, demanded reciprocation surpassing by some degree the utterly meaningless.

The proper thanks I thought would be a demonstration that your offering was not in vain. Yes, maybe some would take your suggested alternative to my gloomy preoccupations as a passive-aggressive jab. But I know you didn't mean it that way. In fact, I'm sure reading about it now is the first time the notion has occurred to you. John, please stop rolling your eyes. The letter is down here.

The gift in this box is a resurrection. I used your present to thread life anew into a tattered heirloom. As long as I can remember, its black, greasy appendages have been tethered limply to its ratty, porous carriage. Too delicate to wash, too dear to discard. I used to love this rabbit. Now he's yours.

I trust you'll find this to be adequately sentimental. Happy birthday.

Rose

> John: Put the bunny back in the box.

Basically, she gives him Frankenstein's bunny. She presents it as a corpse she's cherished since childhood and resurrected for him through sort of an occult knitting ritual. Pretty edgy, Rose. Actually, I'm surprised she didn't go grimdark just writing this letter.

This gift from Rose is so cool. Two sweet bunnies on one birthday?? What are the odds. In a fit of enthusiasm you SHUT UP AND JAM the bunny back in the box, executing a textbook CHAOS DUNK.

Millions would have perished, if everything in the ocean weren't dead already, that is.

> John: Take box.

You gently CHAOS DUNK the fragile bunny back in the box and captchalogue it. It is such a nice present. You will have to write Rose a thank you note and tuck it under her hair band or something. Wait no, that would probably be creepy.

This bunny reminds you that you still have a salamander in your sylladex. She is holding the bunny Dave got you. It's sort of uncanny how similar they are, aside from the knitted enhancements. Seriously, what are the odds?? So weird.

> John: Deploy beloved daughter.

A few people started buzzing about "Shut Up and Jam" the moment Barkley appeared, so I made this Chaos Dunk reference. Do people even know anything about this meme anymore? All things considered, it's kind of one of HS's weaker references, I think. Something feels a little off about its inclusion here, I can't really put my finger on it. Oh well, *Homestuck* lives by the shitpost and dies by the shitpost. That's basically what each update was anyway. It's a tale of 10,000 shitposts.

You release dear, precious Casey. She was probably getting antsy in that card. You think you'll leave her here with Rose. A dangerous quest is nothing to embark on with a sweet, innocent little girl stashed in your inventory.

You aren't actually sure if she is a girl though. You don't even know if salamanders can be girls. Aren't they hermaphrodites or something?

You don't know anything about biology. Unless it is biology that has to do with ghosts and slime. But even then you don't actually know anything, you just sort of like to pretend you do.

Looks like a troll is bugging Rose.

> John: Answer troll.

-- grimAuxiliatrix [GA] began trolling tentacleTherapist [TT] --

GA: Im Supposed To Antagonize A Few Members Of Your Trivial Species
GA: I Have To Start Somewhere
GA: And Somewhen
GA: So I Am Starting With You
GA: And Now
GA: Its Going To Be Pointless And Unpleasant
GA: Mostly For Me
GA: Actually You Know What
GA: Im Not Really Feeling This At All

Finally we understand why Kanaya thought Rose was an idiot during that first impression, and then bamboozled herself into having a very tricky nonlinear conversation with her. It's because this goofball picked up her first troll attempt. So the "trap" Kanaya set by providing Rose with a (possibly) edited version of their first correspondence was a complete waste of time, because Rose was never going to be the one to have that conversation at all. But of course, this all hinges on the fact that Kanaya can't see who she's talking to yet, for some reason... Guess we'll find out what's up with that soon.

GA: Goodbye
TT: she's not here right now, she's asleep!
TT: but ok, see you.
GA: Is This
GA: Your Human Sarcasm That Ive Heard About
GA: That You Always Use
GA: And That Is Basically A Terrible Way To Communicate
TT: umm... no?
GA: I Thought That Was The Thing You Did
GA: The Rose Human Specifically
TT: oh, yeah.
TT: that's me! i am the rose human. look at me, i am so smart with all these snooty words and complicated things to say.
TT: i am the queen of books.
GA: Okay These Are Definitely Insincere Statements
GA: Why Do You Work So Hard At Being So Awful
TT: fffuuhhhhhhhh
TT: i'm so burned, these burns are crazy.
TT: can we just cut to the chase and be friends already??
TT: these cat and mouse games are so dumb, you know we're just going to all be friends at some point anyway.
GA: Have We Spoken Before
TT: i don't know, uh, maybe???
TT: it's hard to keep track with all your time nonsense.
GA: Now That I Think About It It Is Pretty Conceivable That I Will Talk To You Again In The Past After This Conversation
TT: that's because you guys always do things the hard way.
TT: and the dumb way.
GA: I Should Figure Out How The Viewport Feature Of This Application Works
GA: So I Can See What Such A Primitive Creature Looks Like
TT: haha, well i know what you guys look like.
TT: you look kind of like...
TT: howie mandel from little monsters.
TT: even though, to be perfectly frank, he was kind of a big monster.
TT: because he was a big goofy adult.
TT: and fred savage was like his child prankster sidekick.
GA: Is This An Adversary You Have Encountered On Your Quest
TT: no, it's a movie.
TT: you should ask john about it, because he thinks it's awesome, which it is.
GA: It Seems You Put Stock In Johns Assessment Of Things
GA: Even Really Uninteresting Things That Are Pretty Terrible To Listen To
GA: He Is Either The Leader Of Your Party Or You Hold Whatever The Human Equivalent Of Mating Fondness For Him Is

The answer to the question on the previous page is, Kanaya is begrudgingly just starting this trolling campaign on Karkat's orders and hasn't figured out how to use the viewport feature yet. It's impressive that there's such a good explanation to circumvent the crisis in logic that could have otherwise been. It's also interesting that Kanaya knows a few things about the "Rose Human." It invites all kinds of questions. Who talked up Rose to her? Was it Karkat? Was he like, listen, you'll LOVE messing with this one snobby girl in particular. She's right up your alley. Was he...inadvertently setting them up with each other?? That would make sense. He *is* the romance aficionado, after all.

TT: yeah, i got him this really cool bunny for his birthday, and it's really nicely knitted and everything.
TT: because i am basically in love with him, you are right.
GA: Uh Okay
TT: heh, just kidding. i'm sure john knows it's cause i am really thoughtful and i bet he really appreciates the present, and would say thank you if he were here!
GA: Okay Human Courtship Is Definitely A Strange Thing And Its Sort Of Blowing My Mind Listening To This
GA: I Think Ill Talk To Someone Else Now
TT: why don't you talk to john?
GA: Maybe
GA: When Along His Timeline Would You Recommend Communicating With Him
TT: oh man, i don't know.
TT: why don't you pick the time that will make the most complicated mess out of everything imaginable?
TT: you know that's what you're gonna do anyway.
GA: Considering That Youre Obviously Not That Smart
GA: And Basically Understand Whipping Bugwinged Fuckall About Even The Most Elementary Temporal Mechanics
GA: I Am A Bit Perplexed As To Why I Find Myself So Vehemently Fondling The Short End Of The Antagonism Stick Here
GA: Kind Of Irritating
GA: Im Going To Talk To Your Comrades
GA: This John Human
GA: And Figure Out Whats Going On
TT: ok.
TT: if you talk to him in the past...
TT: he'll understand even less buggywhipped fuckall about time, and he'll be confused.
TT: so maybe paste something from this conversation to him? i don't know.
TT: and if you talk to him in the future...
TT: he'll probably know all this stuff, like things you've said to him but haven't said yet!
TT: and then you'll be confused.
TT: sorry, that's just how this works.
TT: don't say i didn't warn you!
GA: Consider Me Fully Briefed On The Matter.
GA: Until Next Time Rose
GA: Next Time In The Past
TT: yeah, bye!
TT: (hehehehehehe)

-- **grimAuxiliatrix** [GA] ceased trolling **tentacleTherapist** [TT] --

The fact that John expresses gratitude in a gracious way for the bunny gift indicates that he is trolling this troll knowing full well that Rose will backread the conversation after she wakes up, thus trolling her by extension as well. His prankster's gambit meter is probably constantly going haywire. It's a shame we so rarely see it.

grimAuxiliatrix [GA] began trolling twinArmageddons [TA]

GA: If Youre Not Too Busy Still Setting Up The Network
GA: Perhaps You Could Come Show Me How To Activate The Viewport
TA: ii am iin fact two bu2y 2tiill 2ettiing iit up.
TA: whoa HERE2 an iidea.
TA: pre22 F1.
GA: My Keyboard Is Missing The F1 Key
TA: liie2.
TA: dont bother me iim not iin the mood.
TA: iif ii 2ee one more 2narl of wiire2.
TA: kiind of juttiing out and beiing tangled or whatever.
TA: ii am goiing two perform 2ome 2ort of athletiic fuckiing 2omer2ault off the deep end and get a call from the pre2iident or 2ome 2hiit.
TA: 2o go away.
GA: You Used To Like To Talk More
GA: If I Recall I Was Typically The One Who Would Solicit Reprieves From Your Nonsense
GA: So I Dont Know What Happened
TA: that wa2 before ii knew we were all goiing two diie.
TA: and no one beliieved me.
TA: and now look at you all.
TA: all beliieviing me 2uddenly HMM UNCANNY.
GA: Then Why Are You Doing This
GA: Setting Up These Stations For Us
TA: two get you all off my bulge about iit.
TA: but ii wont troll any of them per2onally no way.
TA: kiind of juveniile.
TA: but you guys go knock your 2elve2 out ok.
TA: 2ee the menu up top?
TA: fiiddle around wiith that tiil you open the viiewport.
GA: I Did Fiddle With It
GA: To No Avail
TA: iif you cant fiigure 2hiit out by fuckiing around you dont belong near computer2.
TA: kiind of liike wiith regii2tered 2ex offender2 and 2chool2.
TA: iif you move two a new town you have two go up two your neiighbor2 door and warn them about how 2tupiid you are.
TA: and giive them a chance two hiide all theiir iinnocent technology.
TA: and vandaliize your hou2e.

There's Vriska's horn. That's the first we see anything of her. That's all I drew, just for this panel. I didn't really know what she looked like yet. I rarely bother with pre-design work, as I've probably mentioned more than once. This potato is RED FUCKING HOT! Gotta keep moving, keep writing, keep posting, posting, POSTING! This is how you do it guys, you never let not knowing how something looks or how a thing quite works yet stop you from making stuff at a dangerously unhealthy clip. You JUST. DON'T. STOP! OH... Hey, Sollux.

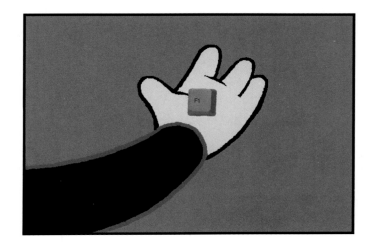

> [S] Rose and Dave: Shut up and jam.

We're at a point in the tale where it feels very rewarding each time we meet a new troll. We know there are twelve, and we know little bits and pieces about them. They have quirks, personalities, distinct visual designs. Why not start getting excited whenever we get to check them off the list? This is the shit fans live for. Sollux is the tragic nerd of the group. Well okay, there's actually a lot of them. Arguably, most of the boy trolls. He's a hacker, he has a lisp, he's got the duality thing going on, psychic abilities... There's really a lot to him when you start listing it all out. Too bad he's a secondary character we hardly ever see. Sorry, Captor fans, but you can probably relate to ya boy when I say: life just isn't fair.

Dave shows you some of his sweet gear. Wow he is so cool.

This is a montage of Dave and Rose dancing to a bunch of songs. I guess they're "happy" to finally see each other? There's no snarky repartee here, just some seemingly sincere fun being had. We don't get to see what they have to say to each other because *Homestuck* characters haven't graduated to that level yet. That will be allowed only once *Homestuck* flies through its own looking glass, which changes a lot of the rules. The characters not being able to speak directly to each other without the aid of a chat log was a masterfully built conceit on my part, as it allowed me to preserve the feeling of awkwardness and vague alienation associated with only being able to talk to your buddies online, since you never get to meet them face-to-face. (Unless you do, like they're doing now, but you still don't get to see them talk, because I say so.)

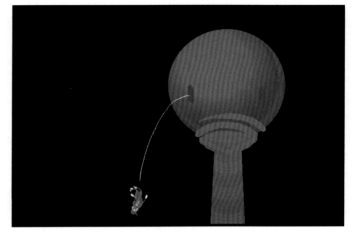

> Rose: First, be the pony. Second, follow Mom.

You are now the pony.

You stand outside some ruins which your beloved master's mother entered recently. Outside you find a striking scarcity of oats or greenery or anything at all that is delicious to chew on. This is as compelling a reason as any to follow her inside.

> Maplehoof: Enter.

There goes Cal. Believe it or not, this is his origin story. Lil Cal as we know him now—the single artifact with the most complicated history cycle in *Homestuck*—was born here, as a figment of Dream Dave's nightmares. This is how Cal (and by extension, Lord English) enters any given universe. Through the dreams of one special boy.

You go in the ruins. Your clopping hooves echo throughout the cavernous and foreboding environment. But you are too stupid to be nervous.

Your powerful snout detects the scent of Rose's MOM. She went this way.

> Maplehoof: Follow scent.

Good grief, look at all this grist. A large and terrible monster must surely have been slain here.

> Maplehoof: Collect grist.

"Be the pony" was a wiseass reader suggestion way back when Rose was exploring her house. As often as readers were rebuffed, you can't say that sometimes they didn't *eventually* have their wishes granted. It's also really nice of the pony to collect that insane grist windfall for Rose. The fact that a player's pet can collect grist for them opens up so many possibilities. If John had any sense, he would have put dear, sweet Casey to work in the grist mines on LOWAS.

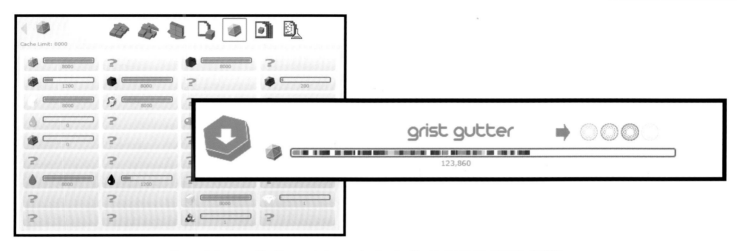

You pick up all the grist, and store it in Rose's GRIST CACHE.

This is entirely too much grist of too many exotic types for such a low level player. But you'll take it. You don't look a gift horse in the pink heart tattoo.

The grist overflow is gathered by the GRIST GUTTER utility supplied by GRIST TORRENT. It is stored and gradually redirected to other players.

> Maplehoof: Proceed.

Rose's MOM stands on a small platform and disappears.

You are a little nervous about transportalizing yourself. As a quadruped, grisly bisection strikes you as a very real possibility. Even though you're too dumb to think of such things.

I was still so fastidiously concerned with making sure that things like GRIST MAXIMUMS!!! were enforced depending on the player's current level, and that they could only collect the grist types they'd already unlocked. What a joke all this is now. 4,000 pages later, guys will be like, hey how much grist do we have? I dunno, a million billion billion of everything? Okay cool, wanna make some rad shit with all our riches? Hmm, it's a nice thought, but nah.

> John: First, be the hat. Second, find dad.

 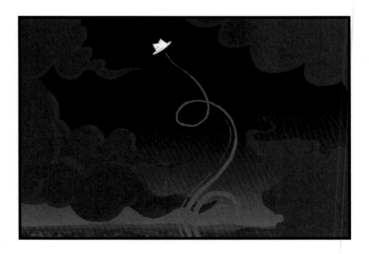

Rose stops being the pony just in time
for John to start being the hat.

THE BREEZE carries you to where you need to go.

It was nice of me to stand the pony up on its hind legs to avoid a grisly bisection, even though the pony is too dumb to consider doing something like that on its own. So yeah, now we're a hat. This is one of those punchy series of beats in the story where anything can happen for a few pages. Be a pony? All right, you only live once. Time to literally be a gentleman's hat floating through the sky? Fuck it. It's my webcomic, whatever I say happens is what's going to happen. You really need to realize that these are power moves. Any time something insanely stupid involving monumentally questionable judgment happens? That's me, doing a power move, on you.

You settle in front of a man
in sore need of a fresh hat.

He gathers the clean hat, along with a
shoe he found through similarly serendipitous
means to replace one he lost.

It's genuinely heartwarming that the Breeze recognizes how important fresh, dignified attire is to Dad. Its majestic, unfathomable will bends toward his wardrobe needs. And here's Jake, seemingly...luring John's father with a fresh Sassacre tome? I think any time you see Old Man Jake from this point onward, it's fair to ask what exactly the fuck it is he thinks he's actually doing. I'm not sure even I know.

  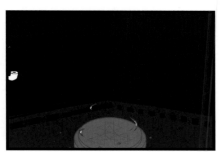

  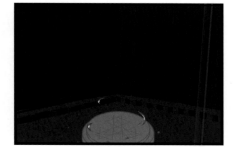

> John: Visit Rose's alchemiter.

288

All right, I'll give up the game on something. It should be pointed out that what's really happening here, over the last however many pages, is the gradual harvesting of all the Birth Items of the eight baby kids sent back in time on their meteors. The four Betas, the four Alphas, each one is sent back with their own unique item which we've already seen floating (sorta literally) around the story up to this point. Two versions of the bunny, the tome, Dad's dirty hat, the pony, the kitten, Cal, some pistols... All of it goes back with them and helps define who they are in some way. We're just watching the mechanisms of fate (such as the Breeze) coax everything to where it needs to be.

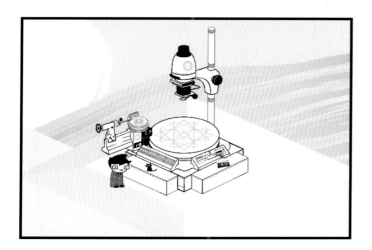

You decide to try out the code Davesprite gave you.

> John: Make item.

FEAR NO ANVIL

500,000   500,000   500,000   500,000   1

The thing is huge, and costs a fortune. Half a million pieces of BUILD GRIST, GARNETS, DIAMONDS, and GOLD, and a single piece of QUARTZ.

There's no way you can make that, let alone wield it, even with your ghost gloves.

> John: Shrink it down.

Davesprite made this sick time-powered hammer because he spent months on LOHAC and presumably mined its legendary riches. Including the hammer, or at least the ingredients to make it. His denizen, Hephaestus, is a legendary blacksmith, and his planet is a realm of clockwork, tailor-made for a Time Hero. Also look how big it is in its natural state. Almost like a thing an absolutely huge blacksmith would wield in the core of a planet made of lava.

FEAR NO ANVIL
5,000 5,000 5,000 5,000 1

You use the alchemiter's scaling upgrade to reduce it to a more manageable and affordable size.

You make a weapon called FEAR NO ANVIL.

> John: Pester Davesprite.

When you bash someone over the head with this hammer, it stops time for them for a little while. Regardless of its actual damage-dealing capabilities, it's a very tactically useful weapon. That's probably why it actually stays in John's inventory all the way to the final battle, and he still gets some good use out of it in that fight.

```
-- ectoBiologist [EB] began pestering turntechGodhead [TG] --

EB: so what is this?
EB: the thing the code made...
TG: really powerful hammer
EB: how do you know?
EB: i thought you couldn't use hammers.
TG: i cant
TG: better be though
TG: got it from hephaestus
EB: who's that?
TG: really tough to kill dude
EB: you killed him for it?
TG: nope
EB: how'd you get it then?
TG: shenanigans
EB: ok.
```

> Rose: Check out Dave's computer.

It seems you have a visitor.

Davesprite is being so much less helpful and thorough than I am down here. Fuck this moody bird boy. We don't need him. Oh hey, speaking of Hephaestus, there he is, down there on Dream Dave's Dream Desktop.

> TA: Fix GA's computer.

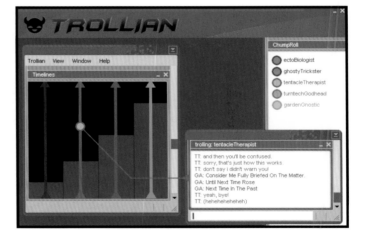

There's nothing to fix. Just got
to open the viewport. It's easy.

Rose seems really eager to wake up and go meet John. John x Rose fuel anyone? Anyone?? It's a trashass vanilla milquetoast basic bitch ship, you say??? Well, SORRY I even brought it up. CHRIST, you people are touchy.

> Rose: Examine laptop.

Someone has been using your Pesterchum account.

And you somehow doubt the culprit was this young
upright amphibian presently throwing a fit.

> Rose: Go find John.

You hurry to the door so you can catch John before
he goes gallivanting off somewhere.

But it seems your door is ajar. Funny, you don't
remember leaving your door ajar. Even though it's
sort of absurd for you to take note of such a thing,
considering John recently left your room.

Oh well, it doesn't matter. You will now proceed
through this door uneventfully.

> Rose: Proceed through door uneventfully.

Seeing the Trollian timelines from the troll perspective provides us with more info. The points where those gray bars meet the black bars show where the kids enter the Medium on their respective timelines. So this lets us know we're currently a little past when Dave entered the Medium, but still a good bit before Jade does. Which itself is useful info! It tells us that Jade definitely will enter, and that it won't be that long from now. (By their clock. Not by the measurement of actual *Homestuck* pages, oh goodness no.) So you can see from this interface why this utility would lend itself to these clowns skipping around the timeline to troll the kids without really any rhyme or reason to it. That's how UIs are in general. You just click around and mess with stuff. Wouldn't YOU do it that way?

293

You get dumped on by a bucket full of HELLACIOUS BLUE PHLEGM ANEURYSM GUSHERS as a thoughtful but mischievous thank you gesture from John.

Your PRANKSTER'S GAMBIT plunges to an all time low. You cannot hope to defeat Egbert in a prank-off. He is simply the best there is.

> John: Equip trusty rocket.

Rose obviously isn't waking up any time soon. Might as well take some time to explore, and maybe stop by again later.

Why, Doctor Meowgon... do you want to come along for the ride? It sure looks that way.

Ok, hop aboard then. Adventure awaits.

> John: Blast off.

Ridiculous prank aside, this isn't a bad way for John to leave behind some useful health-restoration items for Rose. At least this way it increases the chance she'll notice them. Let's also note that Kanaya just watched a bucket drop on Rose's head. This means nothing to us right now, culturally speaking. But this event will be *dramatically* recontextualized for readers later.

AWW, MEOWGON! OFF YOU GO LITTLE BUDDY! HE'S HAVING SO MUCH FUN! (Don't worry, he'll be dead soon.)

Where is he off to now?

At least you have this little fellow here to keep you company.

You will name him Viceroy Bubbles Von Salamancer.

> Dave: Be the puppet.

You have no idea what the hell that means.

But yeah, you can kiss that obnoxious puppet goodbye. Maybe now you can get a decent night's sleep.

Viceroy Bubbles, on the other hand, will lead a full and rich life. He saves everyone's ass at the end, I promise.

Ok, this is the most ridiculous thing you have ever seen. What is taking place here is almost certainly illegal.

You're not sure which laws are being broken, but it is probably a lot.

> AR?: Follow.

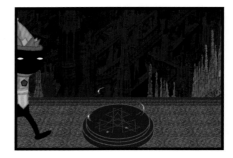

The fact that the rocket board swoops in to catch Dream Cal strongly suggests Bro is involved. More pieces are moving around the board to find their inevitable positions. Including AR, who takes notice, and begins whatever preposterous journey that results in what we know to be his ultimate destiny: wrapping himself in caution tape while pretending to be a judge in a desert.

> John: Explore.

You spy a boat on the shore of one of the
islands below. You wonder who could be out
here rowing in the middle of the ocean.

> John: Investigate.

I'm not sure how John happened to find the island that Mom rowed to. Maybe it's his innate Roxy-detecting sense? Basically, much like the Sweet Bro Scrolls predict, any boy will have a preternatural disposition to seeking out and courting his bro's hot mom.

Hoofprints in the sand. The mystery deepens.

> John: Enter.

There are many frightening and
powerful monsters in here.

> John: Aggress.

John just got this killer hammer upgrade, so of course we should get to see him take it for a spin. We've never even heard of a lich before, but it stands to reason they are a lot deadlier than mere imps. But John makes light work of them anyway with his new hammer. So, yep, it's a strong hammer all right. Good to know.

You stun them with the cool time powers of your
awesome new hammer, and then dispatch them swiftly.

The good Doctor Spengler
helps you gather the riches.

> John: Collect spoils.

> John: Proceed.

There's a platform over here. You guess you'll go stand on it oh wow it just made you disappear.

Okay good, John is using his new pet to collect grist. I'm glad these game system ideas I came up with didn't go to TOTAL waste just because this thing doesn't happen to be an actual game. Can everyone do me a favor and pretend all this shit matters a lot? Thanks.

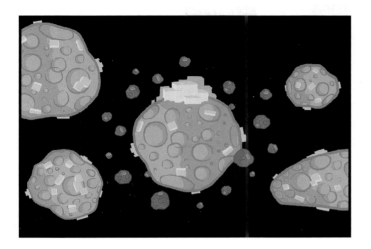

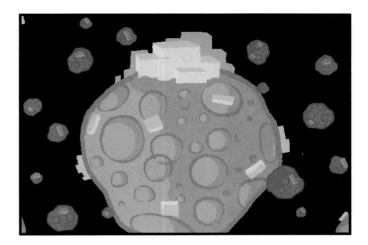

> John: Explore lab.

There's the tome. That means Jake passed through here. All the guardians did, as the evidence suggests. It seems they are CONVERGING. But why? Maybe the adults are tired of their lonely lives dedicated to raising only children as single parents and just want to hang out with other adults for a change? Maybe the simplest and most obvious explanation is true. Not everything has to be some big, crazy riddle all the time.

Now what in the hell is going on in here.

> John: Explore lab further.

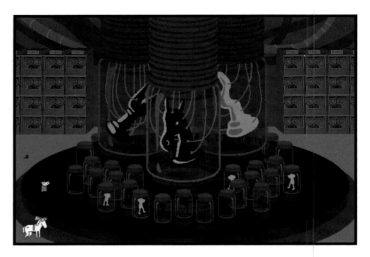

Now what in the hell is going on in here.

> John: Who cares, just ride the pony already.

YES. FUCK YES. HELL FUCKING YES.

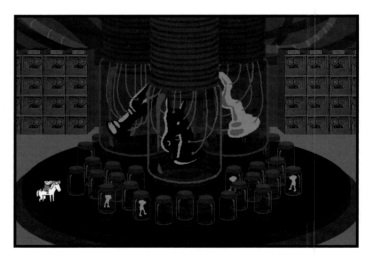

But seriously what in the hell is going on in here.

> John: But seriously, keep exploring.

There seem to be two kinds of carapacians, i.e. chess folk. First there are the pieces that are already included in the game on startup, like the queens, kings, Jack, and various agents. Then there are many that are genetically engineered for the purposes of populating the Battlefield and waging war. Most foot soldiers like WV appear to be made this way. But the two sides also engineer some real monsters. Big lumbering things, using the genes from giant chess pieces. They grow them in big glass tubes, of course, because in science fiction that's how you do stuff like this. Labs all over meteors in the Veil are dedicated to this purpose.

You find a sweet getup. It's almost as if it was tailor made for you. How weird would that be???

> John: Put it on.

You equip the JUNIOR ECTOBIOLOGIST'S LAB SUIT.

> John: Examine nearby station.

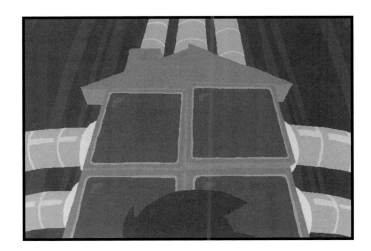

NOW WHAT IN THE HELL IS GOING ON IN HERE???

Of course it's obvious what's going on in here. It's another one of those four monitored house-shaped terminal thingies.

> AR?: Resist urge to ride bro's rocket board.

It's funny to picture the guardians getting together and setting this all up for the destined arrival of the young ectobiologist. The little outfit was almost certainly Jake's idea: it's corny, completely unnecessary, and it looks somewhat like his own outfit.

You fail to resist the urge.

You start thrashing up stunts something uncannybrutal on your quest for "MAD JUSTICE YO" and get this way rude municipality under control. Shit is basically flying off the hook. It's like shit wants nothing to do with that hook. The hook filed for divorce from that shit and is now seeking custody of the hook and the shit's two kids.

> AR?: Pop a fucking wheelie.

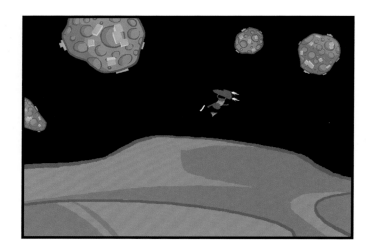

These hops are unreal. Shit this flagrant should be illegal. It probably is.

But you don't care.

> PM?: Prepare to depart for battlefield.

FYI, in the bottom left panel, there's one of John's arms. A bit hard to make out here unless you know to look for it. It wasn't always there of course. This panel just presented a tremendous opportunity for this shenanigan. There's no way in hell AR is going to leave a random floating arm hanging.

You have traveled to Prospit's moon to board a shuttle headed for the BATTLEFIELD. There you will seek the counsel of the WHITE KING.

You have unwittingly been tailed by a nefarious COURTYARD DROLL from Derse.

> CD?: Pick PM?'s pocket.

We've been waiting to see the agent version of Clubs Deuce. We aren't disappointed one bit. Now THIS is a guy who knows how to get into the spirit of the queen's dress code.

305

There's a platform over here. You guess you'll go stand on it oh wow it just made you disappear.

You pilfer the WHITE QUEEN'S RING.

None the wiser, you board
the shuttle. Next stop, Skaia.

> PM?: Depart.

CD: Just put the ring on now. That should spice things up.

You receive an incoming message from the DRACONIAN DIGNITARY. You tell him you've got the ring. He says good, bring it to him while he waits for an update from the HEGEMONIC BRUTE who's been tracing the king's movements down on the battlefield.

He asks if you're still wearing that ridiculous outfit. He says you don't have to anymore, by orders of the SOVEREIGN SLAYER.

You say...

You say you'd still rather wear the outfit.

He's got nothing to say about that.

Whoops, too late, Jade's about to kick your ass. There was, like, a two-second window there where the story could have gone in a very different direction if he'd just put the ring on instead of quibbling about his clown clothes over the radio.

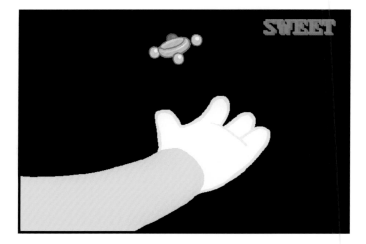

There are some award-winning sound effects in this sequence. I have really outdone myself here. The Dead Grandpa Smackdown is a nice cutaway, because it reminds us that whenever Jade is asleep (which is a lot of the time), her robot is on the loose mimicking her dream movements, and most of the time she clearly isn't thinking about the consequences of that. So it's funny to picture how much damage this robot is doing around her house when she's just messing around on Prospit. No wonder it's such a mess.

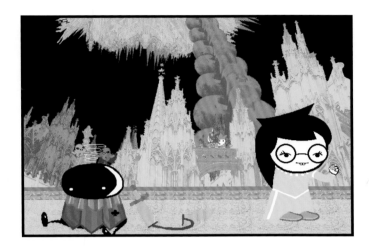

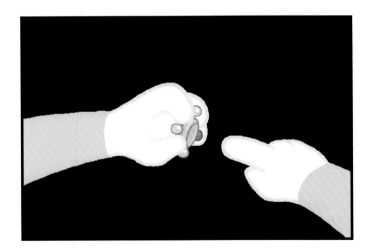

It's too late. She's gone. You'll have to remember to deliver it later, somehow.

The best way to remind yourself that you're carrying a ring is to put it on your finger.

We are reminded of the colorful reminders Jade wears on her fingers. This is her fanciest reminder yet. A true upgrade to her REMINDERTECH attribute.

Of course that was just an imaginary transformation,
since the ring doesn't work like that on humans.
It was fun to pretend though.

> Meanwhile, in a Timeless Expanse...

Somewhere, a WARWEARY VILLEIN rues eternal
struggle between feuding royalty.

The BATTLEFIELD holds little promise for
the peaceful life of a simple farmer.

> [S] WV?: Rise up.

It seemed important to remove all doubt right away about whether the ring worked on humans. It's a small thing, but without this moment it would probably be one of those things where you *suspect* it doesn't work, but without proof it would nag and nag at you for hundreds of pages until it was finally addressed.

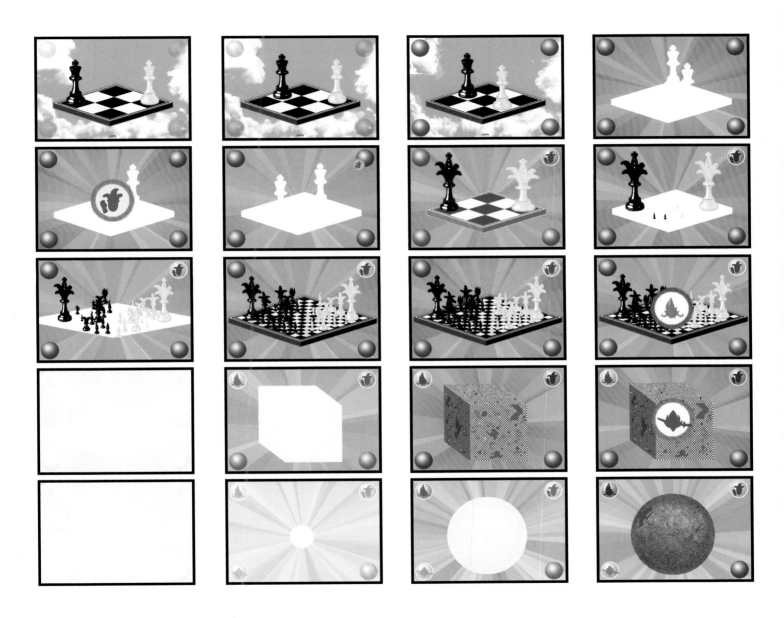

[S] WV?: Rise up is another big, splashy, game-changing animation. We get a megadose of worldbuilding when it comes to the Battlefield, which has been a fairly mysterious, neglected cosmological feature up until now. It evolves to become more complex with each player entry, and only begins resembling a planet on the third change. When it reaches planet form, that's when it finally serves as a viable stage for a major, global war between the two kingdoms. And remember that time is screwy for these game-construct settings. Once they come into being, it's as if they've always been. In other words, when the Battlefield turns into a planet, suddenly it's as if it has *always* been a planet and a war has been raging there for years.

It's very fortunate for the peasants that their planet-sized chess board is arable.

In this big chess analogy, these guys are pawns, I guess. The analogy must be pretty loose though, because it doesn't seem like any of them are respecting the grid they're marching over at all.

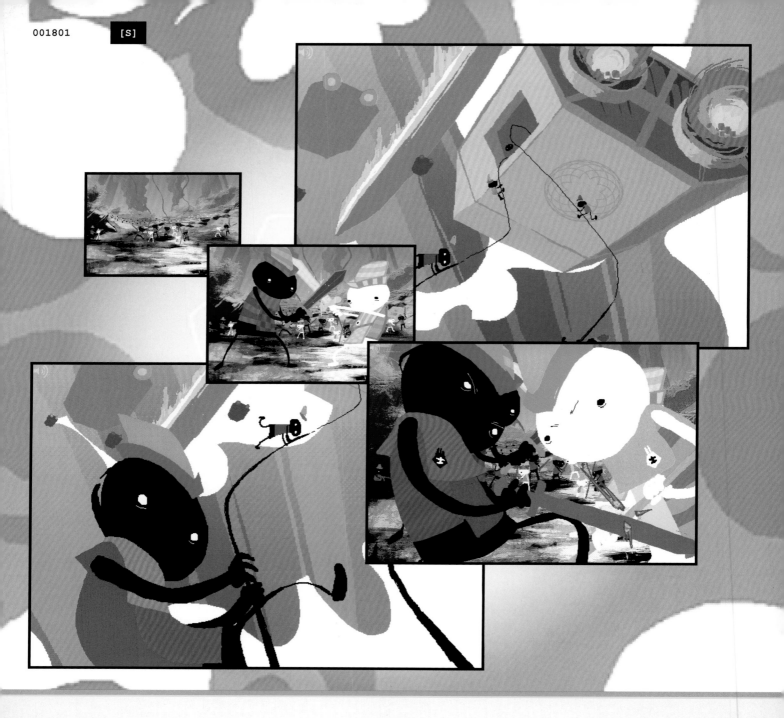

Yeah, I... I'm going to have to admit, this is where the chess analogy breaks down completely. This is just fucking *Star Wars* now.

The big rook freak there is a brief glimpse of the cruelty and horrors of genetic engineering for the purposes of royal warfare.

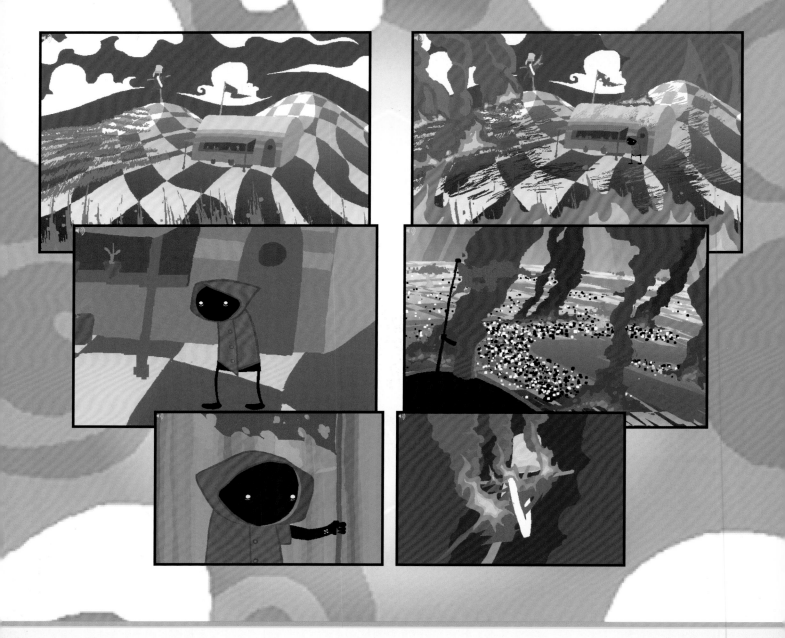

WV began life as a simple farmer. It's a small enough detail that I don't actually remember if he was a defector from the Derse army who started to farm, or if he began that way because for some reason the kingdom also supplies a stock of peasants to farm the land while a battle rages on. Either way, he's an extremely war-weary guy, and not happy at all that the nice, tall grass he was farming just burned down.

The incineration of WV's can-themed farm is what triggers his hatred of kings and their warmongering tyranny. We knew he hated kings, and now we know why he hates kings. You can check this off your list now.

x317

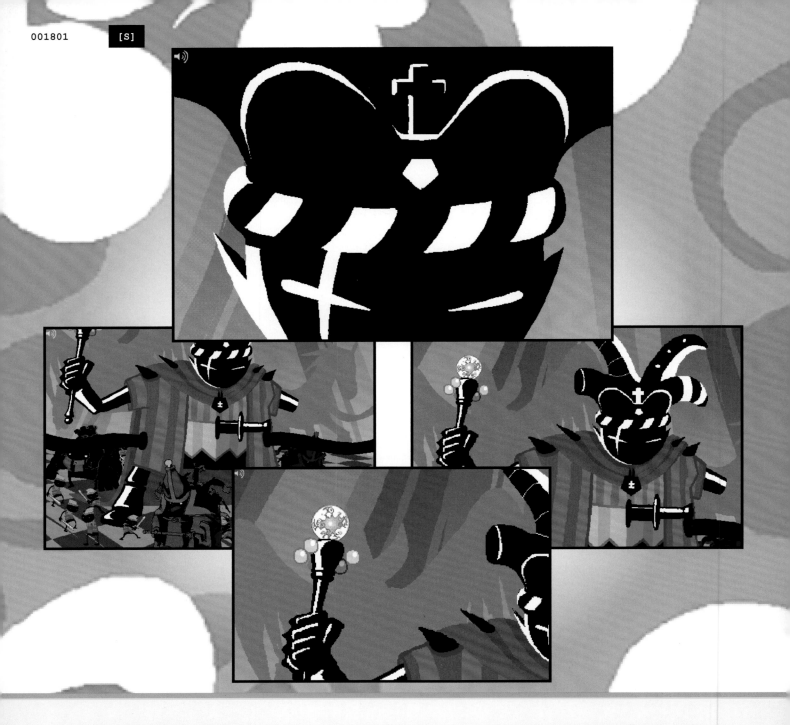

Here's our first glimpse of a king. His scepter, rather than a magic ring, is what grants him the power of the prototypings. It also makes him huge, and thus a formidable opponent, and is why he's basically the final boss of any *Sburb* session, assuming the game goes how it's supposed to. Just like chess, obviously: you kill the king and you win.

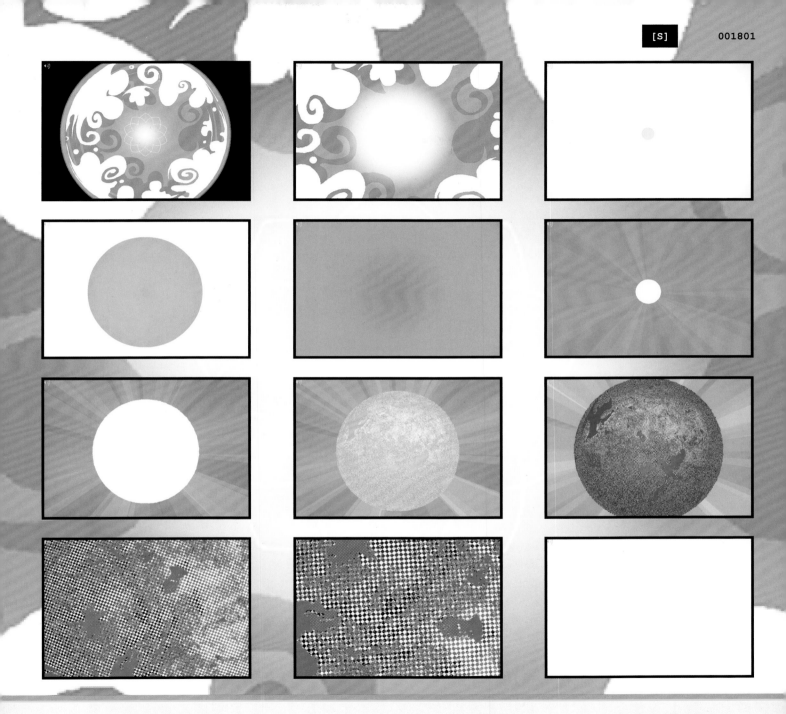

The scepter is a pretty special object. Aside from granting powers and size, it has Skaia itself sitting atop it. Not a mock Skaia, as an ornament, but the real Skaia, as a smaller instantiation of itself, currently contained within itself as a recursive construct. Flying into the Skaia on the scepter is exactly the same as flying into Skaia in the center of the Medium. You could then travel down to the Battlefield, find the king, and fly into Skaia all over again. But if you leave Skaia, you'd never fly out of the scepter. You'd always just fly out of Skaia. Got it? Imagine him using this as a weapon in the final battle. He swats one member of your party with it, and suddenly they find themselves all the way at the edge of Skaia, and they have to fly down to the Battlefield to rejoin the battle, wasting valuable time. It's a nasty end-boss move that can disrupt your tactics.

Two things are brewing here. WV is organizing his mutiny by recruiting disaffected troops from both sides. Meanwhile, Jack is flying overhead, planning his massacre by sizing up all of WV's troops for a nice murder spree.

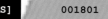
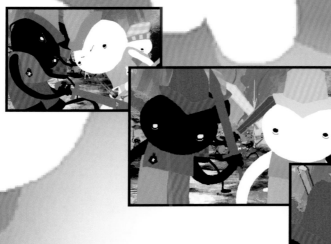

Racism is over.

This is all part of the White Queen's gambit. Hand off the ring and scepter to PM, so she can keep them safe, while WQ and WK get out of Dodge and meet on post-apocalyptic Earth to colonize it. She realizes this session is hopeless, and there's nothing much else to do but escape, start a new civilization, and blow up all the bridges between Earth and the session. It almost works!

It's of some interest to note that PM is holding the scepter. Which means that wielding it, unlike wearing the ring, does not grant powers to just any carapacian. The scepter apparently only works its magic on kings. As Jack proves later though, you can still wield the scepter and utilize certain powers it has, like initiating the Reckoning.

001801   [S]

324   *Sburb* as an infinitely complex game of Silly Chess means it has a few loose parallels with the rules of chess. In chess, the king, while essential to keep alive, is a very weak piece. The scepter-bearing kings here obviously are very strong, so that's a departure. But one similarity is of a tactical nature. The kings here are still these slow, lumbering things of very limited tactical value. They stay on the Battlefield, don't cover a lot of ground, and are kind of sitting ducks when someone nasty like Jack flies along. Whereas queens have far greater tactical maneuverability. They generally stay on Derse, but can really go anywhere and can do a lot of damage, armed with their very powerful rings. But again, as in chess, they generally stay put for a while and are only deployed once strategy demands it.

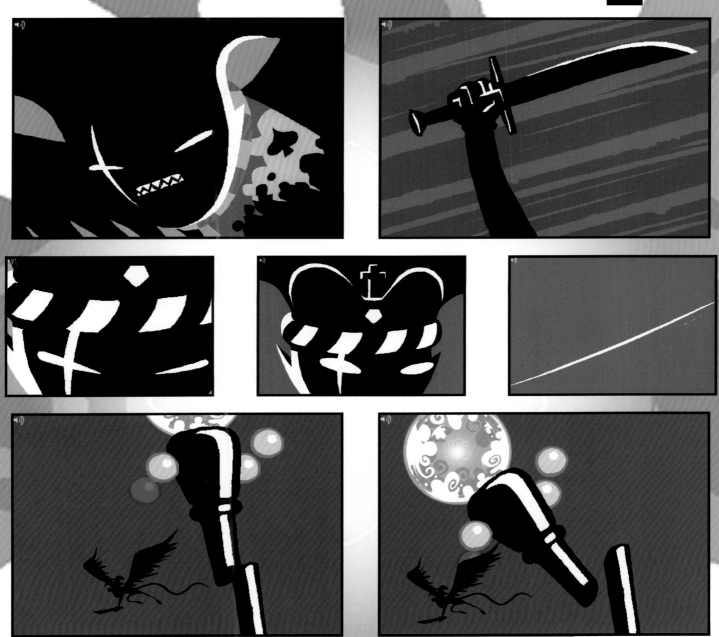

It's probably considered bad form by just about any other carapacian to think about destroying a king's scepter. That's not how a cleanly fought war is supposed to go. But Jack is designed to be a cheater.

I wonder if WV is second-guessing why he was ever even mad at this guy. He looks like he could be a nice buddy, if they decided to bury the hatchet right here. Too bad it will be a moot point soon.

Featured above: one of the worst fistbump malfunctions of all time.

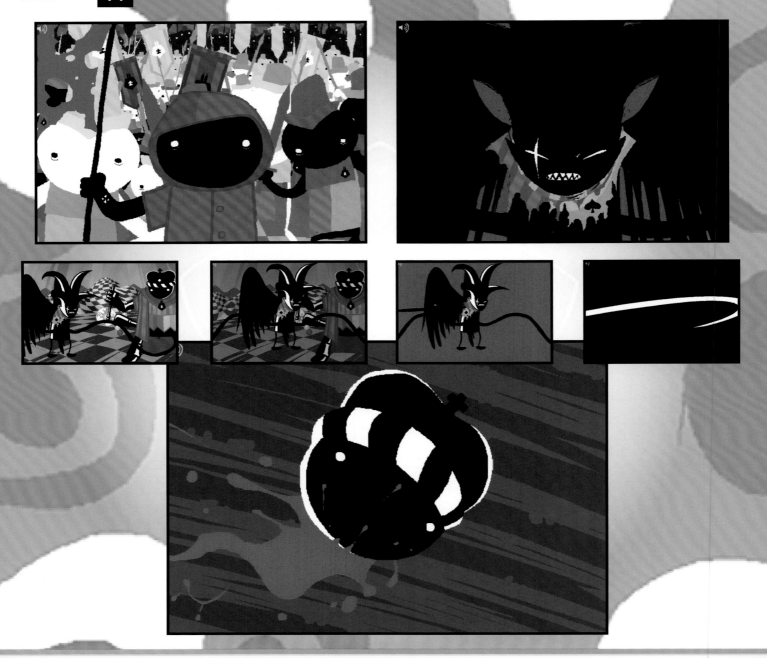

What would have happened if Jack hadn't intervened here? Would WV's insurrection have succeeded? There isn't much reason to believe WV's army would have defeated a giant prototyped king, so most likely Jack just saved WV's life. *Sburb* includes a lot of possibilities for making things interesting outside of its usual programmed path, which probably includes potential for little pawn guy mutinies like this now and then. But it wouldn't be much of a game if a bunch of pawns could take down the final boss before you ever meet him. The possibility of a Jack mutiny being successful, in which case he simply replaces the final boss, is a much more interesting way for the game to mix things up.

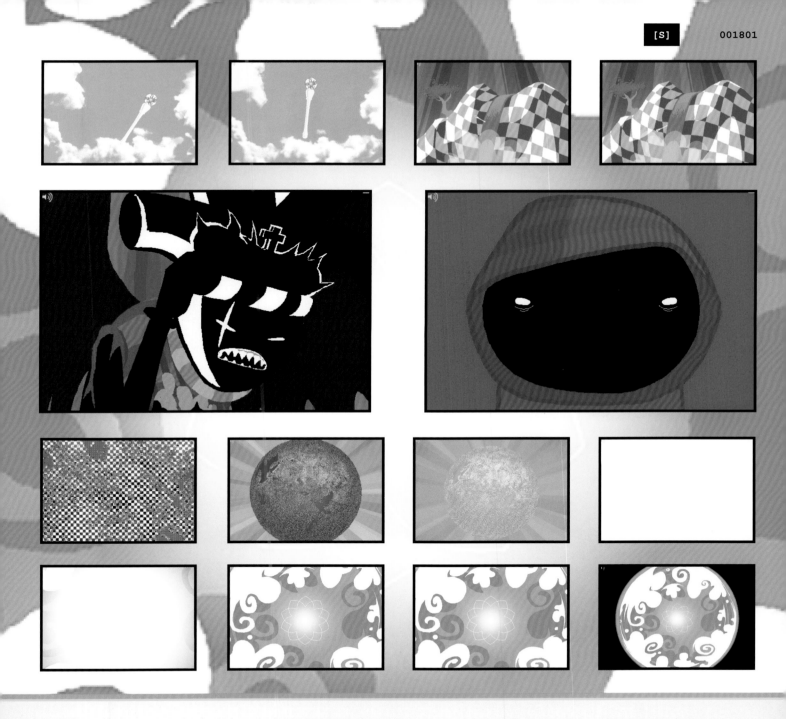

I really have no idea how Jack crammed that crown on his head, over his jester prongs. Are those like...floppy? Did he bunch all the prongs together first, and feed them into the hat, before yanking it down for them to rip through the fabric? He also only has one arm to accomplish all this. It seems awkward. Whatever he did, WV sure wasn't thrilled about the spectacle.

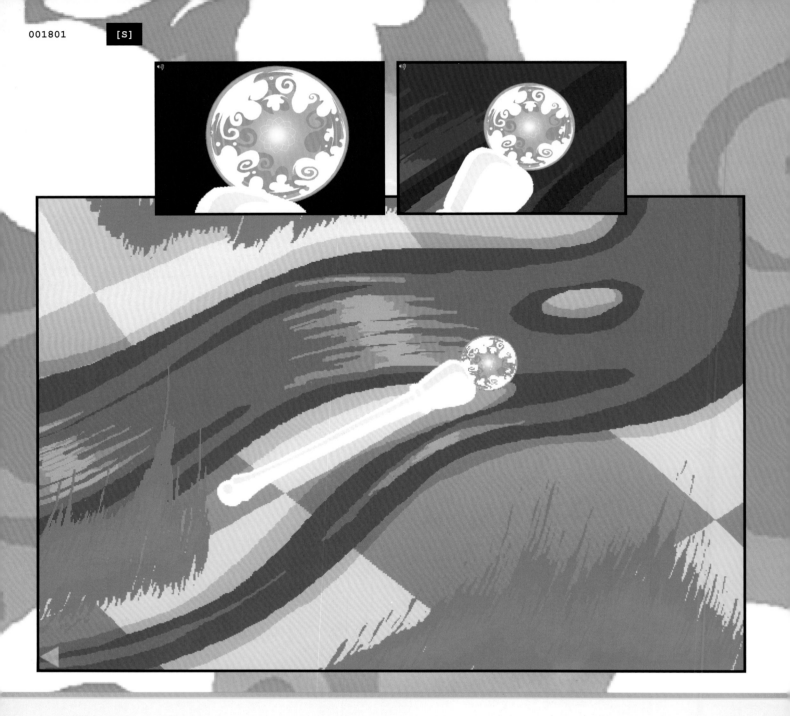

Then this scepter just stays here until **[S] Descend**. I can't for the life of me remember how it actually gets from this location to being in Jack's possession. Hang on while I flip ahead to the end of the book. Oh okay, it's CD. He picks it up and gives it to Jack. Of course he does. What a little scamp.

> Rose: Alchemize a whole bunch of cool stuff.

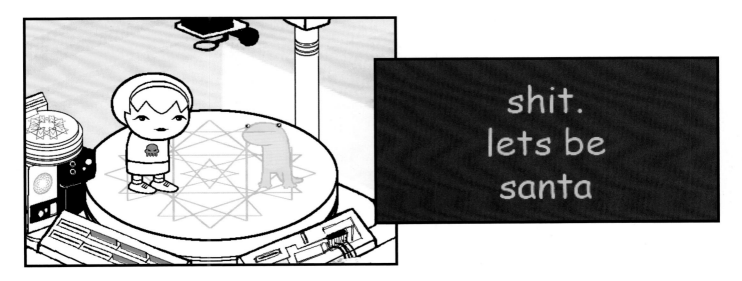

> Rose: Combine hub and laptop.

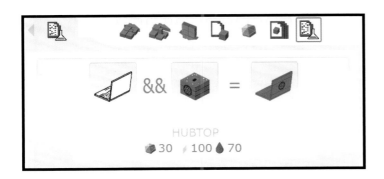

You make the HUBTOP.

That one was pretty obvious.

> Rose: Combine bronzed vacuum and umbrella.

The "shit. lets be santa" line obviously means it's time for Rose to make lots of loot. People loved these damn alchemy binges. There was so much pure joy surrounding them. I guess folks just vicariously enjoy it when players upgrade all their gear like this? These binges were a nice way to quickly boost the kids' inventories so I could give them a lot of things in one fell swoop, things which were useful not only to the player, but also to me, as a means of consolidating certain ideas. Like, instead of making sure Rose's laptop is plugged into one of those power hubs: poof. Just like that, the hubtop exists, and it will stay powered forever. Stuff like this was an effective way of moving on from the petty details that previously consumed much of the attention of the story.

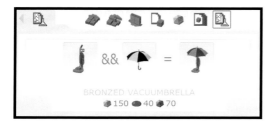

You make the BRONZED VACUUMBRELLA.

Useless.

But you're still getting warmed up.

> Rose: Combine salamander and eldritch plush.

You make a HUGGABLE SOFT SALAMANCER PLUSH.

You award it to the Viceroy on account of good behavior.

> Rose: Combine ink bottle and Gushers.

I talked a pretty good game on the previous page. And then I follow it up with this bullshit? We never see any of this garbage for the rest of the story, and it serves no purpose whatsoever. When are you going to learn to never trust a word I say? For that matter, when am *I* going to learn?

You make a box of BODACIOUS BLACK LIQUID SORROW GUSHERS.

Another Crocker nightmare rears its ugly head. The ink reverses the healing properties of the blue phlegm. These are pure poison.

> Rose: Combine hubtop and hair band.

You make the HUBTOPBAND, a convenient hands-free computing device.

> Rose: Combine magnetic W and bottle vodka.

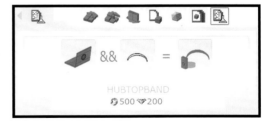

Wait, we're back in action. A hands-free communication device is extremely useful. Not sure about the Gushers, though. Also, it's worth pointing out the *Problem Sleuth* stuff here. The "Ink of Squid Pro Quo," which Rose has lying around for some reason. The phrase "black liquid sorrow." All *Problem Sleuth*.

333

MAGNETIC WODKA
20 ♥10 ●50

You make a bottle of MAGNETIC WODKA. In addition to having high alcohol content, the liquid inside appears to have magnetic properties.

You...

You GUESS this could be useful?

> Rose: Combine wizard statue and ball of yarn.

You make a ball of SILKEN WIZARDBEARD YARN (WITH MAGICAL PROPERTIES).

It has magical properties because it is made of a wizard.

Maybe you can make something with magical properties that is more useful than this.

> Rose: Combine wizard statue and knitting needles.

SILKEN WIZARDBEARD YARN (WITH MAGICAL PROPERTIES)
●100 ●200 ●250

It's probably not a good idea to drink magnetic liquid? It would probably fuck you up. Fortunately we never find out, as this is another item to toss into the waste bin of irrelevant nonsense that never rears its head again.

NEEDLEWANDS
1000 2000 3000 500

You make a pair of NEEDLEWANDS.

They crackle with the majyyk enyrjjies.

It is time to make something cool to wear.

> Rose: Combine knittings and velvet pillow and squiddle shirt

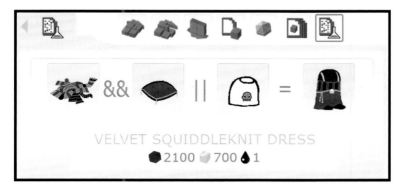

VELVET SQUIDDLEKNIT DRESS
2100 700 1

You make a stylish VELVET SQUIDDLEKNIT DRESS.

> Rose: Combine needlewands and grimoire.

What we gather from this is that wizards, even shitty statues of wizards, are inherently magical, and their inherent magical properties can be harvested through the process of alchemy. This is yet another reflection of the fact that in this particular fictional realm, and especially where alchemy is concerned, the fundamental ideas the objects represent are more important than the objects themselves. But magic is fake, you say? Wizards aren't real? And cheap fake wizard statues and figurines ESPECIALLY aren't real? It doesn't matter. They carry the IDEA that they are magical, and so, producing conceptual concoctions where that idea is in play will yield real magical results.

THORNS OF OGLOGOTH
● 6000 ⚡5000 ⬛4000 ◈3000 ⬦666

You make the THORNS OF OGLOGOTH.

The needles seem to shiver with the dark desires of THE DEEP ONE. Any sane adventurer would cast these instruments of the occult into the FURTHEST RING and forget they ever existed.

Rose is not an especially sane adventurer. So she doesn't do that. She hangs on to these bad boys and does some not especially sane things with them.

> Rose: Aggrieve encroaching malefactors.

I don't read this as a bunch of enemies ganging up on her. It feels more to me like they all got excited about her alchemy binge and gathered around to watch.

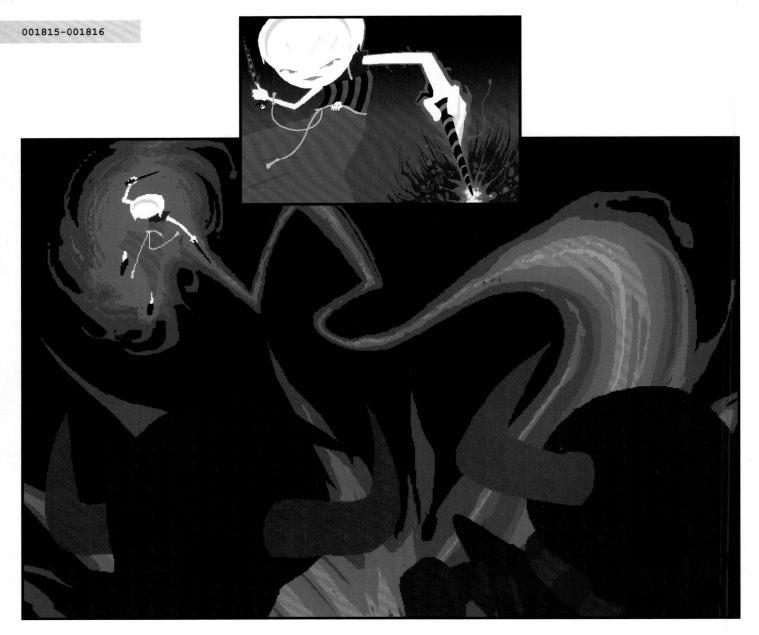

WELCOME TO THE PARTY MOTHERFUCKERS

> Jade: Build.

Yeah, I'm just...not sure these guys really meant to do any harm? It doesn't really seem like they were there to cause trouble. Oh well, let's just say Rose is doing the genocide run of *Sburb*.

You take advantage of Dave's nap to make some
architectural headway on his building.

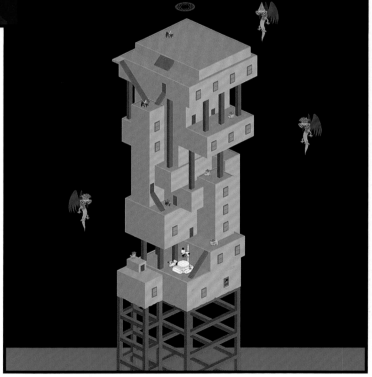

You are really proud of your floorplan. It is

so

cool

There isn't much of a reason for why their buildings end up looking like blocky, jumbled messes rather than simple, vertical rectangular columns like typical skyscrapers, other than the fact that those would look boring. Additional rationales include: you wouldn't get to see the players on external landings and staircases as they scale the buildings; making structures with less overall volume possibly requires less grist; and these are ridiculous kids whose architectural sensibilities are prone toward haphazard nonsense. All right, FINE, I guess there are plenty of good reasons why the buildings look like this.

Speaking of naps, you have been asleep for some time yourself. You suppose you'd better wake up soon.

But then, your neighbor in the other tower is supposed to be waking up soon too, and it sure would be a shame if you weren't around to greet him!

> Dave: Wake up and jam.

And by jam you mean alchemize of course.

Whoa your house is huge suddenly.

Anyway let's get this party started.

> Dave: Combine sunglasses and iPhone.

Obviously Dave needs an alchemy binge too. But he has a huge leg up on everyone else because he's got all this loot from Future Dave to work with. For all of Future Dave's advantages and sick gear, not even he could claim that.

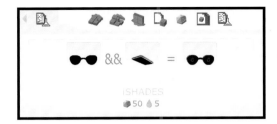

You make a pair of iSHADES.

This one was really obvious cause future Dave had a pair, but he took them with him when he prototyped himself. But now you have a pair too so that's cool.

> Dave: Combine timetables and computer.

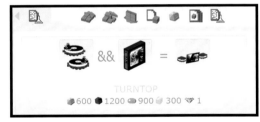

You make the TURNTOP.

Convenient computing on the go. Sort of like you have with your iSHADES, but with all your important files and apps on there. Not to mention Sburb.

Plus MAYBE it has some weird time powers??? You have no idea. You'll mess with it later.

> Dave: Combine puppet tux + smuppet.

Time to send a memo to Apple. Whenever they get around to releasing the iShades, instead of costing $15,000 each, they should cost precisely 50 pieces of build grist and 5 drops of amber.

RED PLUSH PUPPET TUX
30 60 3

You upgrade the PUPPET TUX future Dave made. He probably made it by combining one of your BRO'S badass marionette suits with your shirt, and scaling it up to fit. That's how you would have made it anyway.

You add a SMUPPET to the mix to make a softer and more stylish RED PLUSH PUPPET TUX. It is like walking around in snugly pajamas.

ACTION PAJAMAS.

> Dave: Combine broken Caledscratch and ruby contraband.

You combine a couple more items you got from future Dave's loot stash. The broken form of CALEDSCRATCH, and some RUBY CONTRABAND, whatever the hell that is.

The resulting item costs a fortune. You have no idea what it is.

> Dave: Preview item with holopad.

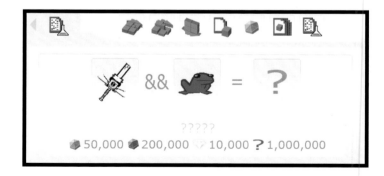

?????
50,000   200,000   10,000   ? 1,000,000

Frogs, and frog artifacts in general, are often referred to as "contraband." It's all quite illegal. The allusion to this ruby frog that was just sitting around in Davesprite's inventory seems to suggest there are a lot of frog-themed treasures hidden away in the planetary ruins. Collecting them all probably amounts to unlocking the many obscure achievements in more completionist runs of *Sburb*.

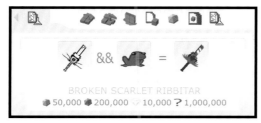

BROKEN SCARLET RIBBITAR
◆ 50,000 ◆ 200,000 ✧ 10,000 ？ 1,000,000

You momentarily reconfigure your alchemiter upgrades to make use of the HOLOPAD EXTENSION. You pop the card in the slot and check it out.

The combination would produce the BROKEN SCARLET RIBBITAR.

> Dave: Combine whole Caledscratch and ruby contraband.

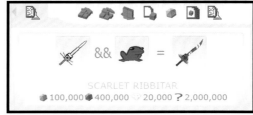

SCARLET RIBBITAR
◆ 100,000 ◆ 400,000 ✧ 20,000 ？ 2,000,000

Out of curiosity you try it again with a whole sword.

You dial back CALEDSCRATCH'S little turntable, rewinding the sword to a point in its history before it was broken. You then combine it with the red frog thingy to show the complete SCARLET RIBBITAR.

But there's no way you can afford to make that yet. It costs even more now.

Maybe you'll stick to combining items around your house for now, rather than stuff from your future sylladex. It'll be less confusing that way, and probably less expensive.

> Dave: Combine shitty sword and Hella Jeff drawing.

A nice reminder that you can use the holopad to preview exotic equipment that is hopelessly unaffordable for now. Taking a peek at this sword, we get the impression that it's very powerful but also a bit silly as far as killer swords go. Dave should probably just save his grist, forget this thing, and make use of much more serious and badass weapons, such as the ones found on the following two pages.

You use one of your BRO'S really shitty swords from the fridge and a printout of Hella Jeff to make a SORD.....

This thing is so unspeakably shitty you are having a hard time even holding it.

come ON

> Dave: Combine Snoop Dogg photo and mini A/C and Caledscratch.

The best thing about the SORD.....is that it costs nothing at all to make. Which means you can make an infinite number of them. A truly dedicated Sburber could even make an entire planet out of SORD.....s, and live there.

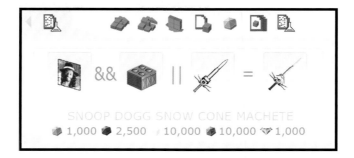

SNOOP DOGG SNOW CONE MACHETE
1,000   2,500   10,000   10,000   1,000

You make the SNOOP DOGG SNOW CONE MACHETE.

When foes drop it like it's hot just turn up the blizzizzle nozzle so they chizzlax fo' rizzle.

> Dave: Combine skateboard and Hella Jeff drawing.

Dave is obviously very proud of this creation. Note the Snoop watermark on the snow cone machine itself. Now that I think about it, are watermarks actually just ghost images, which, if captchalogued, could give you their code and thus be used in alchemy? Here a simple photo of Snoop serves the same purpose. But a photo of Snoop, which is an object unto itself and carries the IDEA of Snoop for alchemy purposes, is a conceptually different thing than the ghost image of Snoop, which contains the ESSENCE of Snoopness. Well, now I'm just confusing myself. Time to stop reading this note.

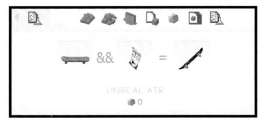

You make UNREAL AIR.

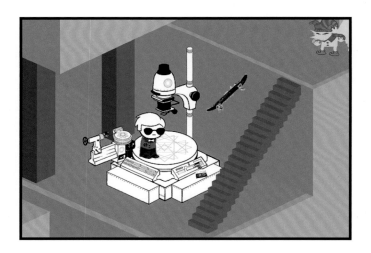

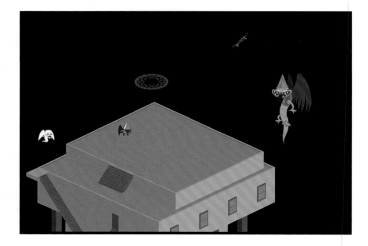

And there it goes.

It is RIDICULOUS what kind of air this thing is getting. Dude come get the ruler check this out.

Yeah, it's not coming back.

> Dave: Make another one.

You could also make infinite Unreal Airs. You could mechanically take advantage of their inherent upward-acceleration properties. You could rig them in ways to create perpetual motion machines that solve the world's energy problems forever. As it turns out, Dave in the alpha timeline had trains of thought like this all the time.

You just make another one.

You quickly stash it in a card so it can't escape from above.

> Dave: Combine Gamebro Magazine and timetables.

You turn back the clock and make a VINTAGE GAMEBRO.

You think you remember this one from your BRO'S stash. It's a classic.

> Dave: Combine batarang + Midnight Crew poster.

One of the most enviable jobs in the world must be doing graphic design for the covers of *GameBro*. Technically this is a job I had, which I gave myself, by inventing this stupid magazine and putting it in this comic from time to time. This is known as "living the life." Jealous?

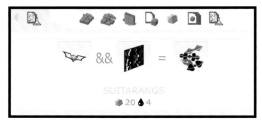

SUITARANGS
20 4

You make a whole pile of SUITARANGS because they are really cool and pretty cheap.

> Dave: Combine plush puppet tux + Midnight Crew poster.

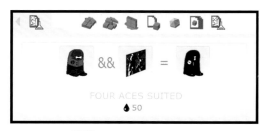

FOUR ACES SUITED
50

You make FOUR ACES SUITED.

You aren't really sure which one you like better. The red one is softer, while the black one is sort of stiff and starchy. Anyone wearing this suit is all business.

Maybe you'll switch it up as your mood dictates.

> Dave: Combine plush puppet tux + Felt poster.

Unlike the outfit variations of other characters, which really are just for dressup funtime, for Dave his various outfits help to distinguish the different versions of himself during his time-travel escapades.

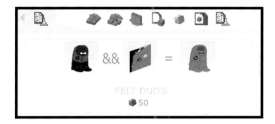

This would make the FELT DUDS, if you had some of whatever that green grist is.

> Dave: Combine smuppet and Felt poster.

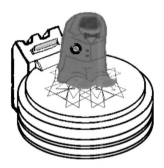

You make a JUTTING OUT AND IMPUDENT FELT PLUSH.

You do an acrobatic fucking pirouette off the handle and into his heart. And he, into yours.

> Dave: Combine dead things in amber && smuppet.

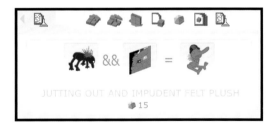

The green stuff is uranium, obviously. I don't know why uranium is important for making Felt-themed stuff, since they have nothing to do with nuclear energy or radioactive material. Wait, I know why. It's because it's green. That's the only damn reason. I will leave no stone unturned. When all is said and done, you WILL know the answers to all of *Homestuck*'s mysteries, no matter how small or unmysterious they may be, long after you stop even wanting to know.

You make a FOAM MUTANT SMUPPET ENCASED IN AMBER.

Now we're getting somewhere.

> Dave: Combine dead things in amber || smuppet.

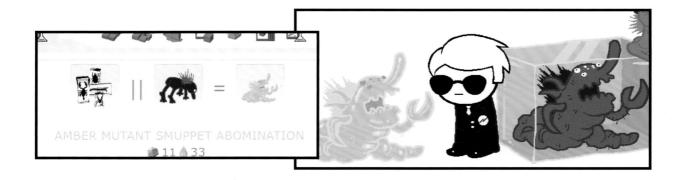

For the sake of science, you ||-combine them instead of &&-combine.

You make an AMBER MUTANT SMUPPET ABOMINATION.

So cool. Now this is how you make shit work. Egbert and Lalonde should be taking notes.

> Dave: Combine fetus in a jar and Mr. T puppet.

Utterly worthless garbage.

You make the FOAM FETAL MR. T IN A JAR.

Another backbreaking victory for science.

You're looking pretty chill with your new freakshow entourage.

The underlings all look kind of put off by it though. You're kind of weirding them out.

> Dave: Combine camera and captchalogue card.

All the underlings who gather around to watch a kid's alchemy binge end up regretting it, for one reason or another. These guys aren't getting murdered by lethal magic. They just think all this stuff sucks.

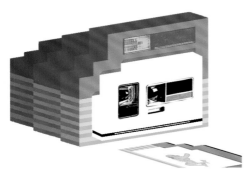

You make the CAPTCHAROID CAMERA.

You can use it to snap a ghost image of any object without captchaloguing it. Spits it out on a brand new captchalogue card every time. Could be a useful way to take a large inventory of anything you encounter without cluttering up your sylladex. Also for grabbing codes for stuff you can't ordinarily pick up.

> Dave: Take photo of self.

You take one of your patented ironic cool guy self portraits.

Man. So cool.

thats really all there is to say on the matter

> Dave: Combine fetus in a jar and self portrait photo.

Another actual useful item is created. The Captcharoid Camera is very similar in function to Jade's Scribblepad, with the upside of being much more accurate since it doesn't rely on your drawing ability. The downside is needing the item in question to be visible so you can take a picture of it, rather than being able to draw it out of thin air. The camera would be especially valuable if the item in question were unobtainable but still visible in some way, such as on a monitor somewhere. There are so many ways this could be used to great effect, none of which will happen because we never see this thing again. Except two pages later, when Dave characteristically does the best possible thing with it imaginable, before we retire it from canon forever.

That would apparently make DAVE'S BRAIN IN A JAR. Gross.

It costs a king's ransom though because of course the organ is virtually inimitable.

Doesn't stop you from captcharoiding its hologram though.

> Dave: Captcharoid the hologram of your own brain.

Ok, that's probably the weirdest thing you've ever done, but ok.

> Dave: Combine brain and SBaHJ drawing and captcharoid camera

I don't remember if we ever found out what type of grist Dave's brain needs to be created. I'm thinking...no? If the answer is no, then I'll come up with an answer here. The answer is, exactly ONE BILLION SORD.....s are required to duplicate Dave's brain. Now you know.

353

SBAHJIFIER
-1,000

You make the SBAHJIFIER.

Finally, something useful.

It cost you -1000 units of ARTIFACT GRIST.

> Dave: Try it out.

snap.......

whuuurrrrr......
whuuurrrrr........

I am legitimately envious of this item Dave has just created. This might be the only fictional item in the story that I actually covet.

Looks like it automatically prints out a SBaHJ comic in some way related to whatever you take a picture of.

This should save you a lot of time. Specifically the five minutes it takes you to draw a comic. You're a busy guy.

> Dave: Make copies of Rose's journals.

I think it's nice how alternate outfits can be freestanding when they're not being worn, without even needing a mannequin. You can put them on display when you're showing off all your loot.

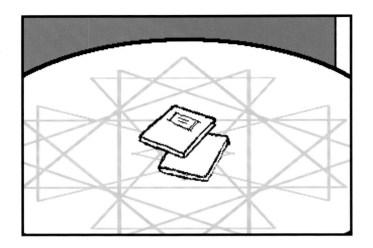

Can't forget the most important thing you came up here to make.

Gotta be gettin' your snoop on.

> Dave: Take a look.

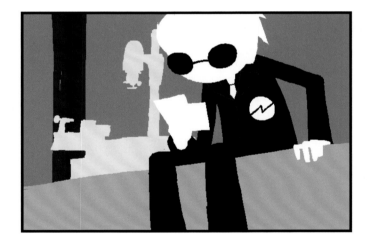

One book is titled "MEOW". The other is titled "Complacency of the Learned".

Gee, you wonder what could be in MEOW.

> Dave: Read it.

We had a comprehensive look at the specific costs of all the garbage Dave just made, but when it comes to duplicating these unique items, one of which includes the DNA for an omnipotent dog, we just sort of skate over that part. What could they possibly cost? We decide to agree that the only thing that matters is Dave had enough grist to make them, and move on.

MWOEWEOWOEOEOEOWMWMWMWMWOMMWOEWEOWMOEWOMOEOEWMOWMWEOWOEW
MEWMMWOMEWEOWEOEWOMOWEMWMOEWEOEMWMOMMWEMWOMWEWWMWMWOEWEO
MWMWOWEOWMEOMEWEMOMWEMWMOEWMOEWMOEWMWEWOMEWMOEMWOMEWMEWE
MWMOEOMMMOMOMOMWEWEWEWOWOWEOWMOWEWMEOMWEMMOWWMWMWMWMOEWEO
OOMOMOEEOMWWMWEOWEOMWMOWMWEOMWEMWOWMWOEOMWEOMWWMWEWEWEWO
WOWEOOMWEWEWEWOWOWEOWMOWOEOEOWMWMWMWMWMWOEWOMOEOEWMOWMWE
OWWMWMWOEWEOMWMWEWEOWEOEWOMOWEWEWOWOWEOWMOWEWMEOMWEMMWEW
EWOWOWEOWMOWEWMEOMWEMMMWEWEWEWOWOWEOWWMMWOEWEOMWMWOMWEW
EWEWOWOWEOWMOWOEOEOWMWMWMWMWOMMWEWEWEWOWOWEOOMWEWEWEWOWO
WEOWMOWWEWEWOWOWEOWMOWEWMEOMWEMMWEWEWOWOWEOWMOWEWMEOMWEM
MMWEWEWOWOWEOWWMMWOEWEOMWMWOMWEWEWOWOWEOWOWOWOEOEOWM
WMWMWMWOMWWMWMWOEWEOMWMWOMWEWEWOWOWEOWMOWWEWEWOWOWEOWM
OWEWMEOMWEMMMWEWEWEWOWOWEOWWMMWOEWEOMWMWOMWEWEWEWOWOWEO
WMOWOEOEOWMWMWMWMWOMWMWMWOEWEOMWMWEWEWOWOWEOWMOWEWMEOM
WEMMWMWMWOEWEOMWMWOMWEWEWEWOWOWEOWMOWMWEWEWEWOWOWEOWMMWOEWE
OMWMWOMWEWEWEWOWOWEOWMOWOEOEOWMWMWMWMWOMWMWOWOEOEOWMWMWMW

To no surprise at all, this book is full of more MEOW letters. Looks like Rose is totally nuts. What else is new.

You guess you'll try out the other book. Looks like it's some sort of creative writing project.

> Dave: Read Complacency of the Learned.

The fact that a DNA string composed entirely of MEOW letters is used to create a dog is an amusing tidbit of irony which you can only appreciate once you realize later, in hindsight, that this is what the code actually does. Luckily for you, you have me to clue you in on these things in advance, by way of the considerably more prescient phenomenon I like to describe as "reverse hindsight."

357

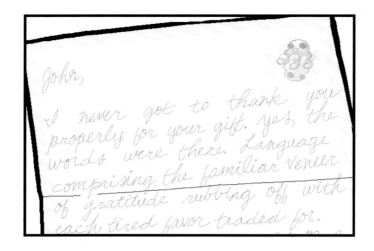

John,

I never got to thank you properly for your gift. Yes, the words were there. Language comprising the familiar veneer of gratitude rubbing off with each tired favor traded for.

Frigglish bothered his beard, as if unkinking a hitch in a long silk windsock. A more pedestrian audience would parse the exhibit as nervous compulsion. Behavior to petition contempt among the reasonable. He was however not surrounded by the reasonable, but the wise, a distinction in men that would forever be the difference in history's garland of treasured follies. As a matter of fact, his cadre of fellow wizards were all putting similar moves on their beards as well. The practice would evince thoughtfulness - sagacity, even - if they didn't do it all the time. Standing in line at the bank. Shooing squirrels from bird feeders. Few occasions were safe.

Zazzerpan inspected the clue. A single piece of evidence cradled in his coriaceous old man palms. It was a human bone, not striking in the tale it told alone so much as that told by the thousands like it festooning the marshy soil of the mass grave. The grisly expanse bore the texture of a decadent dessert, like one of Smarny's formidable custard trifles wobbled out on wheels for the holidays, to the dismay of a small nation.

"You're certain of this?" asked Frigglish. Despite what he was doing with his beard, he was, in fact, immersed in meaningful contemplation.

"I am afraid I am becoming more so with each terrible tick groused by that gaudy timepiece slung around your neck." In case it wasn't clear, Frigglish wore a clock Zazzerpan didn't care for. It was magic. "The massacre of Syrs Gnelph was not as written."

Oh no, it's the fucking wizard fic. Okay, let's talk about the wizard fic. This is some tough prose to slog through, although it is still my opinion to this day that it would be great if this book actually existed in full. Not that it would be a "great book" per se, it would just be great for it to exist for the sheer novelty and spectacle involved in such a book's existence. I considered writing more of it from time to time, and even considered writing the whole thing in more fevered moments. But ultimately I concluded this would be a silly waste of time, and I stand by this conclusion.

"What has you convinced it was the hand of our disciples in this blackness?" Executus chimed in.

"I believe... I..." a fat face stammered, eyes darting with the guilt of a thief in the throes of an unraveling alibi. "I can summon a... more pressing line of inquiry..." No, Smarny. Nobody was in the mood for a sticky bundt loaf just now.

Zazzerpan's ears fell insubstantial to any line of inquiry, pastry-oriented or otherwise. His abstruse contour carved a pondering shape in the fog carpeting centuries-dead. His eleven contemporaries too embraced the muted consternation of their great Predicant Scholar. Few wizards kept sharper adumbratives or read them with such lucidity. When Zazzerpan treated men with silence it was seldom unrepaid by the wise and reasonable alike.

It was harrowing to entertain. Zazzerpan the Learned's storied Complacency of Wizards was marked for grander descendence. Disciples hand-picked, vetted by Ockite the Bonafide and tested by Gastrell the Munificent. The twelve sweetest, most studious children a pair of elderly eyes could give their sparkle. Not the ragged guttersnipe so oft-harvested by the common Obscenity, those vituperative little beggars with hearts to corrupt as dropped bananas brown. That these chosen youngsters would turn was not merely unthinkable, but something of a roundhouse to the temporal bones of the Upper Indifference's high chamber of Softskulled Prophets.

His wisdom-savaged brow pruned further with recount of his many lessons to wouldbe successors. Lessons to advance humanity's elucidation and prosperity, an outcome this bleak trail now painfully obviated. There were few puzzles The Learned could not suspend and dissect in the recondite manifold beneath his extremely expensive pointy hat. Daring to pitch his cherished pupils in with the foul melange of history's rogues, the heretofore abstract scourge that built up civilizations with ungodly magic and tore them down with joyful malice, would prove an intellectual trespass to make his calcium-deficient bones quake.

And more daring yet was the only question that now mattered. Could a bunch of bearded, scraggly old men in preposterous outfits hunt them down? He didn't have an answer. Only a simple observation so blunt and uncharacteristically jejune for the lauded sage it was breathtaking in its selfevidency.

"We're going to need more wands." (Wow. Think of something better.)

This is a good writing style for Rose as a character. Often I had to come up with creative styles for my OCs, like their drawing style or handwriting style, which could be a challenge, and occasionally I had to come up with a creative writing style that would befit a character's personality. The best examples of that are Rose's and Roxy's respective wizard fics, which, while similar in subject matter, are worlds apart in style and humor. But both fics (while entirely skippable, and perhaps advisably skippable, even) do serve as relevant allegories for certain themes and concepts they foreshadow in the HS storyline.

This wizard story seems really involved and kind of confusing. You'll have to save your place and dig into it later, and then maybe ask Rose what the hell the deal with it is.

> Dave: Go get a bookmark.

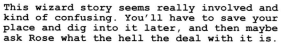

You return to your room in search of a bookmark.

Oh, hey. Finally a use for that pointless juice stained beta that will never serve any purpose, past or future.

You drop it on the john in case you're looking for some reading material later.

> Dave: Check on Rose.

I think Dave is just being polite, getting a bookmark to mark his place. He's probably never going to read this wizard story again. Also, he only made it through two pages, so it's not like it'd be hard to remember where he left off. In truth, what he's probably doing subconsciously is grouping more key items together for their final journey through time, just like the guardians were doing with all those random items in the Veil.

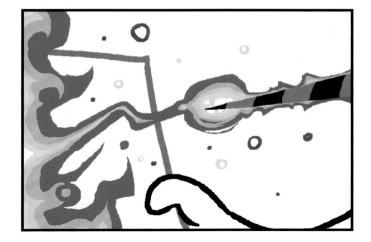

> Dave: Pester.

TG: whoa why are you burning your wizard fanfiction
TT: I'm not.
TT: This book contains a genetic code.
TG: oh ok
TG: then why are you burning that
TT: The gods from the Furthest Ring asked me to.
TG: is that some dumb wizard thing you just made up
TG: or something to do with tentacle monsters
TG: i cant keep track of what you like anymore
TT: How did you know I wrote a story about wizards, anyway?
TG: john told me
TG: he was all snoopin around your room while you were asleep and i was like no man dont
TG: so not cool
TG: then he was like haha dude check it out this book is full of wizard slash
TG: and i was like i dont even want to know this is such a crazy violation of privacy
TT: This story sounds suspicious.
TG: do you want me to chew him out about it i will because that was so outrageous i dont know where he got off being like that
TT: No, I don't actually mind.

The gods seem really desperate to destroy this code and break the endless loop of destruction that leads to the emergence of Lord English, even though they must know they can't stop it. It doesn't seem that clear why they'd be so desperate to prevent something that they know is predestined to happen—until we start seeing some of the destructive potential of LE in Act 6. Then, in Act 7, it becomes *super* clear why they'd want to stop it. In the end, HS is a tragic tale about billions of hideous eldritch monsters who try in vain to avert their own demise, in order to continue being innocently unfathomable and nefarious for eternity. So sad.

```
TT: Too bad I missed him.
TG: i thought you hated wizards
TG: whats the deal with that
TT: I like wizards.
TT: What I don't like is my mother's obsession with feigning interest in them to antagonize
me.
TG: oh man thats so messed up
TG: that you think that
TG: she probably digs wizards for real just like you and youre blowing shit out of
proportion like pretty much always
TG: you and she could probably have been chatting up how awesome wizards were this whole
time but no
TG: youre probably burning your nutjob meow book to spite her too arent you
TT: No, I told you.
TT: It's one of the gene sequences locked in my subconcious.
TT: The gods say it's critical to destroy it.
TG: oh yeah
TG: i thought that was a joke
TG: when did they say that
TT: When I was asleep.
TG: you mean when we were dancing and stuff in our dreams
TT: Yes.
TT: When I flew to your tower, I heard them.
TT: They're far above, in the dark sky.
TG: ive never seen or heard these things in my dreams
TT: Aren't you often distracted?
TT: By music and puppets?
TG: uh yeah
TT: Have you ever looked into the sky without your shades?
TG: no what a ridiculous question
TT: Maybe you should try it some time.
TG: ....
TT: You're the prince of the moon.
TG: ........
TT: I'm sure they've been meaning to seek a royal audience.
TG: .........................
TT: What do all these dots mean........
TG: dunno
TG: anyway yeah i guess ill do that
TG: get some sky monsters to boss me around sounds cool
```

> Davesprite: Also pester.

She and her mother absolutely could have been chatting up how awesome wizards were this whole time. But no.

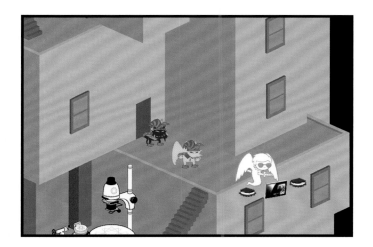 

TG: so really why are you burning that
TT: I just explained this to Other Dave.
TT: Do I have to explain everything to you twice now?
TG: no i know
TG: im using daves spare computer i saw the whole conversation through his pesterchum account
TT: Oh, I see.
TT: So instead of having to double explain, I merely have to put up with being double spied upon.
TT: What a relief!
TG: i just mean
TG: you didnt burn that book in the future
TG: that book was completely pointless
TT: I know.
TT: But now it's not.
TT: You appeared to make it relevant by traveling to the past.
TG: so does that mean the sleeping thing worked
TG: you remember the future
TT: I remember some things.
TG: ok cool
TG: so why is the cat code so terrible now
TT: I don't know.
TT: But the gods were pretty emphatic about it.

Rose seems intuitively more sensitive to Davesprite's existential crisis than either John or Dave are for some reason. She refers to him as Other Dave, instead of Real Dave. Maybe she isn't the warmest person, but perhaps due to spending a lot of time ruminating on grim subjects, she finds herself in a natural position of empathy for people in grim circumstances.

TG: well ok i guess its done but why are you so sure theyre right
TT: Have you ever known them to be wrong?
TG: i guess not
TG: but they sort of freak me out
TG: i mean listening to gross space mutants all day isnt my idea of an awesome time
TG: especially the ones that sing oh god
TT: Is that why you always kept the music turned up?
TG: no i flip out to ill jams because they kick ass
TG: obviously
TT: I guess we'll chalk another riddle up in the solved column.
TG: yeah case the fuck closed

TG: are you talking to future me
TT: Yes.
TG: ok im out of the loop again
TG: between you taking orders from dream beasts and bird wing me with like
TG: future secrets
TG: im doing some sort of spectacular fucking jackknife off the loop and getting a wink and a nod from barack obana
TG: im coming upstairs
TT: Ok.

> Dave: Chill with Davesprite.

Here comes DD to steal the MEOW code to create Bec which will lead to a massive upgrade in Jack's powers eventually. So who ordered him here? Is it Jack? Or is it Vriska? (The answer to everything is always Vriska.)

DAVE: so it was pretty funny how i made a copy of roses evil
book right before she burned it and now she doesnt know about it
DAVESPRITE: i know its crazy what kind of foresight this guy has
DAVESPRITE: im telling you coincidences like that are unreal
they dont even happen
DAVESPRITE: most of the time
DAVE: the best thing about how i did that is how it in no way
will ever come back to bite us in the ass ever
DAVESPRITE: dude our shit is SAFE
DAVE: so safe
DAVESPRITE: gonna sleep pretty sound tonight
DAVESPRITE: with that big fucking payload of safety you just got dropped on us
DAVESPRITE: gonna be all huggin my pillow and shit
DAVESPRITE: grinning like a goddamn bear full of honey
DAVE: safer than some flintstone vitamins in a bottle
DAVE: keep twisting junior all you get is clicks
DAVESPRITE: asshole thinks its candy
DAVESPRITE: doesnt even know he just stepped on a security rake and got a face full of
fucking safety
DAVE: yeah
DAVE: anyway guess ill go back down and burn that book
DAVESPRITE: alright

> Dave: Go back in time and stop the thief.

I wonder when this Flintstones Vitamins safety bottle reference is going to become dated. Are we there yet? Do kids get this joke? Do the fucking Flintstones even still exist? Who would have thought that a fictional family of cavemen would be anything other than a perfectly timeless cultural touchstone forever.

365

It looks like you already tried that.

Whoever took those books was a pretty cold blooded dude.

You figure you'll cool it on the time travel for a while. Don't want to see the Dave corpses start to pile up. Especially if one of them winds up being you.

> Dave: Throw yourself out the window.

You ditch the body before Jade sees it. That would probably freak her out.

> John: Press a button on the control panel.

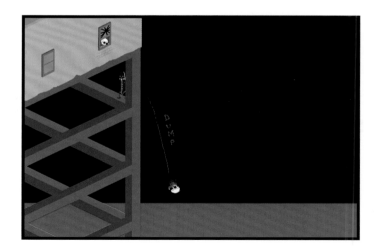

Sure, he's dumping his own corpse out the window because JADE is the one at risk of freaking out. Whatever you say, Dave.

366

You push one of the nearby buttons. It activates the upper right monitor. The view is locked on to a particular location on Earth at a particular date and time.

Whoever was in the lab appears to have recently calibrated this device.

> John: Examine monitor.

The monitor displays a town on the west coast of the United States. It appears to be your old neighborhood. But there is a factory there you do not recognize. The date is December 1st, 1995, a few months before you were born.

> John: Zoom in.

12/01/1995

John had no idea Crocker used to own this town. When the factory was destroyed, it probably led to a brutal depression of the local economy. I'm sure this is what he's thinking right now.

367

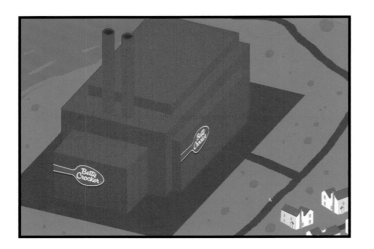

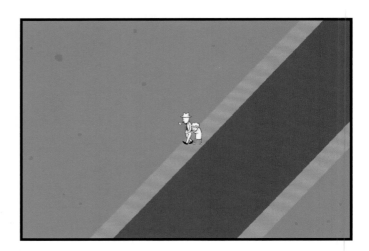

An old woman is escorted by her son on a lovely day. A target has been locked over the gentleman's mother.

A meteor overhead looms unnoticed.

Grandma Jane seems perfectly happy as she walks by the factory, which belies her dark personal history involving this brand. How much has she told her son of her troubled past? Probably not much.

They witness the destruction of the facility. Collateral damage to a corporation owned by a renowned billionaire explorer.

A mystery begins.

> John: Press blue button.

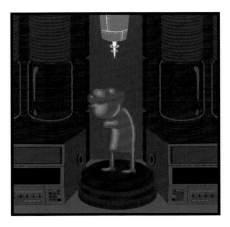

John is a true ectobiology genius. Look at him push that big blue button. It's literally the only thing he can do with this machine, and it was set up so that he would do it, at the exact moment he needed to do it. Incredible work, John.

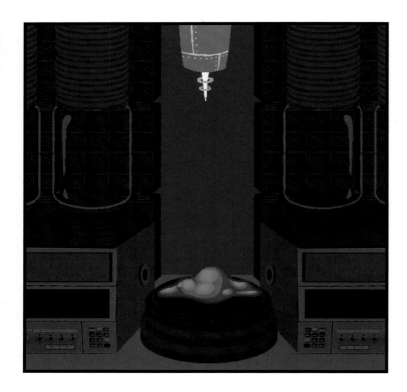

You create a PARADOX GHOST IMPRINT of the
woman you recognize to be your grandmother.

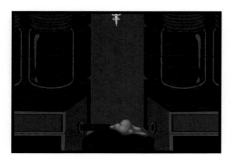 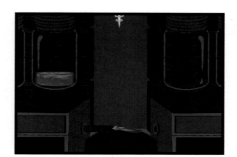 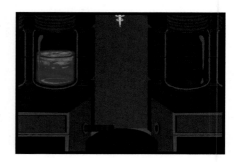

John: Refill the lab's Slurpee machine.

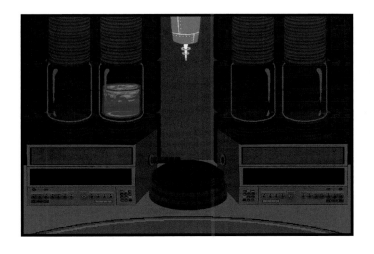

The ghost sludge is sucked into a glass tube.

> John: => SWITCH 4

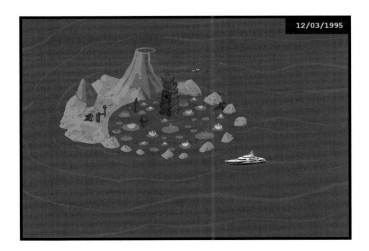

12/03/1995

You switch to a monitor displaying a view of a
remote island in the Pacific, on December 3rd, 1995.

> John: Zoom in.

It is a little-known canon fact that Old Jake Harley has had dozens of children with many families strewn all over the world over the course of his very long life. Yet his final child, an adopted baby Jade he retrieved from a crater, seems to be the only one he was ever actually proud of. Enough to name a boat after, at least.

A renowned billionaire explorer approaches on his yacht. An old factory lost two days prior, but a new shipmate gained. Together they settle the island and plunder its secrets.

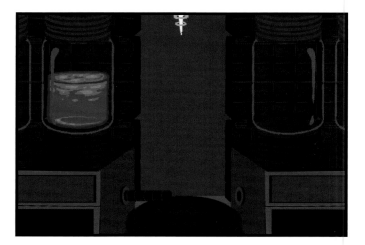

A meteor overhead streaks unnoticed, headed toward an unseasonably warm city in the central United States.

> John: Press blue button.

It's also possible he's not really proud of his new daughter Jade so much as he's just excited to finally be journeying to the place he's been spending most of his life looking for. The mysterious island with the ULTIMATE ruins to plunder, and home to the demonic, omnipotent reincarnation of his childhood dog.

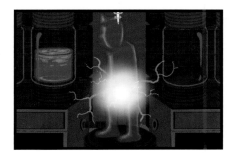

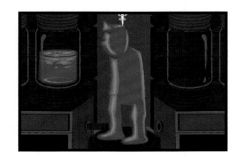

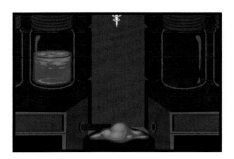

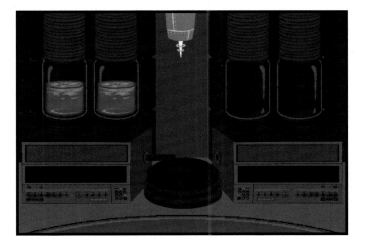

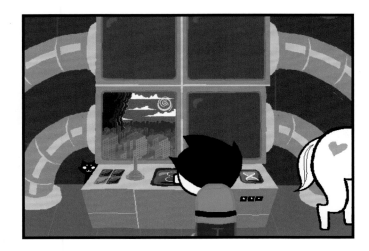

You create a PARADOX GHOST IMPRINT of the
man you spotted in the woods with your book.
The ghost sludge is collected.

> John: => SWITCH 3

You switch to a view of an unseasonably warm city in
the central United States, on December 4th, 1995.

> John: Zoom in.

John talks about him like he still doesn't realize this is obviously Jade's grandpa. Come on dude, try to connect some dots here. Baby Jade was RIGHT THERE
ON THE SCREEN.

 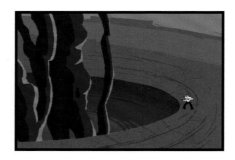 

An outrageously awesome dude stands before a crater where his favorite record shop stood one day prior.

He is prepared for the occasion with a small pair of outrageously awesome shades.

A meteor overhead races unnoticed, headed to a lake near a laboratory on the east coast of the United States. No aquatic life would survive.

> John: Press blue button.

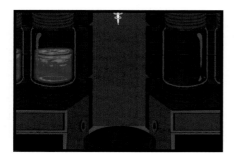 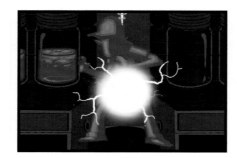 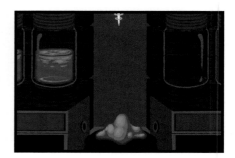

Here's Bro, ready with a tiny pair of shades. What an amazing fatherbrother he's surely going to be to this craterbaby.

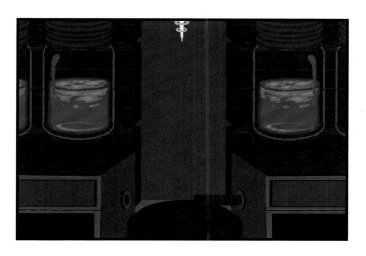

You create a PARADOX GHOST IMPRINT of the outrageously awesome dude. The sludge is allocated to one of another pair of tubes.

> John: => SWITCH 2

You switch again to a view of your neighborhood, on April 13th, 1996. It is the day of your birth.

There is more real estate you do not recognize near the recently devastated baked goods facility. It is a shopping mall you have never seen before.

> John: Zoom in.

I wonder what else was in this doomed shopping mall. A Blockbuster Video, maybe? I guess it was doomed in more ways than one.

Mom sure traveled a long way with her new daughter just to stand idly by a joke shop, cast a flirtatious glance at the owner's dapper son, watch the store blow up, and then peace out. Of course this isn't actually that confusing. The next page just says what's going on. Jake told her to do this. She's been working for him for a long time. Mystery solved.

A professional lady and new mother has traveled from
the opposite coast at the behest of a famous and
wealthy scientist to study one of numerous recent
celestial anomalies while he is on expedition.

She notices a meteor overhead, on collision course
with a quaint family joke shop. A distinguished
gentleman notices the lady and comes outside to
greet her, oblivious to the threat above. The
gentleman's mother remains inside, busying herself
with a tall bookshelf, a ladder, and a rather hefty
unabridged joke book.

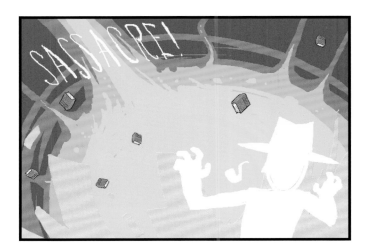

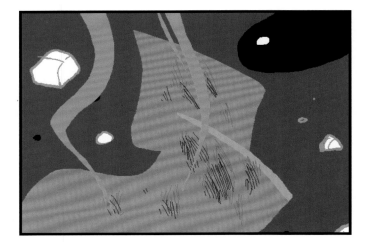

An old mother lost today, but a new son gained.

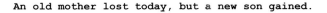

Since the beginning, we've been led to believe that Nanna died when she fell off a ladder and the Sassacre tome fell off the shelf and crushed her. This explanation seems to get debunked here, because clearly her shop has just been blown up by a meteor. But then later it gets undebunked, when we find out John was on that meteor, riding a copy of the tome, which did in fact end up crushing her.

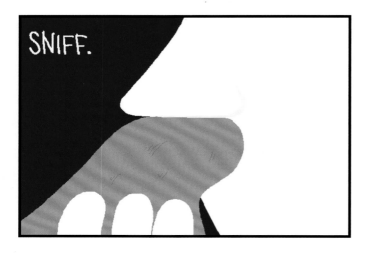

The gentleman discovers a clue. A powerful
nose detects perfume. The lady has fled.
The mystery deepens.

But the monitor has not lost track of the lady.

> John: Press blue button.

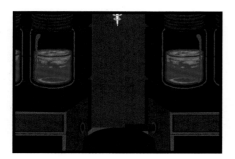

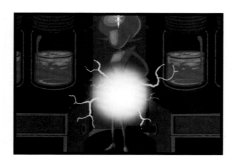

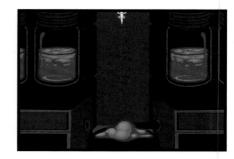

This Dad x Mom thing really is the chief romantic subplot at this moment in the story. I had yet to open the floodgates on your shipping grids. There really wasn't much going on except for this, and maybe some really vague nods to Dave x Rose before I cracked open the incest situation (which is literally happening right here, on these pages). So forgive me for milking this a bit.

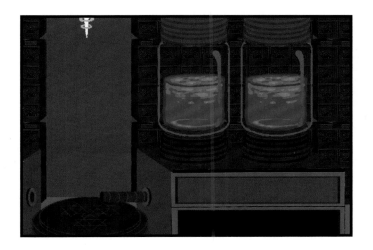

You create a PARADOX GHOST IMPRINT of the professional lady. The sludge fills the final tube.

Once all the tubes are filled, an automated sequence begins to execute.

Four young PARADOX CLONES are created.

> John: There's one more button to push.

If you're a *Homestuck* veteran, then at this point you probably take for granted as a basic premise that all these characters are slime clones of themselves, and the original four are slime kids of the slime clones, and it's one big, weird paradoxical incest slurry of intermingling familial nonsense, which then pitches the entire narrative in the direction of the heroes understanding themselves in relation to their star-crossed, same-age siblings and parents. But while this was all unfolding originally, it's hard to convey how baffling it all was to the readers as it was playing out. In many ways, HS is a completely different story before these slime shenanigans fully contextualize who all these people are and where they actually came from.

Ectobiology sure does involve a lot of button pushing. At least it does when you're a junior ectobiologist.

Your loyal assistant Dr. Meowgon is all over this one.

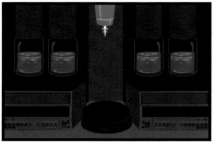

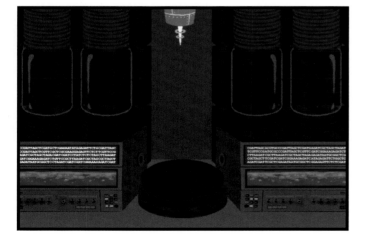

One pair of tubes empties the sludge into the chamber below.

The other pair does as well.

Another sequence is activated.

I guess this means Meowgon is technically responsible for breeding all their parents? Makes total sense when you think about it.

> John: Scale echeladder.

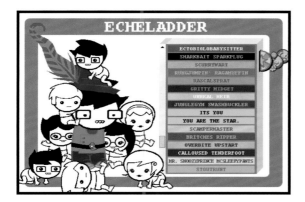

You storm up your ECHELADDER to claim the coveted if difficult to pronounce rung: ECTOBIOLOBABYSITTER.

Your ladder is absolutely hemorrhaging the boondollars. Just what your porkhollow's fat ass needs.

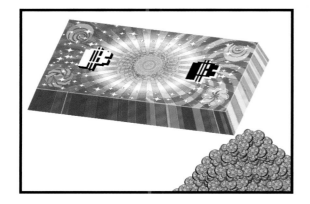

You surpass ONE MILLION BOONDOLLARS and trade them all in for a single whopping BOONBUCK. This is of course going directly into the college fund for these youngsters.

Sure is heavy. Into the hollow it goes.

The boonbuck looks like a really satisfying object to obtain. I'm surprised I never thought to sell these. As like, paperweights I guess? Or maybe chocolate bars. Yeah, that's a good idea.

> Navigating the veil nearby...

An old man has much to do before he returns to Earth, dies, gets stuffed by his adopted-yet-biological daughter-slash-grand-daughter, and stuck in front of a fireplace.

Taking priority at the moment is shipping two passengers long overdue for a reunion.

This, I guess, is a ridiculous way to show that the porkhollow has outlived its purpose. It simply can't fit all the riches John will accumulate from now on. Meanwhile, Jake gives up the game, and admits to the fact that he/I am literally shipping Mom and Dad.

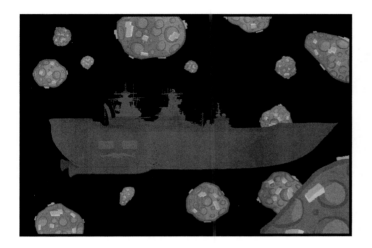
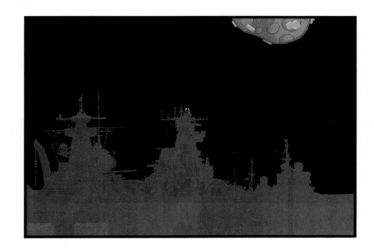

I honestly have no idea how Jake got this huge floating battleship, or made it. Possibly via some in-session alchemy? But I will say the blunderbuss propulsion system is a nice touch.

> CG: Troll John.

Roxy was so transparent. Like, WHOOPS! My scarf. How CARELESS of me. If only a handsome gentleman would return it thirteen years from now on a romantic cruise through a meteor belt.

CG: SEE THIS IS A CASE IN POINT.
EB: what point?
CG: THE POINT I WAS JUST MAKING.
CG: ABOUT THE ULTIMATE RIDDLE.
CG: YOU BLITHERING FECULENT SHITHOLE.
CG: OK THAT'S YOUR CUE TO LAUGH AT ME SOME MORE I GUESS.
CG: BECAUSE YOU SEEM TO REALLY GET OFF WHENEVER I FLAME YOU.
CG: HUMANS ARE DERANGED.
EB: oh man, i must be getting closer to the conversations where you're trolling me harder!
EB: this is pretty exciting, i can't wait to see what you've got up your sleeve.

CG: YOU SEE WHAT I MEAN??? FUCK YOU ABOUT THAT.
EB: anyway, you weren't making a point about the ultimate riddle, dude.
CG: YES I WAS, AND NOW I'M LOSING MY TRAIN OF THOUGHT DIPSHIT.
EB: nope, we never talked about it.
EB: yet...
CG: OH HELL, THAT'S RIGHT.
CG: DAMMIT, I GUESS THIS IS GOING TO BE CONFUSING.
EB: oh, you're just starting to figure that out now?
CG: SEE I KIND OF PAINTED MYSELF INTO A CORNER.
CG: I STARTED TROLLING YOU AT THE END, JUST BEFORE THE RIFT.
CG: AND THEN JUMPED BACK A LITTLE.
CG: AND NOW I GUESS I'VE BECOME RAILROADED INTO WORKING BACKWARDS HERE.
CG: UNLESS I WANT TO DO THE SORT OF DUMB SCHIZOPHRENIC HOPPING AROUND LIKE THE OTHERS.
EB: oh my god, i know, you've already told me like a million times!!!
CG: I HAVE?
CG: WOW I CAN'T WAIT FOR ALL THESE AMAZING CONVERSATIONS TO TAKE PLACE.
CG: IT'S GOING TO BE LIKE THAT HUMAN VACATION WITH THE GIANT RED CHIMNEY ASSHOLE UP IN HERE.
CG: YOU KNOW, THE ONE WHERE A BUNCH OF MOANY NOOKSUCKERS SING AT A LITTLE PINE TREE I THINK.
EB: man, i've got to say i'm a little disappointed by this "masterful trolling" you were bragging about.
CG: I WAS BRAGGING?
CG: WHY WOULD I BOTHER WITH THAT SORT OF PEDANTIC HUMAN HORSESHIT.
CG: MAYBE YOU SHOULD CONSIDER THAT I WAS BRAGGING TO GET YOUR HOPES UP IN THE FUTURE.
CG: ONLY TO LET YOU DOWN.
CG: AND THUS TROLL YOU MASTERFULLY IN THAT RESPECT.

Karkat talks about Christmas like it's this weird human thing but doesn't mention trolls have their own very similar holiday, called Twelfth Perigee's Eve. The Christmas tree is literally just a huge pile of shit their lusus drags in, and they festively decorate it together. Karkat should recognize the similarity that Christmas has to his beloved holiday, while marveling at how stupid it is that humans lug a tree into their house instead of doing the wholesome thing, which is obviously to bring home a giant turd.

EB: maybe, but that would be pretty weak too!!!
CG: YOUR BRITTLE HUMAN CALCIUM BASED SKULL IS WHAT IS WEAK, AND IF YOU AND I WERE IN THE PROXIMITY OF A BLUNT INSTRUMENT I WOULDN'T HAVE MUCH TROUBLE PROVING IT.
EB: w/e.
EB: so what was the "case in point" you were making, anyway?
CG: I WAS SCROLLING BACK AND NOTICED YOU WERE IN THE VEIL.
EB: whoa, i am?
CG: YEAH DUMBDUMB, YOU'RE TUMBLING AROUND ON A BIG GODDAMN METEOR.
CG: AND YOU JUST CREATED YOUNGER VERSIONS OF YOURSELVES AND YOUR GUARDIANS.
CG: PROBABLY BY MUCKING AROUND WITH THAT THING LIKE A DOOFUS.
EB: wait...
EB: these are baby versions of us?
CG: HAHAHAHAHAHA, SO CLUELESS.
CG: WHAT DID YOU THINK YOU WERE DOING THERE ANYWAY.
EB: well...
EB: i saw footage of my nanna, and some other people who i am pretty sure were like jade's grandpa and rose's mom and stuff from a long time ago.
EB: and then...
EB: there were all these little guys scurrying around.
EB: so they are like cloned copies of us?
CG: NO.
CG: THEY ARE LITERALLY YOU AND YOUR GUARDIANS.
CG: PARADOX CLONES.
EB: huh?
EB: what do you mean they are literally us?
EB: do they go back in time?
CG: YEAH, OBVIOUSLY. GREAT GUESS BRAIN HERO.
CG: BUT TECHNICALLY THEY AREN'T EVEN SENT BACK IN TIME BECAUSE WITH RESPECT TO THE MEDIUM YOUR UNIVERSE'S TIMELINE IS MEANINGLESS.
CG: SERIOUSLY WHY WOULD IT GIVE A CRAP ABOUT EARTH'S PAST OR FUTURE OR WHATEVER, FROM IT'S PERSPECTIVE IT'S JUST A BUNCH OF POINTS TO CHOOSE FROM.
CG: JUST LIKE YOUR CHRONOLOGY IS FROM OUR PERSPECTIVE.
CG: BUT I GUESS THAT'S A BUNCH OF SEMANTICS. WITH RESPECT TO YOUR PERSONAL CHRONOLOGY YEAH THEY GO BACK IN TIME.
CG: A PARADOX CLONE IS BY DEFINITION A CORRECTLY CLONED DUPLICATE THAT WILL INEVITABLY GO BACK IN TIME AND BECOME THE ORIGINAL TARGET THAT WAS CLONED.
CG: IF IT'S A MALFORMED CLONE, IT'S JUST A MEANINGLESS MUTANT THAT HAS NO BEARING ON THE STABLE LOOP CONTINUUM.
CG: I DON'T SEE ANY TENTACLES OR EXTRA EYEBALLS OR WARPED BONE BULGES, SO THOSE GROSS LITTLE THINGS THERE ARE ALL YOU GUYS, WAITING TO GO TO EARTH AND GROW UP AND BECOME THE INSIPID BUNCH OF GRUBFISTED DOUCHEBAGS YOU ALL ARE NOW.
CG: AND THIS WAS THE POINT I WAS TRYING TO MAKE ABOUT THE ULTIMATE RIDDLE.
EB: what is the riddle anyway?

386   Karkat helpfully removes all doubt that these babies grow up to be our heroes, and that they aren't just some copies John made. When telling a complicated story, generally it's a good idea to absolutely corner the reader into understanding exactly what is and isn't happening. And even then, they often still don't understand. You can lead a horse to water, etc., etc. Paradox clones are just standard clones, except that, paradoxically, the DNA comes from the very person they eventually grow up to be. So where did the DNA come from in the first place? It somehow spontaneously generated itself in paradox space, I guess. Or was "fundamental" to it in some unfathomable way. Just like the self-originating bullshit all these kids bicker at each other about in these stable time loop conversations they're having.

EB: maybe i can guess, i am good at riddles!
CG: HAHAHA, THINK AGAIN IGNORAMUS.
CG: IT'S NOT EVEN THAT GREAT.
CG: OR EVEN MUCH OF A RIDDLE AT ALL.
CG: IN THE COURSE OF YOUR ADVENTURE YOU WOULD HAVE ENCOUNTERED ALL THESE FRAGMENTS OF LIKE WEIRD POEMS AND SHIT.
CG: YOU FIND THEM ALONG YOUR QUESTS, WITH CLUES AND STUFF BURIED IN THEM TO HELP YOU SOLVE PUZZLES AND MOVE HUGE STONE COLUMNS AND MAKE STAIRCASES APPEAR AND LOTS OF NONSENSE LIKE THAT.
CG: AND IT'S ALL MASKED IN THIS FLOWERY SORT OF FROTHY POETIC JACKASSERY THAT NOBODY REALLY CARES ABOUT.
CG: AND I SURE AS HELL DON'T CARE ABOUT SPOILING IT FOR YOU.
CG: BUT WHAT ALL THESE LOFTY SYMBOLIC ALLUSIONS BOIL DOWN TO IS SOME GRANDER STATEMENT ABOUT WHAT YOU SEE HAPPENING HERE.
CG: THAT YOU WERE ALWAYS THE KEY TO SEEDING YOUR OWN EXISTENCE THROUGH THIS GAME.
CG: AND ANY HOPE THAT IT COULD HAVE PLAYED OUT DIFFERENTLY OR THAT YOU COULD HAVE AVOIDED THIS WHOLE MESS WAS ALWAYS JUST A RUSE.
EB: a distaction, perhaps?
CG: WHAT?
EB: nevermind.
CG: BECAUSE IF IT DIDN'T GO DOWN THIS WAY THEN HOW WERE YOU EVEN BORN, GET IT.
CG: WHICH IS ESPECIALLY PATHETIC SINCE PARADOX SPACE APPARENTLY WENT TO ALL THIS TROUBLE TO MAKE YOU JUST TO HAVE YOU FAIL AND DIE.
CG: REALLY THERE'S NOTHING MORE TRAGIC THAN THESE NULL SESSIONS FULL OF KIDS ENTERING THE GAME AND FULFILLING SOME COSMIC DESTINY SHIT JUST TO GET WIPED OUT AND LEAVE BEHIND AN EMPTY POINTLESS INCIPISPHERE FOR ALL ETERNITY.
CG: ACTUALLY IT'S SORT OF HILARIOUS.
CG: OR IT WOULD BE IF IT DIDN'T AFFECT ME PERSONALLY.
CG: BUT ANYWAY, THERE'S A LOT MORE TO THE RIDDLE THAN JUST THAT, LIKE WHAT WE WERE JUST TALKING ABOUT LAST TIME WE TALKED.
CG: BUT THAT'S SORT OF THE GIST OF THE THEMES IT DEALS WITH.
EB: ok.
EB: well, if i run into some salamanders who tell me all about this riddle and get really excited about it, i will try to act surprised.
EB: so this is the same kind of thing you went through?
EB: with, like, being your own paradox clones and creating your own parents and stuff?
CG: YEAH.
EB: how did that even work, with 12 of you?
CG: IT WAS REALLY FUCKING COMPLICATED AND I'M NOT GOING TO GET INTO IT.
CG: OUR FAMILY STRUCTURES ARE ALREADY WAY MORE COMPLICATED THAN YOURS WITHOUT EVEN GETTING SPOOKY TIME SLIME INVOLVED.
CG: BASICALLY WE HAVE NOTHING IN COMMON WHATSOEVER.
CG: EXCEPT MAYBE THIS...

The Ultimate Riddle is one of those things the exact definition of which is kind of a moving target throughout the story, due to its mysterious—you could say, riddle-like—nature. Kind of like the way the Mirthful Messiahs can refer to different "mirthful" pairs of people, depending on at what point in the story the idea is discussed.

CG: I WAS THE GUY IN YOUR POSITION, TO MAKE ALL THESE CLONES, AND FRANKLY IT ALL KIND OF FREAKED ME THE HELL OUT.
EB: huh...
EB: yeah, i guess now that you mention it, i am finding it all a little strange...
CG: OH, ONLY JUST NOW???
CG: FUCK YOU ARE FAST, I HOPE YOU GOT THE MAD BOONBUCKS TO PAY OFF THOSE SPEEDING TICKETS.
EB: no, no, i mean the ghost stuff and paradoxes are one thing of course...
EB: it's something else.
EB: it's just...
EB: this is really weird...
CG: WHAT'S SO WEIRD ABOUT IT.
EB: well, normally humans hatch...
EB: from like these slimy pods.
EB: then we wriggle out as a little pink larva.
CG: OH REALLY.
CG: HUH, MAYBE WE HAVE MORE IN COMMON THAN I THOUGHT.
EB: (hehehehehehehe)
CG: MAYBE THOSE REALLY ARE MUTANT CLONES AND THEY AREN'T GOING BACK TO SEED YOUR PLANET???
EB: um...
EB: sure...?
CG: HELL, I'M CONFUSED NOW.
CG: NOT THAT I GIVE A SHIT ABOUT YOU AND YOUR POINTLESS AWFUL LIVES.
EB: hey, i have an idea.
EB: why don't you get back to me in a few minutes?
EB: i mean like a few minutes of my time, not yours.
EB: all of these little pink monkeys are getting way out of line and i have to tend to them.
EB: if you message me in a couple minutes, we can continue conversing in a sane, linear fashion for a change!
CG: UM, OK?
EB: and then after that you can keep going backwards and then make fun of me riding my little red rocket.
EB: you can tell me i look like a silly little paradox clone fresh out of my slime tube and this is just all a big nurseytime recess jamboree.
EB: that would burn me good!
CG: OK THAT IS PRETTY GOOD.
CG: BUT I CAN'T USE IT, BECAUSE YOU SAID IT, AND THEN LATER, I.E. RIGHT NOW, YOU WOULD GET THE SATISFACTION OF KNOWING YOU WERE THE ONE TO COME UP WITH THAT BURN.
CG: SEE, YOU ARE DEALING WITH A PRO, YOU CAN'T OUT TROLL ME SO JUST FORGET ABOUT IT AND STOP TRYING.
EB: (hehehehehehehehehehe)

> John: Tend to little pink monkeys.

Of course Karkat is the John of the group. He's the main guy, for one thing, so duh. Second, he's a "geneticist," where John is a "biologist." The "carcino" suggests his influence in the process was cancerous or defective in some way, except that's more of a "Karkat's bad self-esteem" thing than anything actually supported by the text. Anyway, all I really want to do is take a moment to appreciate Karkat's nod to the absurd speeding ticket system in *Sburb* that I have been low-key roasting myself over throughout much of this book.

They're scramblin' all over the place!

They appear to be preoccupied by some of the objects littered around the lab. At least it is keeping them busy.

> John: Get trolled by CG again.

They are all naturally, and very conveniently, gravitating toward their predestined Birth Objects. Luckily, most of these objects present some attraction to their innate personalities. Well, maybe the Dave/pony pair is kind of a head-scratcher. Except when you consider that Dave probably wouldn't hesitate to ride a pony down to Earth, if given the choice.

CG: OK IT'S A FEW MINUTES LATER.
CG: LOOK HOW SANE AND LINEAR WE ARE BEING.
EB: yeah!
CG: OK AWESOME, NOW FUCK YOU AND GOODBYE.
EB: wait!
CG: WHAT.
EB: i was just looking at all these rascals, and i was wondering...
EB: how they go back in time and become us and stuff.
EB: does it have something to do with the reckoning?
CG: HOW DO YOU KNOW ABOUT THAT.
EB: you told me.
EB: we had this great dare going.
EB: to see who could be the least helpful and informative.
EB: and you totally lost, dude!
EB: you were hella helpful.

CG: I WAS OBVIOUSLY JUST SPITING YOUR STUPID POINTLESS HUMAN DARE.
CG: WHAT IS A DARE ANYWAY, IT'S NOTHING.
CG: SOMEONE SAYS DO SOMETHING AND THEN, OH LAUGH LAUGH, YOU LOSE IF YOU DON'T DO IT.
CG: THAT ISN'T ANYTHING THAT DESERVES A WORD.
CG: WE DON'T EVEN HAVE A WORD FOR DARE IN OUR LANGUAGE.
CG: THE CLOSEST APPROXIMATION WOULD BE "WORTHLESS FUCKING BULLSHIT WASTE OF TIME FOR SILLY LITTLE CHILDREN"
EB: oh, wow.
EB: is that the title of a movie too?
CG: YES, IT'S THE TITLE OF EVERY DUMB MOVIE YOU EVER LIKED.
EB: ha ha, that isn't even true and doesn't make sense!
CG: ANYWAY, HOW COULD WE HAVE MADE A DARE IF I'M MOVING BACKWARDS ON YOUR TIMELINE.
CG: YOU WOULD DARE ME TO DO SOMETHING, THEN I WOULD DO IT NEXT TIME, BUT THEN YOU WOULDN'T EVEN REMEMBER THE DARE.
CG: BECAUSE WE DIDN'T MAKE IT YET.
CG: THAT'S WHAT ISN'T TRUE AND DOESN'T MAKE SENSE YOU DAMP BAG OF PUKE.
EB: well yeah, the dare never happened, i was joking around and made that up to give you hard time.
CG: YOU HAVE SOUNDING STUPID DOWN TO SUCH A SCIENCE.
CG: WHERE IS YOUR LAB COAT AND TEST TUBES DOCTOR BRAIN PROFESSOR?
EB: i am wearing a lab coat!
EB: sort of...
CG: YOU LOOK LIKE AN ELF.
EB: that's bullshit!
CG: YOU LOOK LIKE YOU SHOULD BE BLOWING INTO A FUNNY LITTLE SHELL, AND LIMBERING UP FOR A SILLY COOKIE DANCE.

Karkat destroying John over his stupid outfit might be the first time he officially owns Jake. Actually, we can see Jake, right there. You might be inclined to think he is looking adoringly up at John, but no. It's more likely he's admiring that stupid outfit his future self left there for John.

EB: do you even have elves?
CG: YES, LET'S COMPARE WHICH FANTASY CREATURES THAT DON'T EXIST WE BOTH DO OR DON'T NOT HAVE.
CG: WHAT A GREAT FUCKING IDEA, JOHN!
EB: uh, what?
CG: YOU ASKED ABOUT THE RECKONING, SO WHY DON'T WE TALK ABOUT THAT INSTEAD OF ALL THESE PRETTY MUCH TERRIBLE THINGS.
EB: ok.
CG: YEAH, SO WHEN THE RECKONING STARTS HAPPENING, ALL THESE PARADOX CLONES GET SHIPPED OFF TO METEORS, FLUNG THROUGH SKAIAN DEFENSE PORTALS, AND SENT BACK TO EARTH.
CG: END OF STORY I GUESS.
CG: BYE.
EB: wait!!!
EB: so that means...
EB: we are all sort of like superman?
CG: UH YEAH, I GUESS.
EB: cool!
CG: YOU ALL TRACE THE MYTHOLOGICAL FOOTSTEPS OF YOUR BELOVED HUMAN SUPERMAN WHO'S REALLY JUST A MUSCULAR CAUCASIAN ALIEN.
CG: IT'S HILARIOUS HOW HUMANS WORSHIP HIM AS A PINNACLE OF HUMAN HEROISM AND VIRTUE BUT HE ISN'T EVEN HUMAN.
CG: ACTUALLY IT'S INCREDIBLY PATHETIC.
CG: BUT ALSO IN A WAY KIND OF ADMIRABLE.
CG: BECAUSE IT MEANS DEEP DOWN YOU ALL MUST REALIZE WHO YOUR DADDY IS.
CG: WE ARE, BITCHES.
EB: yeah, superman is pretty cool, i guess.
EB: did you know nicolas cage was almost going to play superman one time?
CG: OH MY THROBBING PHLEGM LOBE, WHO GIVES A BARFING FUCK ABOUT THAT.
CG: JOHN EGBERT, YOU HAVE ASSASSINATED MY PATIENCE.
CG: ADIOS LOSER.
EB: wait!!!!!!!!!!!!!!!!!
EB: get back to me in a couple minutes, ok?
CG: SD;LKFJSD;LKFJSDLFKJ;
CG: FINE.

> AR?: Shred.

Since Karkat refers to Superman as a "MUSCULAR CAUCASIAN ALIEN," we can interpret this to mean via *Homestuck* nomenclature that Superman is actually in Trickster Mode. I think you will agree this is a really, really interesting train of thought. Who is Superman the Trickster Mode version of? Is Superman actually Trickster Batman? It kind of makes sense. Superman flies around, is ridiculously overpowered, solves problems without much effort, and has kind of a saccharine attitude about justice and all compared to Batman.

This is definitely the worst author note in the book. None of my other bad notes can even hold this one's jockstrap.

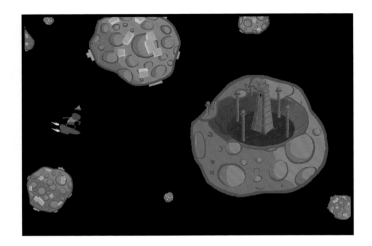

You are ripping up so many hellaceous shreds this fierceshitty biznasty is getting so deliriously rudebrazen it...

Ok you lost the handle on that sentence.

Oh my god, is that what you think it is?

This thing is so completely illegal.

How could this atrocity be floating out here unnoticed all this time?

You are going to throw whoever is responsible into the slammer.

You always call jail the slammer when you are extra angry at crimes.

> AR?: Go in.

I wonder, since parking violations are so prevalent in the Medium and agents are authorized to write tickets...are there tow trucks too? Or tow shuttles? If so, AR should just call a fleet of them out here, and have this OUTRAGEOUSLY illegal meteor hauled back to Derse and impounded forever.

There is a large elevator platform ahead.

> AR?: Go down.

Below there is a dark cavernous room.

Near the platform is a TIME CAPSULE. It has deployed a SEED, and waits
for something to be deposited, and for the clock to be set.

It is all harmless enough. Still no sign of any perpetrators.

> AR?: Search premises.

We can now deduce that this is how AR got stuck in these ruins on post-apocalypse Earth for all those years. And because Karkat just told us how the Reckoning works, we can also deduce how these ruins got there in the first place. (Though we have yet to see its collapsible design for travel purposes.) There is something fairly bracing about the reading experience toward the end of Act 4, in MY humble opinion, as you start to get a sense of its design and the pacing of certain deliveries. With these swift narrative karate chops, one after another, this act answers so many of the questions that have been dangling out there for a long time now. There aren't too many patches of *Homestuck* quite like it, where there's a distinct feeling of a big, multifaceted puzzle being solved in a rapid succession of reveals. The tail end of Hivebent? Maybe Cascade too? I don't know. Beyond that point I'm not sure it even counts, because it starts being more teen soap opera and less a huge, creative game of fucking Vulcan Galaxy Brain Death Jenga.

393

Deeper into the darkness of the room there is some complicated lab equipment. Again, nothing particularly unusual for this jurisdiction.

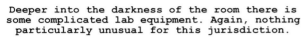

> AR?: Examine equipment.

There is a large monitor. Displayed on it is a small human girl in a fancy house. The date is April 21, 1910.

Eight days prior, the orphan girl was taken in by an aristocratic southern colonel and legendary humorist. He recovered the young lady from a crater where a bakery once stood, operated by the man's wife, a notable baked goods baroness.

There's clearly still more cloning work to do. But this time it'll happen at the lab inside the frog temple, which has a special purpose. All the planets that spawn *Sburb* need a First Guardian. There's Jane, and Sassacre, who is obviously just Mark Twain, and who for some reason uses Dad as a sprite base. Why not. Jane grew up here in Crocker Manor, along with Betty Crocker herself, and I think you probably know who that is. I actually came up with this extremely elaborate backstory explaining the decades leading up to this moment and the decades after it. The whole "Crocker's Schemes on Earth" backstory. This probably sounds like something you want to read. But trust me. It really isn't.

There is an explosion in the colonel's back yard.

Land sakes alive, we are cooking with petrol now!

The colonel and his new grand daughter investigate.

The impact site is where a dog house stood moments ago. It was the magnificent abode of the man's beloved pet, HALLEY.

He takes a belt from the old julep flask. He'd sooner perish himself than lose that dear animal.

Twain was born in a year Halley's Comet came by, and died the next time it came. So his dog is named Halley. His death, as seen on the next page, was also triggered by a considerably more stupid cosmic event: the arrival of Jake, who promptly murders him and steals his dog.

395

People would think reports of the man's death were greatly exaggerated.

But they weren't.

This is exactly why babies should not be allowed to dual-wield flintlock pistols.

An old colonel lost, but a new brother gained.

Good work, Jake.

Ah ha! There's HALLEY. The youngsters adore their new guardian. Good dog. Best friend.

The young boy has difficulty pronouncing the name though. Sounds more like "Harley" when he says it.

> AR?: Fast forward.

Thirteen years later, the boy develops a taste for adventure. He and his guardian bid farewell. His sister is sad. She will be left all alone with the wicked pastry baroness. She can handle it, he tells her. He believes in her.

This is why Jake took the name Harley, and therefore why it's Jade's name too. Just another mystery that wasn't even a mystery, which nobody was on the lookout for answers to, but I'll be damned if I wasn't going to shoehorn some retroactive logic into the story to offer a half-decent explanation for why he had that name when he was born into a family named Crocker.

This all seems pointless to you, and immaterial to the crime that has been committed.

Though you do find it odd that the appearifier target has been fixed over that especially stupid looking animal.

You hear the elevator platform. Someone is coming.

It is a high ranking agent from your kingdom.

Could he be the man behind this crime? Could his intent be mutinous?

You know the agent to be far too dangerous to take into custody.
You hide behind some equipment and observe.

Is this REALLY an act of mutiny? It's a fair question. All he is really doing here is ensuring the creation of the First Guardian, which was necessary to Earth and a functioning session regardless of Jack's mutinous intent. And yet, Bec's existence nevertheless proves important to Jack's rise... Welp, even I'm stumped. DD is a tough nut to crack.

He appears to be holding some notebooks. Also what appears to be a pair of juice-stained envelopes.

Only one of the books is useful to him. The envelopes are useless. And he couldn't make it through more than a paragraph of the other book. Some weird thing about wizards. He discards them.

The spare notebook lands on the floor. The envelopes land in the SEED.

The TIME CAPSULE stores the seed, and on account of some default setting, is programmed to bloom several hundred million years from now.

The capsule then readies a new seed.

I think the important takeaway here is that DD actually tried to read an entire paragraph of *Complacency of the Learned*. This tells us he is not a man who is completely unamenable to trying out any given wizard fic he might find randomly somewhere during his travels, but he's not going to waste too much of his time on it if it doesn't pass muster. Which begs the question: if he'd actually liked it, would he have been sucked into it for an hour or two down here while he was supposed to be cloning a really important dog?

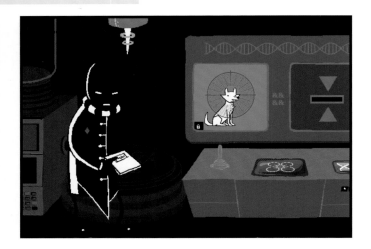

The agent approaches another device near the large monitor.

> John: Get trolled by CG in sane and linear manner.

CG: OK, I GOT BACK TO YOU.
CG: ARE YOU HAPPY.
EB: sure, i guess.
CG: YOU DON'T EVEN KNOW IT YET.
CG: BUT YOU ARE ABOUT TO START PASSING OUT BUNNIES LIKE THEY'RE CHEAP CIGARS.
CG: IT'S GOING TO BE AN EMBARRASSING DISPLAY.
EB: what are you talking about?
CG: YEAH, EXACTLY, NUMSKULL.
CG: LET'S JUST HAVE OUR CHAT, THEN IT CAN NATURALLY OCCUR TO YOU TO BE AN IDIOT IN THE DUE COURSE OF TIME.
EB: ok...
EB: i was sort of mulling it over while looking at all these babies with guns and sitting on ponies and things...
EB: and how the reckoning takes them back.
EB: and how you said our reckoning starts sooner.
CG: YEAH.
EB: are you sure it has to start so soon? can't we delay it?
CG: HAHAHAHA.
CG: IT STARTS IN A FEW MINUTES STUPID.
CG: SEE THAT COUNTDOWN CLOCK OVER THERE?
CG: YOU AREN'T DELAYING ANYTHING.
EB: oh... dang!

The design of the device tells us some things. It was built not just to target a source creature to base the First Guardian on, but also to accept some form of literature containing the needed DNA code. Which means that in every session of *Sburb*, at some point, one or more players will have unwittingly taken to transcribing the code in some written format. Keep this fact in mind for later, when Doc Scratch explains the hell out of his own origin story.

EB: i guess i better get off this meteor then!
CG: WELL I MEAN IT DOESN'T HAPPEN ALL AT ONCE.
CG: FIRST SOME SMALLER METEORS GO.
CG: THEN BIGGER ONES.
CG: SPREAD OUT OVER LIKE 24 HOURS OR SO.
CG: IT'S SUPPOSED TO BE LIKE...
CG: GO TIME.
CG: WHEN IT STARTS.
CG: LIKE IT'S TIME TO HURRY UP AND STOP FUCKING AROUND AND KILL THE BOSS, GET IT?
CG: THE ROCK YOU'RE ON DOESN'T BLAST OFF RIGHT AWAY.
CG: TOO BAD, BECAUSE IT WOULD HAVE SPARED YOU FROM MAKING A FOOL OF YOURSELF IN A COUPLE MINUTES, AND MORE IMPORTANTLY, SPARED ME FROM HAVING TO WATCH.
EB: ok, well you keep saying how doomed we are and how all this bad stuff happens sooner, but you never say why!
EB: what happens in our game that's different from yours that makes things go so badly?

CG: JACK NOIR.
EB: who is jack noir?
CG: AN AGENT OF DERSE.
CG: WHO FLIPPED OUT AND ROSE TO POWER.
CG: HE KILLED YOUR BLACK QUEEN AND KING AND NOW HE'S IN CHARGE.
EB: so you didn't have him in your game?
CG: NO, WE DID.
CG: BUT HE WAS HARMLESS.
CG: ACTUALLY, HE WAS AN ALLY, SORT OF.
CG: HE SETTLED A GRUDGE AGAINST THE QUEEN BY HELPING US DETHRONE AND EXILE HER.
CG: AND THEN HE WOUND UP EXILED HIMSELF, AND SORT OF KEPT HELPING US THROUGH A COMMAND TERMINAL ON OUR OLD PLANET.
CG: HE'S KIND OF A HUGE ASSHOLE THOUGH.
CG: BUT BECAUSE HE TOOK THE QUEEN OUT OF THE PICTURE, WHEN WE GOT TO SKAIA WE ONLY HAD ONE MONARCH TO DEAL WITH INSTEAD OF TWO.
CG: OF COURSE IT WAS A NASTY GIANT 12X PROTOTYPED BLACK KING THAT TOOK FOREVER TO KILL, JUST BARELY IN TIME BEFORE THE BIGGEST METEORS CAME, BUT STILL.
EB: i see.
EB: so after he got exiled and all that, he came here into our game and caused all this trouble?
CG: NO, GOD.
CG: EGBERT YOU ARE THICKER THAN THAT HIDEOUS JOKE BOOK YOU WADDLE AROUND WITH.
CG: TRY TO THINK MORE ABSTRACTLY.
CG: THINK ABOUT VIDEO GAMES.

With dialogue foreshadowing stuff like this, I get to sort of craft a crude sketch of certain future story events for myself. Vague enough to allow some flexibility in how it all plays out when I make it, but specific enough to point in a certain direction and arrange other stuff. So when I tackle Hivebent next, and somehow get my arms around a plot dealing with twelve players and all the ridiculous shit that involves, I have some things to work with already. Like the fact that, as Karkat reveals, their Jack was an ally who helped them exile the queen. His account also mixes in some points we know already, like the fact that Jack served as Karkat's exile, and the queen was exiled too and joined the Felt for some reason. But now knowing they both got there as part of a mutiny plot to assist the trolls adds some texture to their backstory, and explains why Slick and Snowman still have this contentious thing going on.

```
CG: WHAT'S AN EARTH GAME YOU LIKED TO PLAY?
CG: NAME ONE.
EB: ummmm...
EB: crash bandicoot?
CG: OK I DON'T KNOW WHAT THAT IS, BUT I HAVE A FEELING IT'S A REALLY LAME EXAMPLE, BUT
THAT'S FINE, IT'S NOT THE POINT.
CG: SO LET'S SAY YOU PLAY YOUR BANDICOOT AND I PLAY MY BANDICOOT.
CG: THEY ARE ESSENTIALLY THE SAME BANDICOOT, SAME APPEARANCE AND DESIGN AND BEHAVIORS.
CG: BUT THEY ARE STILL COMPLETELY SEPARATE BANDICOOTS ON SEPARATE SCREENS.
CG: SO WE BOTH HAVE OUR OWN ASS BANDICOOTS TO OURSELVES, THE SAME BUT DIFFERENT.
CG: OUR JACKS ARE THE SAME BUT DIFFERENT TOO.
CG: SAME GUY, DIFFERENT CIRCUMSTANCES AND OUTCOMES.
CG: OUR JACK TRUMPED THE QUEEN, BUT GOT NO FURTHER.
CG: YOUR JACK GOT THE BEST OF BOTH OF THEM, AND IS NOW SOMETHING HIGHER THAN A QUEEN OR A
KING...
EB: like an ace?
CG: SURE OK.
EB: ok, i think i get it.
EB: but how did he do that? what was different about what we did versus what you did?
CG: FRANKLY I HAVE NO IDEA WHAT THE ORIGINAL THING THAT TIPPED THE SCALE WAS.
CG: IT IS UNDER INVESTIGATION.
CG: BUT IT DOESN'T REALLY MATTER.
CG: THE WORST IS YET TO COME.
CG: FOR YOU.
EB: oh no!
EB: what is the worst thing?
CG: ALREADY TOLD YOU.
EB: dammit!
EB: oh, hey...
EB: sorry, hold on, this little lady is bugging me about something.
CG: YEAH YEAH, YOU MIGHT AS WELL GET IT OVER WITH AND GIVE HER THE LOUSY RABBIT ALREADY.
EB: oh!!!!!
EB: oh man, i just had THE BEST idea, this is so perfect.
EB: a blonde mother and daughter together, this is totally perfect.
CG: PERFECT FOR WHAT, FLEXING YOUR FORMIDABLE MENTAL HANDICAP LIKE A FUCKING HEAVYWEIGHT FOR
THE NEXT SEVERAL MINUTES?
CG: OH WAIT, LET ME CHECK, THE ANSWER IS YES.
EB: it is like that scene in con air, i will give her the bunny like i am nick cage fresh
out of the slammer.
CG: FUCK.
EB: i wish i had a filthy wifebeater on, oh well.
```

I actually have strong doubts that John liked to play *Crash Bandicoot*. In fact, according to me, the guy who wrote this, there is a reasonably high probability that he never played it at all.

CG: JUST...
CG: AUGH.

> [S] John: Reunite with your loving wife and daughter.

Now we get to "watch" the goofy *Con Air* animation without the critical musical accompaniment, Bowman's cover of Trisha Yearwood's "How Do I Live." The animation experience is an emotional rollercoaster. A cumulative celebration, if you will, of *Homestuck*'s whimsical essence and its uncompromising spirit of absurdity. Now, here in this book, examining the frames will be more of a somber, meditative practice. I invite you to quietly behold Nic Cage's face for several minutes. Reflect on his visage the way one shows reverence for a religious icon during moments of silence in a church. You will come to understand that this sequence doesn't need funny music at all, and your appreciation of the content will be all the richer for it.

This does admirably explain how Rose and Jade got these bunnies as their Birth Objects. It wasn't their own attraction to the bunnies, which wouldn't have made a lot of sense. It was John's attraction to the idea of performing this stupid skit at a highly inappropriate moment, which resulted in them being shipped off to Earth with a couple of ratty bunnies, thus setting the stage for them to grow up and regift the bunnies back to John in the first place.

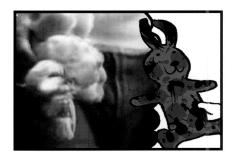

The official *Con Air* bunny I own is not the one pictured in the upper left corner. That's the ruined one at the end of the movie. I don't know where that one is, or frankly, if it even survived the shoot. The one in my possession is the bunny still in its original package, which Nic Cage buys for his daughter at the beginning of the movie. I'm just assuming that at some point in the future, I will have to travel back in time and give Cage the bunny for him to use in the film in the first place.

The skit is essentially complete once Rose gets the bunny. But Jade gets one too, as kind of an afterthought. John does have another bunny to spare, so why not? That way these three young ladies all go home with something nice. Jane, however, gets fuck all, since she's offscreen at the moment, having decided to crawl into a man's filthy hat.

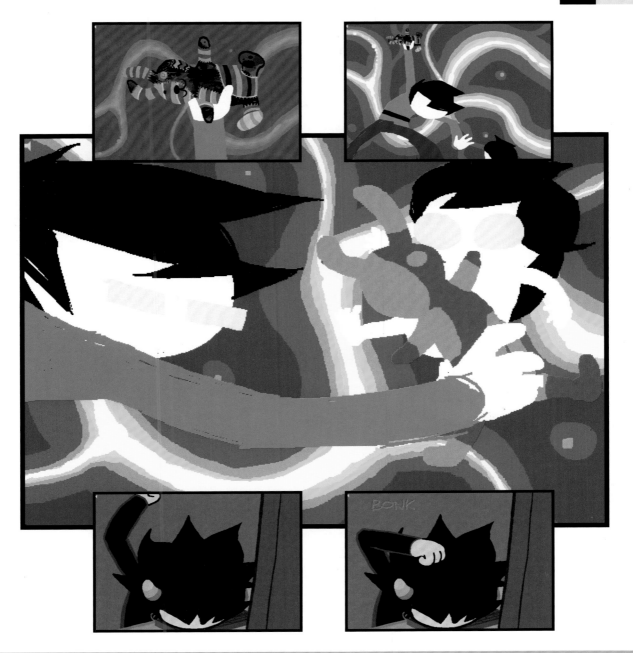

Karkat is being melodramatic and pretending not to enjoy every minute of this spectacle. We don't know it yet, or have the context for understanding what it means, but at this moment he has a hate crush on John. It was hate at first sight. Every morsel of conversation we have read between these two has been driven by these feelings. What he is doing here now, bonking his own head, is nothing more than an act of powerful sexual frustration.

The scribbled sequence above is misleading. By the time the plane crashes into the giant guitar in Vegas, the sports car it was keeping in tow had long since been severed. Also, there's another floating arm. What a great place to sneak an arm in. Generally when I was retconning arms into the story, the more surreal and incomprehensible a location was for John's arm to show up, the better. Not only did this moment not even take place inside the canon of the comic, it didn't even take place in the canon of the movie. It truly happened nowhere. And yet, there is his arm.

There is nothing remotely stupid about any of this.

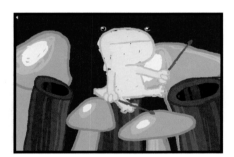  

John, his name is Bubbles Von Salamancer now. Respect his new identity.

Roxy seems to be really getting into that hug there. I think I did a tremendous job in seeding her overwhelming attraction to Egbert men here in Act 4. Stick this fact in your pipe and consider smoking it toward the end of Act 6.

HERE COMES THE GUITAR SOLO

There's a part in *Con Air* when John Malkovich holds a gun up to the bunny during a tense moment and says don't move or the bunny gets it. Or something like that. The rowdy criminals like to keep things loose and fun up there on the jail plane, as you will know if you have seen the film, which you have, at least a hundred times. Don't deny it.

> END OF ACT 4

At some point in this song cover, there's a guitar solo. But nobody is playing a guitar. It's just some guy making jackass noises with his mouth. So John here is working his air guitar to go along with that riff. Actually it makes sense that a Hero of Breath would play an air guitar. I really do think of everything... It's incredible.

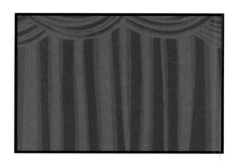

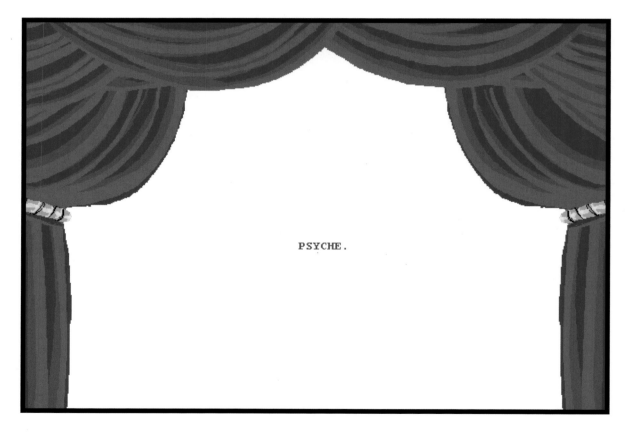

PSYCHE.

It'll be a few more pages.

This was an End of Act psyche-out. I doubt anyone would have had a problem if it were the real End of Act animation, because it was pretty good by just about any standard. But I was just pulling people's chains, as some say I am wont to do. Psyche-outs were effective tools in the real-time delivery of these pages online. Anything could happen. You just never knew, and all you could really do was wait a while for the next update to come, to see if you were getting played. Here in a book though, this doesn't work at all, does it. You just coast on through the fakeout. In fact, you can see the next page over to the right before you can even process the fact that this was supposed to be a fakeout. Everything is RUINED.

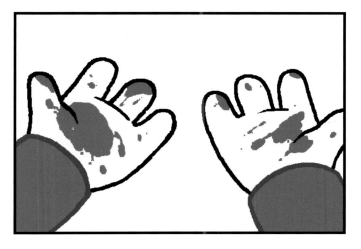

> Dave: Get trolled by GC.

```
GC: D4V3 WH4TS 1T SM3LL L1K3
TG: what
GC: YOUR BLOOD
TG: fuck off
GC: D4V3
GC: G1V3 1T 4 L1TTL3 T4ST3 FOR M3
GC: T3LL M3 WH4T HUM4N BLOOD T4ST3S L1K3
GC: 1V3 B33N SO CUR1OUS >:]
TG: youre the annoying blind one arent you
GC: Y34H
TG: dave told me about you
GC: GOD
GC: TOO M4NY D4V3S
GC: 1TS L1K3 TH1S B1G 4SSHOL3 4ND COOL GUY P4RTY
GC: BUT SOM3ON3 FORGOT TO 1NV1T3 4LL TH3 COOL GUYS
GC: >;]
TG: man im telling you burns like that are unreal
TG: where do you even get a burn thats that sick
GC: I B3T YOU C4NT W41T TO B3 4 US3L3SS P13C3 OF SH1T 4LL D4Y 4ND F4LL DOWN 4LL TH3S3 BURNS
TG: no you messed that up
```

Dave stands on a toilet transfixed by his own blood. At this point in the story, during the herculean ramp-up of its many concepts, systems, character profiles, puzzles, and mysteries, it's still kind of hard to get a feel for what any one protagonist's longform arc is supposed to be. But you do start getting little glimpses of things that snowball later. Like hints that Dave has suppressed certain traumas he struggles with, and works very hard not to think or talk about them.

GC: D4V3 D4V3
GC: 1S TH1S YOU
GC: http://tinyurl.com/PUR3D4V3
TG: uh
GC: PFF4H4H4H4H4H4H4H4H4H4H4H
GC: H4H4H4H4H4H4H3H3H3H3H3H3H3H3H3H3H3H3H3H3H3H3
TG: did you try to draw shades on his face and miss
TG: whats even the point hes already wearing shades
GC: H4H4H4H4H4H4H4H4H4H4
GC: 1TS SO P3RF3CT TH4T 1S SO YOU
GC: H3H3H3H3H3H3H3H3H3H3H3H3H3H3H3H
TG: this is moronic
GC: D4V3 T3LL M3 WH4T YOUR BLOOD SM3LLS L1K3
GC: OR 1LL M4K3 4NOTH3R ON3
GC: 4ND 1 KNOW TH3S3 HURT YOUR F33L1NGS
GC: >:D
TG: i dont know what it smells like or tastes like
TG: but i sure as hell know what it looks like
TG: like a fuckin symphony on my retinas
TG: shit is beautiful like a little vermilion picnic on my hands
TG: every day i open my eyes i find poetry in even the simplest things
TG: just one of those little joys in life you take for granted you know
TG: this miraculous gift of vision
GC: D4V3 D4V3
GC: CH3CK 1T OUT
GC: 1 F1GUR3D 1T OUT
GC: TH1S H4S GOT TO B3 YOU!
GC: http://tinyurl.com/TH1S1SSOOOOD4V3

For a little while, mining the internet for examples of these "Cool Kids" was kind of a hobby. It seems to be a whole genre of marketing out there, particularly within a certain range of time periods. Terezi seems to have made this observation as well in her brief study of Earth culture, and correctly pinpointed it as the perfect material to troll Dave with.

```
GC: 444444444H4H4HH4H4H4H44H444H4HH4H4H4H4H4
GC: H3H3H3H3H3H3H3H33H3H3H3H34H4H4H4H4H4H4H4H4H4H4H4H4H4
TG: i could give myself a hernia trying to be as big a douche as that guy
TG: i could try but it would wind up like a motorcycle stunt gone horribly wrong
TG: my broken body would flop and tumble around like a rag doll
GC: H4H4H4H4H4H4HH4H4H4H4H4H4H4H44H4H4H4H4H
GC: OH GOD 1 C4NT BR34TH3!!!!
TG: and yet as much as that guys the tooliest dude i could ever hope to meet he and i would
still get along famously
TG: cause we can both see
GC: H3H3H3H3H3H3H3H333H3H3H3H3H
GC: H4H4H44H4H4H
TG: just him and me
TG: havin a see party
TG: like a couple of eagle eyed bros peepin shit up into the wee hours
GC: D4V3
GC: C4N 1 COM3 TO YOUR S33 P4RTY?
TG: i guess but youll have to be careful not to stumble around bumping into all the gorgeous
masterpieces hanging around everywhere
TG: god so beautiful to look at with my perfect eyesight
GC: C4N 1 L1CK TH3 P41NT1NGS?
TG: yeah thats fine
```

> Jade: Get trolled by AT.

```
-- adiosToreador [AT] began trolling
gardenGnostic [GG] --

AT: jADE, hI, iS YOUR ROBOT NEARBY,
GG: ummmmmmm.....
AT: wHERE YOU CAN TYPE, bECAUSE YOU
ARE ASLEEP,
GG: oh! yes it appears so!!!
AT: oK, uHH, iN THAT CASE, aRE YOU
HAVING A PLEASANT NAP,
```

Tavros's Trollian window predictably is a stupid disaster of concurrent chat sessions. He's got two open with Dave and Rose in the past, one open with Jade in the future... Get it together, man.

GG: i guess! ive been pretty busy here
GG: ive had to stay asleep for a long time because john is supposed to wake up soon
GG: but he just wont wake up!!!!!
GG: im pretty sure im supposed to be the one to wake him but i dont know what to do :(
AT: uHHHHH,
GG: huh??
AT: oHH, sORRY,
AT: i WAS LOOKING TO SEE IF i COULD SEE HIM BE AWAKE IN THE FUTURE,
AT: bUT i CANT SEE IN HIS DREAMS, oR ANYTHING,
GG: oh......
GG: well thanks for trying anyway!
AT: bUT YOU WILL WAKE UP SOON, iT LOOKS LIKE,
AT: sO MAYBE THIS MEANS YOU HAVE SUCCESS,
GG: i hope so!
GG: what am i doing when i wake up?
AT: oH, gOODNESS, tHERE IS SO MUCH GOING ON, aND THERE IS A LOT OF TROUBLE THAT YOU ARE IN,
GG: oh no!!!!!
AT: bUT, wHAT IT COMES DOWN TO IS, iS THAT YOU DON'T HAVE MUCH TIME ANYWAY,
AT: tHIS IS YOUR LAST DAY,
AT: bEFORE YOU MAKE THE RIFT,
AT: aND THEN i CAN'T SEE WHAT HAPPENS AFTER THAT, aNYMORE,
AT: wHICH IS OK, wITH ME, bECAUSE, tO BE HONEST,
AT: sEEING YOUR WHOLE BIG CONFUSING FUTURE AND PAST IS, kIND OF OVERWHELMING,
GG: yes i know what you mean....
AT: iTS SO COMPLICATED, aND, i DON'T EVEN KNOW WHAT i SHOULD BE ACCOMPLISHING,
AT: i THINK,
AT: uSING THESE GADGETS AND THINGS, aND MY TIME LINE ADVANTAGES, tO PLAY PRANKS ON YOU,
GG: that sounds like it would be fun!
GG: but you guys never even played pranks on me, you were always just kinda mean D:
AT: sORRY, }:(
AT: i THINK,
AT: tHE IDIOTIC THING ABOUT TROLLIAN IS,
AT: iF YOU USE IT TO TROLL PEOPLE, i THINK YOU ARE JUST AS LIKELY TO GET TROLLED YOURSELF,
AT: mAYBE EVEN MORE BADLY,
AT: wHICH i THINK IS WHAT IS GOING ON HERE, jUST BETWEEN YOU AND ME,
GG: well i know i havent trolled you guys!
GG: or not yet........
GG: heheheh
AT: nO,
AT: bUT YOU SORT OF ARE,
AT: mY FRIEND IS GOING CRAZY, hE WANTS TO TALK TO YOU,

If you use Trollian to troll people, you are only likely to get more trolled yourself if you suck and have no idea what you're actually doing, like Tavros and Karkat. On the other hand, Terezi and Vriska are great at trolling people with Trollian, as well as with other trolling-based formats. This completely debunks Tavros's pathetic, self-pitying theory.

AT: hE LEFT YOU A MESSAGE, a LONG TIME AGO ON YOUR TIME LINE,
AT: tO TALK TO HIM, wHEN YOUR ROBOT BLOWS UP,
GG: oh yeah!
GG: i totally forgot about that
GG: does it really blow up or was that another trick?
AT: uHHHH,
AT: i DON'T KNOW, i CAN'T SEE IT BLOW UP IN YOUR FUTURE,
AT: nOT ON SCREEN,
AT: i MEAN,
AT: tHERE ARE LOTS OF EXPLOSIONS, aLL THE TIME, aNYWAY,
AT: tOO MANY EXPLOSIONS,
GG: hmmmmm
GG: you could ask me in the future!
AT: oK, i WILL ASK,
AT: oK,
AT: yOU SAID, yES, iT DID BLOW UP, aND YOU TALKED TO HIM,
AT: aND, uHHH,
AT: tHEN YOU SAID HE WAS ACTUALLY A PRETTY NICE GUY, wHICH i THOUGHT WAS WEIRD,
GG: is he not a nice guy?
AT: nOT, rEALLY,
GG: hmmm....
GG: well maybe hes just been through some tough times
GG: maybe we should give him the benefit of the doubt?
AT: uHHHH,
GG: for whatever its worth i think youre a pretty nice guy too!
AT: oKAY, tHANK YOU,
GG: also you seem to be the only one who ever thinks to talk to me while im asleep!
GG: why is that?
AT: oH, i GUESS,
AT: tHAT IT MAKES SENSE,
AT: bECAUSE YOU HAVE A ROBOT, tO LET YOU SAY THINGS THAT HAPPEN, oN PROSPIT,
AT: aND i'M CURIOUS,
AT: bECAUSE THE ONLY TIME i EVER HAD FUN PLAYING THIS GAME WAS WHEN i WAS ASLEEP,
AT: bUT NOW ALL OUR DREAM SELVES ARE DEAD,
AT: }:'(
GG: oh no!!!
GG: dream selves can die?
AT: yEAH,
GG: i never knew that
GG: or even thought about it....
GG: i guess it makes sense though

Jade, do yourself a favor and stop fucking around with this idiot. He ends up getting your grandfather killed.

> Rose: Get trolled by GA.

There is a very misleading line of analysis that suggests Tavros loved his time flying around on Prospit so much because he was paralyzed, and therefore enjoyed the freedom and mobility that flight as his dream self allowed. This is wrong, because it was clear from his backstory that he loved Pupa Pan, and always dreamed of flight even before he was paralyzed. So please, let's not woobify this guy any more than is absolutely necessary, okay?

-- grimAuxiliatrix [GA] began trolling tentacleTherapist [TT] --

GA: Hello Again
GA: Are We Friends Yet At This Point In Time
GA: I Would Speculate That If We Are Not By Now Then It Is Probably Not To Be
TT: Pardon?
GA: Furthermore Which Rose Have You Chosen To Be This Time
GA: The Stupid Rose Or The Smart Rose
TT: I'm a little busy.
GA: It Sounds Like You Are Attempting To Be The Smart Rose This Time
GA: Please Take Note Of The Subtle Scorn Underlying The Selection Of The Word Attempting
GA: Smart Rose Should Get A Kick Out Of That
GA: Smart Rose Is All About Subtle Scorn Isnt She
TT: That sounds about right.
GA: Whereas Dumb Rose Doesn't Capitalize Letters Even When Discussing The Proper Names Of Human Monsters In Earth Cinema
GA: I Think You Should Establish A Greater Commitment To A Single Roleplaying Scenario
TT: Honestly, I was looking forward to playing along and reading your Dumb Rose script for our next conversation.
TT: But it turned out there was a perfectly logical explanation for it all.
TT: Imagine my disappointment.
TT: While I imagine yours, once you finally catch on.
GA: I Suddenly Dont Understand Anything
GA: What Are You Talking About
TT: I'd love to explain in detail and cause some sort of time paradox.
TT: But you see - and this revelation may be as startling as any -
TT: I'm a little busy.
GA: I Believe I Understand
GA: It Was I Who Did Something To Provoke Your Scorn In A Previous Conversation
GA: One Which I Have Not Had Yet
TT: Yes, that is definitely a conclusion you have just now drawn.
TT: The only thing left to do is ride out the next several conversations while you maintain that understanding.
TT: And while I maintain the chilly facade you have grown to so enjoy from Smart Rose.
TT: Which shouldn't be too difficult, because... have I mentioned?
TT: I'm busy.
TT: Goodbye.
GA: Fine

> Dave: Keep getting trolled by GC.

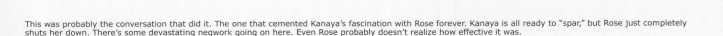

This was probably the conversation that did it. The one that cemented Kanaya's fascination with Rose forever. Kanaya is all ready to "spar," but Rose just completely shuts her down. There's some devastating negwork going on here. Even Rose probably doesn't realize how effective it was.

```
GC: D4V3 D4V3
GC: 1 F1N4LLY GOT 1T
TG: oh hell
GC: 1 F1N4LLY F1GUR3D 1T OUT
GC: ONC3 4ND FOR 4LL
GC: TH1S 1S YOU!!!!!!!
GC: http://tinyurl.com/D4V34NDBRO43V3R
GC: FFFF44444444444H4H4H4H4H4H4H4H4H4H474H4H4H4
GC: H4H4H4H4H4H4H4H4H4H4H4H4H4H4H4H4H4H4H4H4H4H4H4H4H4
TG: that
TG: ok thats pretty amazing
GC: 4H4H4H4H4H4H44H4H4H4H4
GC: OH GOD 1T 1S SO P3RF3CT
GC: JUST 4 COOL DUD3 4ND H1S BRO R1GHT TH3R3
GC: 4DV3NTUR1NG THROUGH T1M3
GC: 4ND PL4Y1NG P1NB4LL
GC: 1N BRO H34V3N TOG3TH3R
GC: T3LL M3 TH4T 1SNT SO FUCK1NG P3RF3CT
GC: >8]
TG: hey speaking of which
TG: where is my bro anyway
TG: havent seen him at all since i got here
TG: davesprite doesnt know
TG: you can see everything that goes on right
TG: or like smell it or whatever
TG: how does that even work
TG: how do you use a computer and know whats going on it doesnt make sense
TG: my face doesnt make sense
GC: D4V3 YOUR *F4C3* DO3SNT M4K3 ......
GC: D4MM1T
```

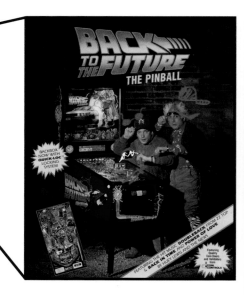

The *BTTF* pinball thing frankly isn't even a great example of Cool Kid Marketing. I guess it's in the ballpark. I mainly just thought it was an incredible graphic resource that absolutely needed to be included somehow. Terezi found it somewhere online too, and yet again proves that she agrees with me on matters such as this.

TG: hahaha
GC: BUT 4CTU4LLY YOUR F4C3 *DO3S* M4K3 S3NS3
GC: TO MY NOS3
GC: 4ND MY TONGU3 >:P
TG: ew
GC: 1M SORRY D4V3 TH4T YOU W1LL N3V3R 3XP3R13NC3 TH3 S3NSORY BOUQU3T TH4T 1 3NJOY 3V3RY D4Y
GC: TH4T 1 3NSCONC3 MYS3LF 1N L1K3 4 W4RM 4ND COMFY B4THROB3 M4D3 OF FL4VOR 4ND M3LODY
TG: oh ok
TG: so the dumbest and most far fetched explanation imaginable ok got it
GC: 4NYW4Y 1 DONT KNOW WH3R3 YOUR BRO 1S
GC: 4S F4R 4S 1 C4N T3LL YOU N3V3R S33 H1M 4G41N B3TW33N NOW 4ND TH3 R1FT
GC: TOO B4D H3 WONT B3 4ROUND TO B41L YOU OUT 4G41N L1K3 H3 D1D WH3N YOU 3NT3R3D!!!
TG: man dont remind me about that
TG: so embarrassing
GC: 1TS OK 1 WONT T3LL JOHN 4BOUT 1T
GC: 1 KNOW TH4TS WH4T YOUR3 WORR13D 4BOUT
TG: ok cool
GC: BUT LOOK YOU DONT N33D TO B3 UPS3T 4BOUT NOT H4V1NG YOUR BRO TO L34N ON 4NYMOR3
TG: whos upset
TG: bout time the dude gave me a little space
GC: BLUH OK WH4T3V3R YOU S4Y BUT TH4TS NOT TH3 PO1NT
GC: TH3 PO1NT 1S 1 W1LL H3LP YOU 1NST34D D4V3
GC: 1S TH4T COOL >:]
TG: i guess
GC: 1 KNOW 3V3RYTH1NG TH4TS GO1NG TO H4PP3N TO YOU
GC: 1 C4N T3LL YOU B3FOR3 1T H4PP3NS
GC: SO YOU C4N B3 R34DY
GC: 4ND NOT H4V3 TO GO B4CK 1N T1M3 4ND G3T K1LL3D 4LL TH3 T1M3
GC: 4ND ST4ND ON 4 TO1L3T LOOK1NG 4T YOUR OWN BLOOD FOR T3N M1NUT3S
TG: alright so whats next
GC: F1RST YOU GO THROUGH TH3 G4T3
GC: 4ND WH3N YOU GO THROUGH YOU W1LL GO TO 4NOTHER PL4C3 1N YOUR W1LD CH3RRY L4V4 L4ND
GC: 4ND YOU W1LL QU1CKLY M33T SOM3 FR13NDLY CROCOD1L3S
GC: TH3Y W1LL TRY TO 34T YOU
GC: BUT TH4T 1S JUST TH31R W4Y OF B31NG FR13NDLY!
GC: YOU SHOULDNT B3 SC4R3D
TG: why would i be scared
GC: D4V3 PL34S3
GC: YOU 4R3 CRY1NG L1K3 4 L1TTL3 BOY
GC: 1TS 1S H4PP3N1NG R1GHT H3R3 1N FRONT OF MY NOS3

```
GC: YOUR T34RS T4ST3 D3L1C1OUS
GC: K1ND OF L1K3
GC: L1K3 SOM3TH1NG YOU WOULDNT KNOW 4BOUT
GC: 4 TROLL D3L1C4CY C4LL3D COTTON C4NDY
TG: we have cotton candy dumpass
GC: >8O
```

> [S] Descend.

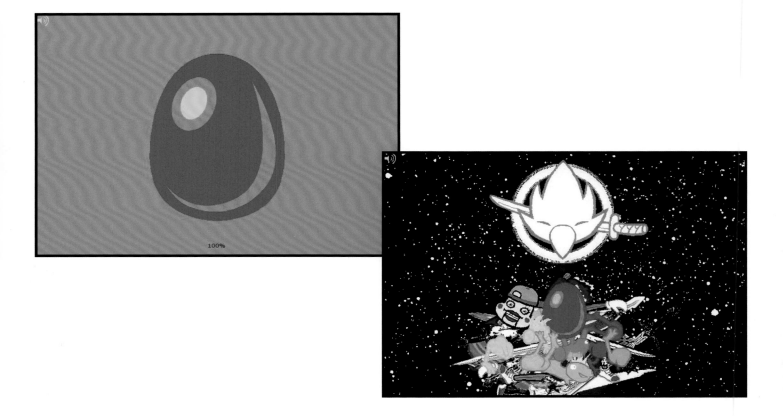

[S] Descend is the longest animation up to this point, at about four minutes (and thirteen seconds iirc). There are a few other significant escalations of animation gravitas in this act, but then this one comes along and dunks on them all. It's a little different from previous animations which in general tend to have more of a singular focus, with a few subplots sprinkled in. This one is all over the place. It covers a lot of ground in the plot, switches between many different frames of reference, everything is explosive, and it all sort of glides from one scene to another in sync with a fairly ambitious (at the time) musical medley by Toby Fox, who titled the song "Descend." So that's what I named the animation as well.

424

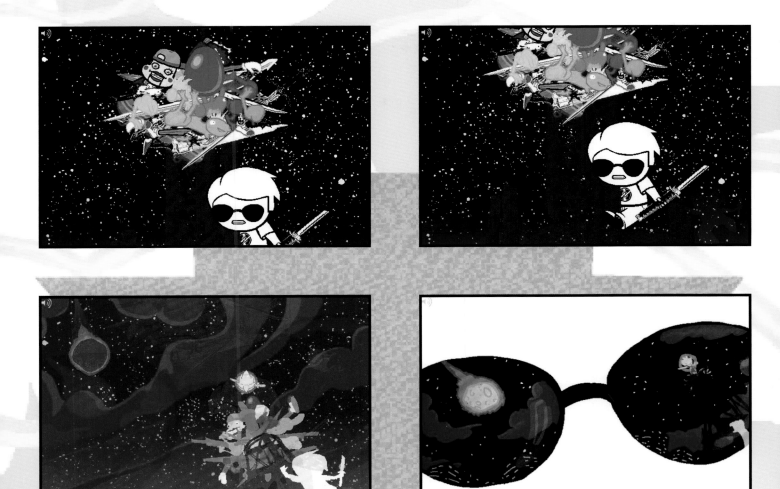

There's another animation in HS that fits the previous description but is much longer. In a way, **Descend** is like **Cascade** Lite. Or **Cascade** is **Descend** Heavy. Anyway, as with almost all HS animations, the song existed well before I ever started animating and usually informed the ideas I would have for it, including how all the action was paced and arranged. So the fact that this particular song was so eclectic, jumping all over the place a lot more than other songs tended to, led to this sort of action-collage feel to the way it plays out. Suddenly we're here, then we're over there, then whoops something blows up, and we're back over here, and now there's... wait, what? Squiddles?? Oh never mind, back to some other important stuff. It's a wild way to end a wild act, but as usual when it comes to anything ambitious and unprecedented in HS, it just turns out to be a warm-up for even crazier things down the road.

425

We finally rewind so we can see the famous "embarrassing entry incident" with Dave. Was it absolutely necessary to do this? No, I guess not. It probably would have felt like a strange missing chunk of the story, though. I think what this segment primarily accomplishes is demonstrating the fact that Bro is capable of chopping a meteor in half with his sword. That's quite a Big Fact.

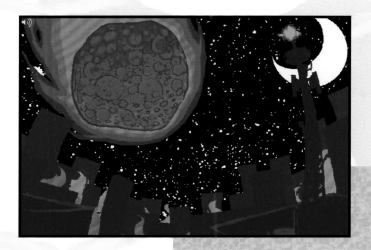

So the "incident" really is just that Dave gets pecked on the head and falls. Not all that embarrassing, honestly. Dave has been blowing this out of proportion, as one might guess. This moment does give us another example of the fact that not all contact with a sprite will result in prototyping. Often minor points of brief or light contact with the sprite won't do it. Like passing your hand quickly over a candle before it burns, an analogy I may have used before.

It seems absolutely crazy that Bro's standing on a meteor and riding it down to Earth. Until you realize (later in this very animation) that they all came down to Earth that way as infants. So it's second nature to them in a way, and they seem inoculated to the ill effects of riding a flaming meteor, for reasons that defy any remotely defensible explanation grounded in even the most desperate feats of authorial asspull logic. So I will not offer any to you at this time. But do not take this as an admission that I COULDN'T. I'm just kinda busy, that's all.

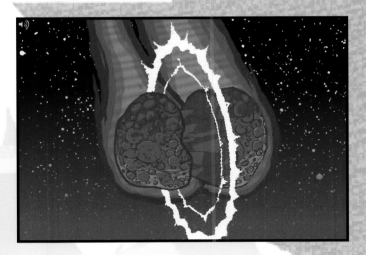
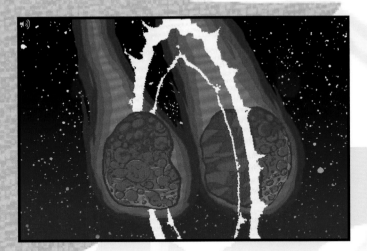

Don't worry everybody, Bro is here to save you all. By...splitting the meteor in two, so there will be two devastating impact sites instead of one. But the important thing is, this buys Dave a few extra seconds. Also, I don't think we see the egg hatch here? It hatches in the animation. Basically the idea was, there was never anything for Dave to do. He just had to wait for the egg to hatch in a warm environment when it was good and ready, under stressful circumstances. A simple test of patience.

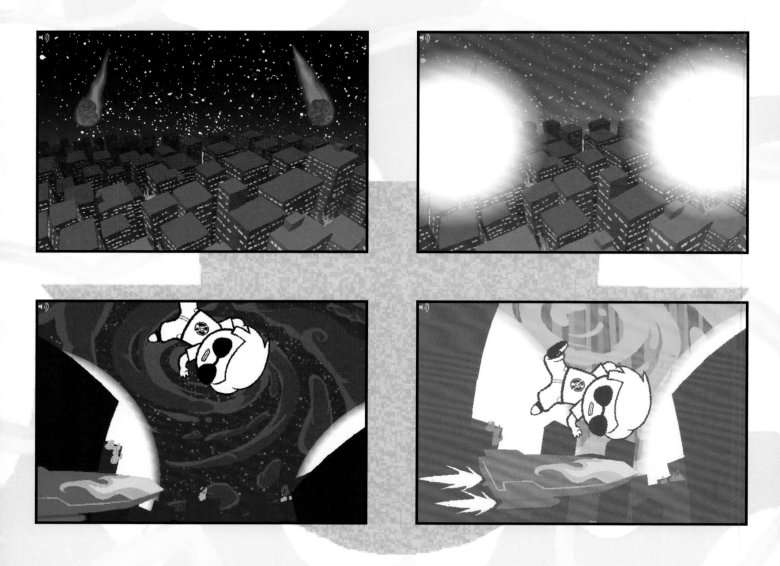

I wonder how Bro's board knows what to do. Some sort of AI embedded in it? That explanation wouldn't be totally baseless. He did program a lot of chat room bots, lusty for puppets.

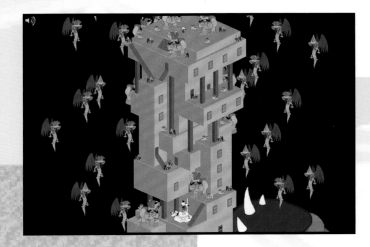

SMASH CUT to Dave where we left him, being guided by Terezi to enter his first gate. Where will it take him? Somewhere on LOHAC, where his unconscionable dollarcrimes may begin.

Mom and Dad, armed to the teeth with their weapons of choice, proceed to Skaia for reasons unknown. I think...maybe they just got married?? We didn't see what happened, but they might have gotten married, guys, just a head's up. So this is their honeymoon destination. A romantic getaway to the Battlefield. Hope nothing goes wrong!

Jack just wants the peasants to kiss his ring. Is that too much to ask? Or his sword. With their torsos. Actually that's probably what he wants. Forget the thing I said about kissing his ring. He'll kill you if you try to do that.

433

Here's a different art style. Starting with the Battlefield scene where Jack kills the king, I got pretty fast and loose with the art styles because I was trying out the idea of an "art team" for these longer animations. A few people chipping in art assets, no matter how different or crazy the styles get, just to shorten the amount of time needed to make more ambitious pieces like this. **[S] Descend** only took about a week, which is a stupidly short period of time to make and release content like this. I was always looking for shortcuts to keep the pipeline SPITTING FIRE, and one idea was to start using contributions from others no matter what the style. Getting a group to stay "on model," editing, and retouching stuff eats up too much time. I said what was needed, people made stuff, I tweaked it a little in Photoshop, and slapped it in there. Instant animation studio.

434

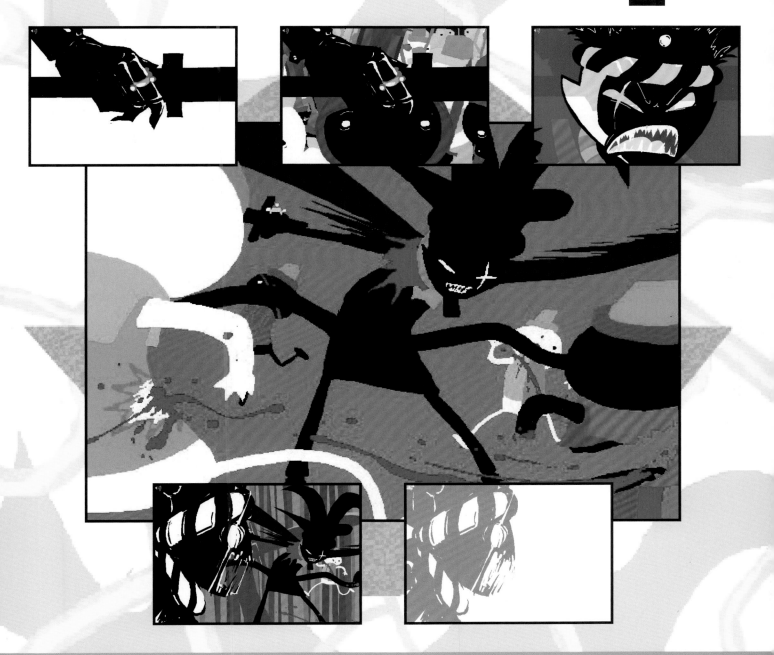

Meanwhile, WV...heroically shuffles to the back of the crowd while his loyal rebels get slaughtered? What is he doing?? Shaking my damn head over here.

435

Karkat once said Jack stabs you to say hello. I guess this is his formal mass-greeting ritual. Everyone bleeding on the floor should feel honored.

Oh, I see how it is, WV. You scurry to the back of the crowd, wait until Jack kills everyone, run forward again and pretend you were there all along, and now you're just SHOCKED that he did this. SHOCKED, you say! Actually, a less cowardly explanation might be something like this: *Sburb* seems to designate certain figures like him as "special" pawns, who are reserved for doing important things later, whatever they might turn out to be. Like being an exile or something. Since Jack and other agents are constructs too, maybe they can "smell" special pieces and avoid killing them? Maybe that's why HB only punched PM instead of eating her head. If certain constructs are built in certain ways to mix things up and keep the game's "plot" interesting, it doesn't really serve that purpose if they indiscriminately kill each other off before they've had a chance to do whatever curveball things they were built to do.

We don't know it yet, but this attack is called Red Miles. It shoots miles and miles of deadly red stuff out of his ring. Just another reason the ring is powerful, which is a fact we learn right now. It helps you picture why, under ordinary circumstances, the queen would be a formidable adversary for players to defeat. That's one reason why it pays to get deeper into the political strategy of *Sburb* and try to stage crafty ousting operations like the trolls did. If you're a *Sburb* player, why would you want to mess around with shit like this?

Yeah, I don't know what the hell these things are. I guess dead is what.

We are still dealing with countdowns. Not countdowns to entry into *Sburb* this time, but a Reckoning countdown. Countdown-based tension will continue all the way until the end of Act 5, when a bomb called the Tumor finally blows up. After that, we chill out with the countdowns mostly. The countdowns are replaced by a lot of other stuff. Like, for instance, several dozen intermissions, and Too Much Gamzee.

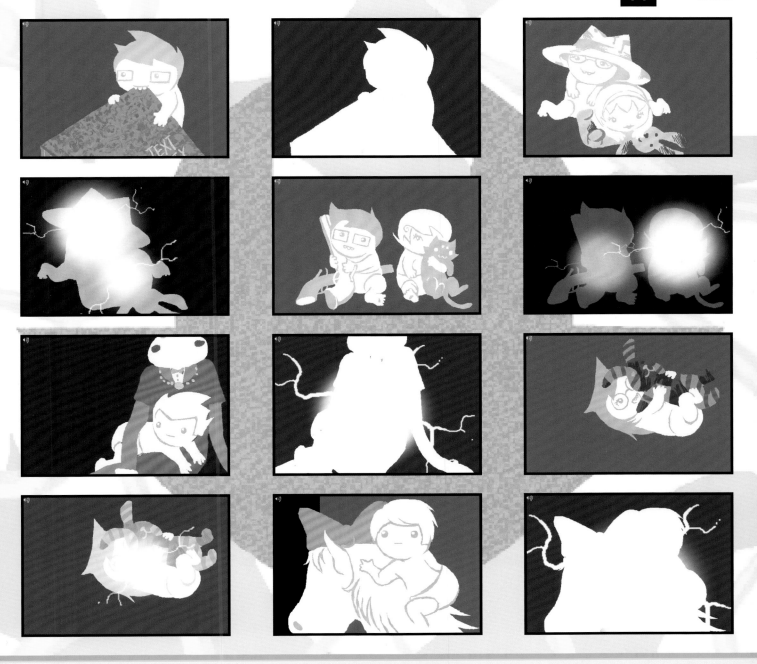

There they go. This is the last time you will ever see that pony and kitten alive. Rest in pieces, dear friends.

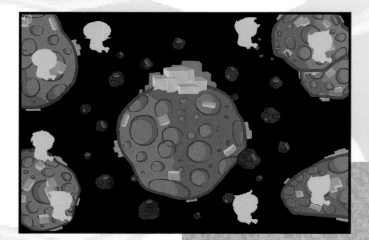
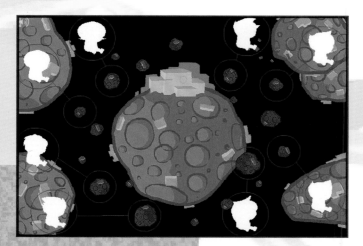

That big Prospitian bomber is pretty cool. It does make me wonder why they decided to build conventional aircraft to mix in with all their clearly superior *Star Wars* space ships. You never know with these chess guys.

Jack is taken aback by the moxie of this rifle battalion. I guess I am too. I forgot there were guys with rifles? I'm just going to be the one to say what we're all thinking. These chess armies are ridiculous.

CD is always the guy who's there at the exact right time, holding the exact right thing when the boss needs it. He's loyal and reliable to a fault, if a bit simple-minded, and extremely literal in the interpretation of his orders. We see him play this role again just before **Cascade**, when he drops several tons of shaving cream on Jade. He really believed it was what the boss wanted him to do. But that time, it was not.

444

Jack is initiating the Reckoning. It's unclear why he wants to do so. When in doubt, the fact that he likes to destroy things, murder people, and cause problems will suffice for any explanation of his motives. This is the crisis Karkat was alluding to. The Black King would observe better form and would wait much longer before doing this. He'd want to allow the kids to make it much further in the game, and get close to challenging him directly before turning on the heat of an imminent meteor shower. He's programmed to be a much better sport than Jack.

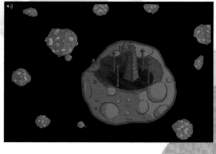
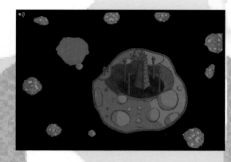
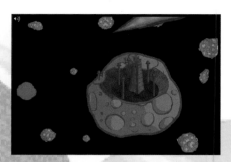
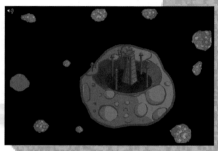
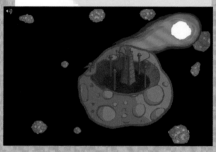
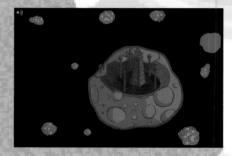

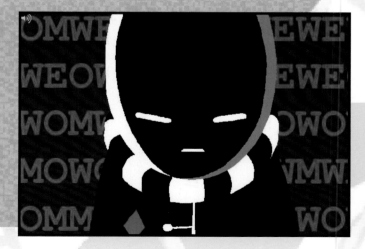

The scepter "summons" the meteors, and they start to fly toward Skaia one by one. DD meanwhile doesn't have much time to finish his work here unless he wants to get stuck in these ruins with this dang dog and AR. That would turn into an awkward roommate situation on post-apocalyptic Earth. There probably wouldn't be enough caution tape for the two of them.

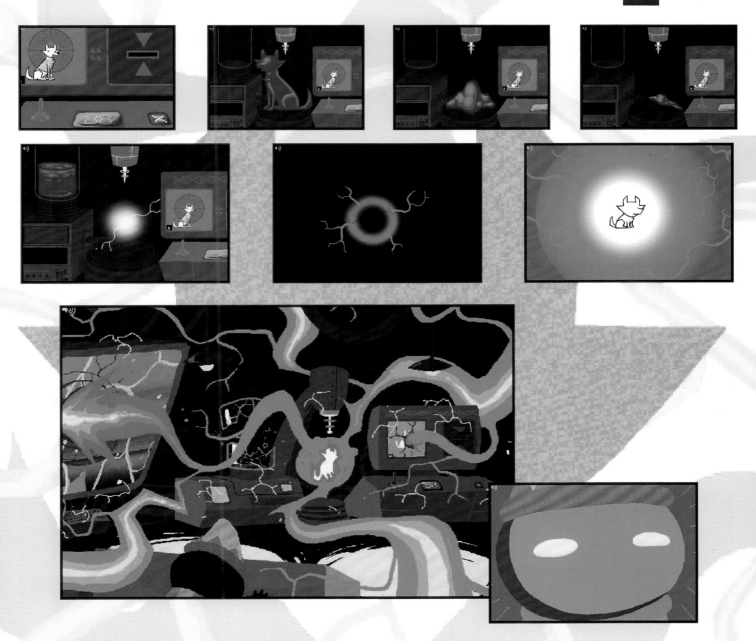

We could already infer this was going to happen when we first saw this machine locked on Halley a while ago, because we are smart. Also this helps us understand why AR recognized the Bec shape carved on the pumpkin and regarded it with possibly some combination of fear and reverence. It would also not be too illogical if carapacians were programmed to recognize and respect a First Guardian, or in some cases, to go to the bother of cloning the guardian in the first place. As DD does here, and the queen does later with Doc.

447

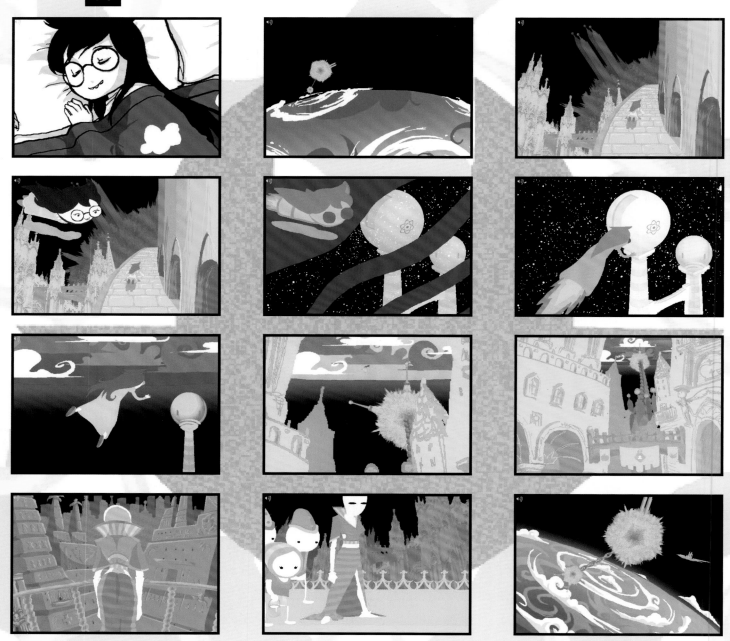

Ms. Paint is ready to go. Her proximity to the queen suggests she has a prominent position in the royal hierarchy. As she very well should. Anyway, this is just a quick glimpse of the queen and her entourage evacuating, heading to Earth to rebuild civilization and preserve Prospitian culture.

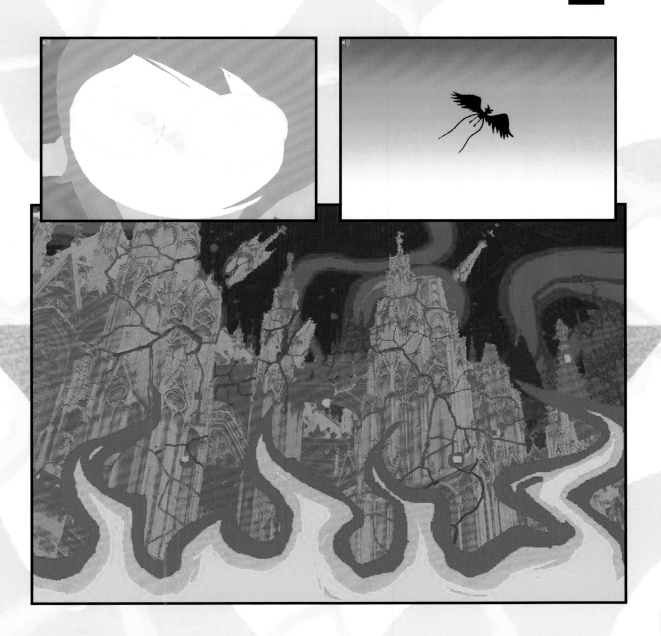

Very strong smash cut. We don't need to see what he did. It's just on fucking fire. NEXT!!!!!

001940 [S]

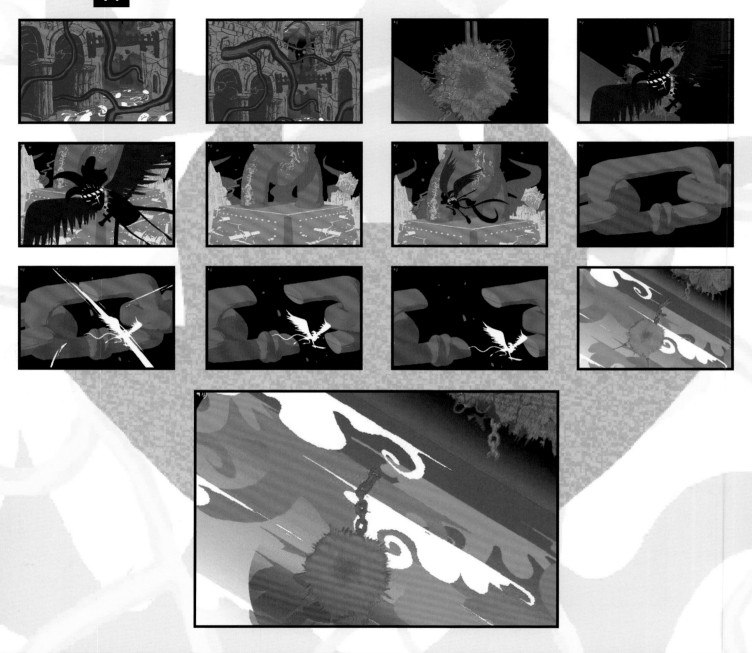

This proves the chain is definitely keeping Prospit's moon in orbit and isn't just for show. Which means if the chain is severed, the moon just gets launched along whatever trajectory it was headed on, like a stone launched by a slingshot. So, that's what happens. Also, it's kind of interesting how if you view Skaia as if it were a planet, and you were hovering over its surface looking at the horizon like this, all its clouds are upside down. That's because Skaia is a big ball of pure sky, and the sky is up. You aren't supposed to STAND on it, like some kind of FOOL. You look UP at it, from a place like Prospit.

450

Jack seems to know exactly where to go in order to find the biggest badass he can throw down with. It probably took a while to get to LOHAC, but this anime dude's ass isn't going to kick itself.

We just saw exhibitions of both these guys' power. Bro sliced a meteor in half, Jack spewed a bunch of red junk from his ring and chopped a giant chain. So we know they're heavyweights. But this is just a taste. A duel that ends in a stalemate. Round Two comes later.

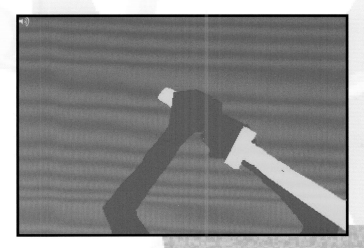

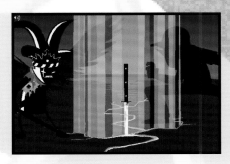

It seems Bro's main goal here isn't to duel so much as get the Scratch started. If not literally, then to leave a clue for the other kids to figure out. Because of course he can't just come out and TELL the kids, hey guys, you're screwed. You're going to need to scratch this giant record to reset things, and here's how exactly. Mysterious ninja bros don't explain stuff, it cramps their style. They mostly communicate through interpretive sword fights.

453

This is the Squiddles intermission. I spent some time joking about how there would be a huge Squiddles intermission, with like a forty-eight-player Squiddle *Sburb* session, and we would get to know each one in great detail. I threatened this more than once, I think. But in the end, this three-second clip of nonsense was probably the closest we ever got to that. Sorry, buddies, you will be fondly remembered for the useless and utterly unwanted subplot you could have starred in.

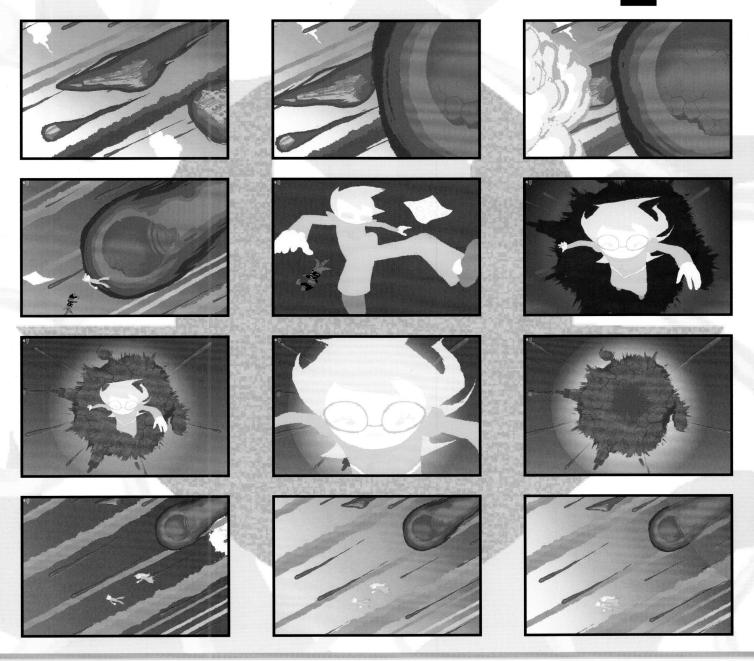

Every now and then, between the thousands and thousands of pages of sobbing teens complaining about their feelings and being basically useless, I fuck up and make one of them do something truly heroic.

Jade, this is no time to be giving your dear brother John a savage pair of purple nurples. Why don't you try waking him up instead?

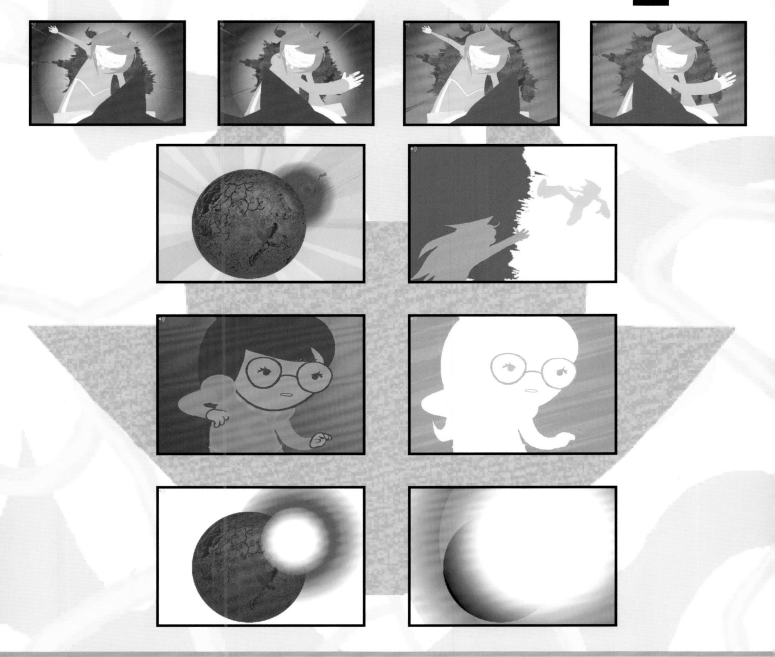

Jade shows off her quarterback's arm, which appears to be capable of hurling John entirely outside the blast radius of an explosion that's about the size of the planet.

Here we catch up to this milestone moment, the mysterious incident Karkat refers to when Jade's robot blows up. Now we know its circuits overload or something because Dream Jade dies. Keep that in mind as a precedent. When Dream You dies, Robot You blows up. Jade told Karkat to contact her after this point because it's a significant, conspicuous moment that clearly delineates two distinct phases of her journey: the one where she's got all the answers due to being able to see cloud visions from Prospit, and the one where she doesn't know anything and is at a loss for what to do next. The future isn't her business anymore. The trolls have completely taken over that racket.

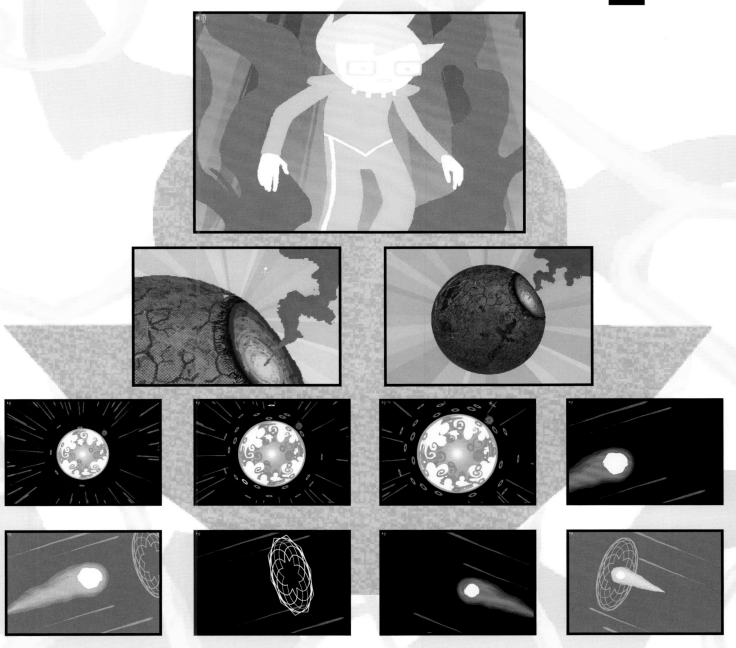

Skaia activates its defenses in response to the Reckoning. The fact that the portals send things back in time, toward Earth, is a secondary purpose. The primary purpose is just to catch meteors and protect the Battlefield, allowing the players as much time as possible to defeat the king and create the universe. But the longer the Reckoning goes on, the more meteors come, and the more Skaia struggles to defend itself with portals. Unfortunately, every meteor it successfully diverts is sent to Earth, which is another nail in its coffin. Skaia sacrifices the planet of origin so that its child (a new universe) may have a chance to be born. But it simultaneously seeds the dead planet with the potential for new life and civilization (exiles), and retroactively seeds the planet with the children who would fertilize Skaia with the new universe. This is the essence of the universal creation cycle. Sacrifice the old to make way for the new. Life rises again from the ashes of the old. Rinse and repeat. Something else to wonder: how often has Earth itself been through this process before humanity came along?

Maybe it says something about Dirk that he is easily the most contented with his particular Birth Object. He doesn't care that he's riding a meteor. He just wants to snuggle up with his new puppet dad and take a nap.

Rose starts to go a little nuts here. It might be that her partial union with her future dream self's memories has started to breed an intense hatred for this game and its cruel manifold futilities, and this one spontaneous decision to blow up her gate sets her on a path of recklessness and destruction. It's also possible she's just being a shitty teen. As a general rule in this story, never rule that out.

462

This is a pretty good explosion graphic/animation. You can tell I felt that way, because I reused it a bunch of times in later panels. But maybe that isn't saying much, because I reused almost everything, even bad things.

Descend was a good note to end on because it spins out a lot of exciting plot threads for the next time we check in with all these guys (which, don't worry, won't be until after we slog through about 600 pages of Hivebent). Dave enters his gate, Rose blows up her gate and flies away like a lunatic to do god knows what, Jade is falling from her room which just exploded, and John is floating around in his pajamas looking dumber than usual, wondering why there's a huge flaming crater on a planet he doesn't recognize. So you can imagine why there was some grumbling from the peanut gallery when immediately after this we start lurching through the introduction of all twelve trolls for several months. Too bad for all those suckers that everybody loved the trolls, and my ludicrous pacing decisions were absolutely vindicated, as they always are.

463

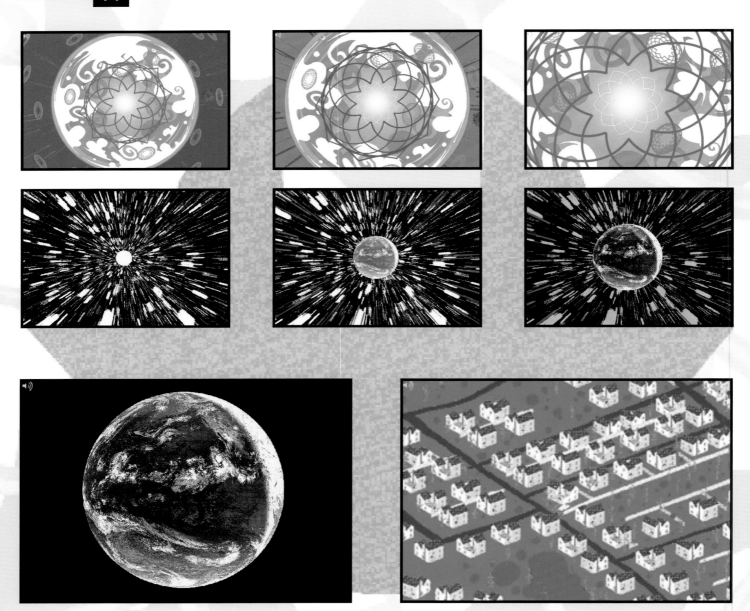

Me, from my director's chair: Okay, activate the Meteor POV Camera...now! And, scene. Several moments of silence. Someone on the set begins to slow-clap. It turns out that's me. I'm doing the slow-clap.

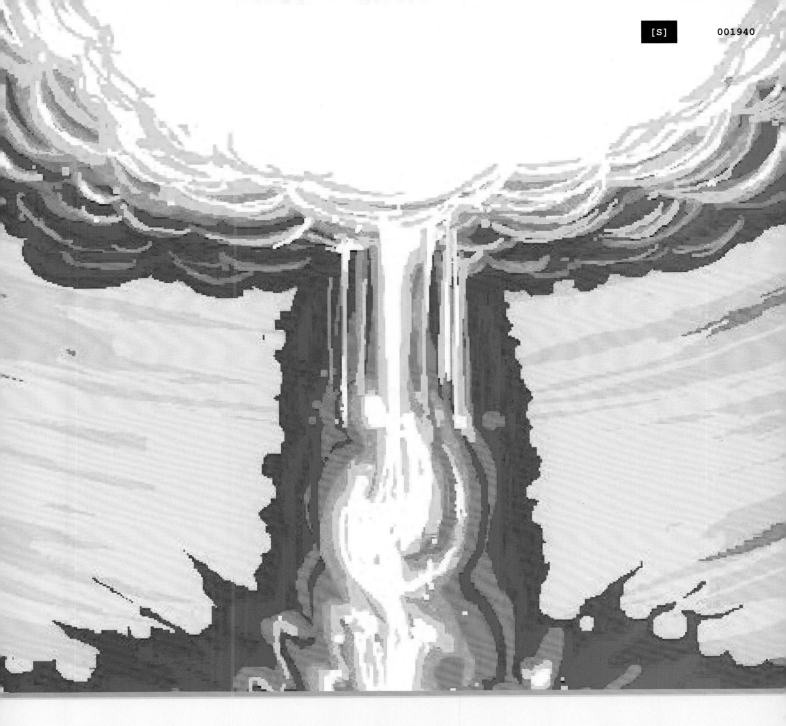

Well, that's the end of Act 1. See you next time, everybody, as we begin our journey through Act 2.

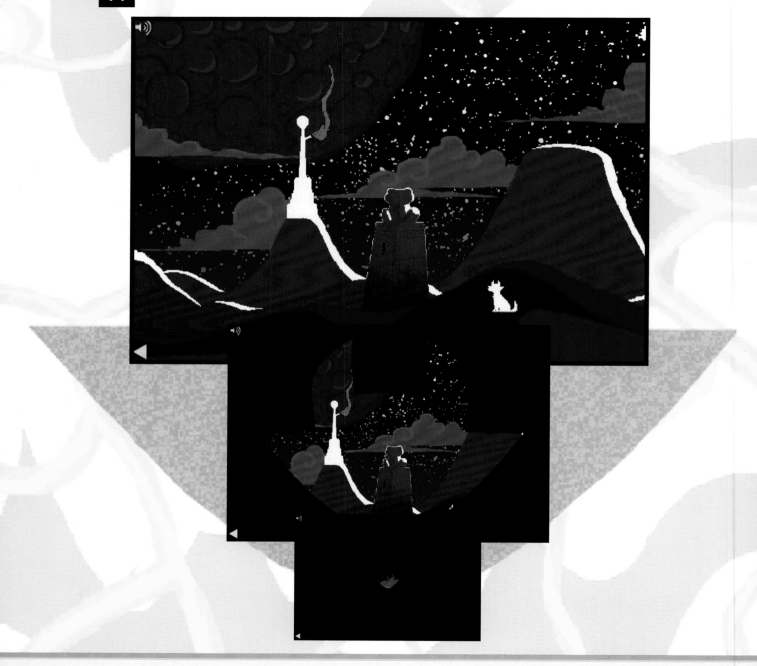

Just joking, this is the end of Act 4, not Act 1. We're going forwards, not backwards, silly. Tune in next time, for Act 5, when we go way, way backwards, and meet Karkat at the beginning of his journey. It'll be great. Wait, there are still some more pages in this book?? Goddamn it.

More magic numbers. Seriously, don't even ask me how I pulled stuff like this off. It just worked out a lot of the time. The next magic number introduced is 612, because that's the date when Act 5 began, 6/12. There's a lot to say about that magic number, like how the group of kids are four thirteen-year-olds, and the group of trolls are twelve six-sweep-olds. Lots and lots of stuff like that, but wow, I really should consider shutting the fuck up already and save some material for the next book.   **467**

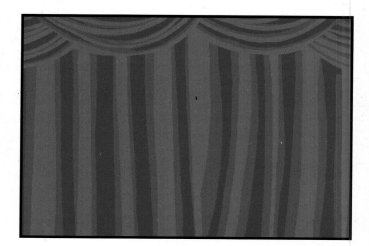

Before we go, let's make one more note about how huge Jade's meteor is. This is the big one, the Extinction Level Event meteor. Just as the Reckoning escalates and becomes harder for Skaia to stave off the longer it goes on, the deeper we get into the meteor shower on Earth the more apocalyptic the meteors get. Note that Bec is standing there, watching, like a very good dog, and we close out on the Bec head shape. This suggests things are going to start getting very, very Bec-y. But not until after Hivebent, which, as I have warned, is a significant haul. It should be an entire book's worth of content, if I am not mistaken.

END OF ACT 4

And as it happens, here's the end of Book 3. As if the partitioning of *Homestuck*'s structure wasn't already baffling enough, with all the Intermissions and Act Act Acts. Now there are book numbers to consider, and as the series rolls on, the book numbers will start to have virtually no relation to the Act and Intermission segments they contain. But the most important thing we both agree on is that you will definitely own all of them. For until you have read each and every one of my precious Author Notes, you will never be able to claim to truly "understand *Homestuck*," and therefore you will not know peace in this lifetime or beyond. Tune in next time for Hivebent, wherein twelve alien adolescents spend about 600 panels screaming at each other, using an array of typing quirks that are virtually unreadable.

ART CREDITS

[S] WV?: Rise up.
Michael Firman, Nic Carey

[S] Descend.
Brett Muller, Eyes5, Jessica Allison, Lexxxy,
M Thomas Harding, Nic Carey, Paige Turner,
Richard Gung, SaffronScarf, Vivus

SBURB CLIENT   ✕

SBURB version 0.0.1

SKAIANET SYSTEMS INCORPORATED. ALL RIGHTS RESERVED.

SBURB client is running.

Homestuck
Book 3
Part 1: Act 4

VIZ Media Edition

By Andrew Hussie

Cover Art — Adrienne Garcia
Book Design — Christopher Kallini
Cover & Graphic Design — Adam Grano
Editor — Leyla Aker

Printed in China

Published by VIZ Media, LLC
P.O. Box 77010
San Francisco, CA 94107

10 9 8 7 6 5 4 3 2 1
First printing, October 2018

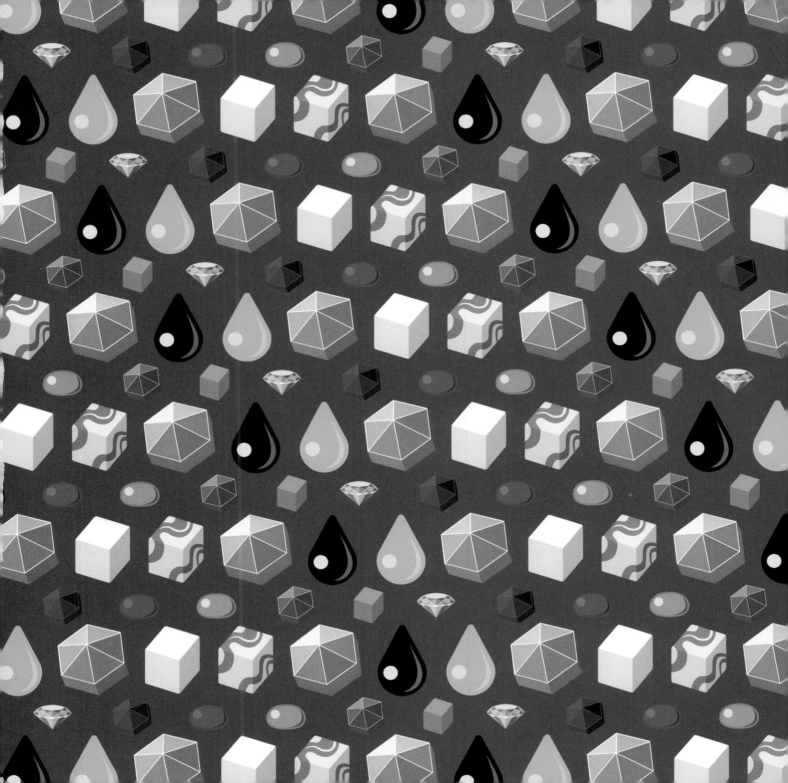